T0078016

One Bipolar
CURE!

28 Years without an Episode!

Hugh Drummond Fulcher

authorHOUSE®

AuthorHouse™
1663 Liberty Drive
Bloomington, IN 47403
www.authorhouse.com
Phone: 833-262-8899

Published by AuthorHouse 04/25/2022

ISBN: 978-1-6655-5752-8 (sc)
ISBN: 978-1-6655-5751-1 (e)

Contents

List of Figures

DISCLAIMER

This book is intended to inspire innovative thinking about the mind, life, and God and is not intended to be a substitute for professional medical services. Neither the author nor the publisher is responsible for consequences experienced, or not experienced, if using the author's alternative mind healing exercises and processes. Practicing alternative healing exercises, given herein, are at the discretion, risk, and responsibility of the reader. Bold processes and exercises have only been practiced and proven beneficial by the author.

TEASER, AND WHY READ?

D o you have bipolar, or other mental, disorder or want to understand and help someone who has? Learn how a physicist/nuclear engineer has healed his bipolar disorder using conflicting exercises for extending his mind to emotional survival limits, and meditation to calm back down. It is life changing not worrying about going manic.

The author experienced 17 years of sporadic manic episodes even with psychiatric medications. He has been mania free for 28 years.

Bipolar Disorder is caused by stress beyond ability to cope with feelings of no way out. Normal thinking within social and challenging limits is overridden by high energy survival thinking. The manic mind goes out of control beyond emotional limits. Experience manic thinking.

With conflicting exercises, the mind learns to control itself at limits. We learn the most about our minds at limits. Exercises release small discrete trauma scar energy from the neck, throat, and brainstem, releasing tensions in related areas of the brain. The mind becomes less emotional and easier to control. Trauma scars are like cancers sporadically firing and causing the overall energy of the brain to remain at high levels. Athletes extend minds and bodies to limits to be all they can be.

Facial meditation reduces mental energy and subconsciously

tenses muscles on the sides of the temple and scalp renewing facial, and facial skin, muscles. The face looks and feels younger.

In the author's first manic episode, he needed to learn of God's origin. His imaginary manic models *explain* God's origin and his infinite abilities. Working to finish his first healing book, he received an inner voice: *"Don't Leave God Out."* His first book became and later books were spiritual. Christianity and science were important in mental healing and spiritual beliefs.

ACKNOWLEDGEMENTS

I thank my Savior, Jesus Christ, and God for sharing so many ideas. I am eternally grateful to my parents, Lewis Page Fulcher, Sr., and Frances Drummond Fulcher, (both deceased,) for their love and guidance when I had mental difficulties. They fought for me, and saved my life, when I was unlovable and "expecting death." In heaven, they remain the love beneath my wings.

My children, Keston Hugh Fulcher, PhD, and wife Meghan, Kara Fulcher Hawkins, M.D., and husband, Andy Hawkins, M.D., have been supportive in many ways.

I thank computer builders and software developers for tools that have made writing and editing easier.

Note: This mind healing and spiritual book is experimental and controversial. I have not asked for nor received medical assistance from my daughter, son-in-law, or son.

DEDICATION

One Bipolar Cure!/18 Years Without an Episode! is dedicated to those who have supported my writing and life, and to those I hope to assist in living healthy, confident, and spiritual lives. Specific dedications are:

My parents, Frances Drummond Fulcher (deceased) for her patience, and Lewis Page Fulcher, Sr. (deceased) for his wisdom, and both for their love;

My Uncle, O. Hugh Fulcher, MD (deceased), former Head of the Georgetown University Neurosurgery Department, who instilled confidence in reasoning about the brain;

Thomas M. Fulcher MD (deceased) who took such an interest in my writing; My children, Keston Hugh Fulcher, PhD, and Kara Fulcher Hawkins, MD;

My double first cousin Barbara Fulcher Mays and husband Carlton (deceased) have always been supportive of me, my family, and my endeavors.

All readers coping with abuse, mental pain, disorders, and uncertainties; Everyone who loves, cares for, and shares with, others.

VITA

Hugh Drummond Fulcher graduated from Virginia Tech, B.S. in Physics, and M.S., in Nuclear Engineering. He was a licensed operator for the Virginia Tech experimental nuclear reactor and studied at Argonne National Laboratory.

He was a university physics and engineering instructor for Virginia Tech and Danville Community College. As a nuclear engineer, he has designed nuclear reactor cores, developed nuclear monitoring software, performed nuclear safety analysis; and, as a Software System Engineer, he has implemented numerous engineering design systems into mainframe computers.

Mr. Fulcher has worked with nuclear reactor design and consulting companies, nuclear utilities, and National Laboratories.

Conversations on neurosurgery with O. Hugh Fulcher, MD, an uncle and former Head of the Georgetown University Neurosurgery Department, "expected death," and experience modeling complex nuclear reactors, inspired Mr. Fulcher to model the brain, mind, and God, from a science-spiritual perspective of the *human* experiment.

He founded a leasing company in 2004 and is a member of *Who's Who in America.*

ABSTRACT

BACKGROUND

A physicist and nuclear engineer became bipolar due to bullying throughout childhood but mostly due to a frigid, abusive, and deceptive wife. With conflicting physical exercises, he carefully and briefly extended his mind to emotional limits to release small localized trauma energy. Reducing the energy of the brain and extending the brain and mind briefly to limits heals the brain and mind and maintains control at expanded emotional limits. He experienced 17 years of sporadic severe manic episodes even with medications. He has practiced conflicting psychiatric exercises for 28 years with medications. He healed his disorder using conflicting physical exercises not chemistry. Athletes extend minds and bodies to limits to be all they can be.

CAUSE

Bipolar Disorder is caused by stress beyond ability to cope with feelings of no way out. Symptoms began with deep depression that exploded into manic episodes at emotional *survival* limits. Normal everyday interactions and coping skills are overridden by high-energy emotional survival thinking. *Survival* thoughts override attention for reasoning with others. The manic mind becomes overactive and out of control.

NORMAL THINKING

The book examines everyday *"normal thinking"* in some depth in early chapters to show credibility as healing and spiritual models in later chapters include manic imagination and creativity to assist psychiatric healing and beliefs. Thinking about thinking and God is healing.

CURE

My unusual cure uses conflicting neck exercises to briefly stress the mind to emotional survival limits. With careful practice the mind learns to think, cope, and control itself at emotional limits. Conflicting neck exercises release discrete trauma scars from the upper neck, upper throat, and brainstem. Releasing tensions in the neck and throat releases tensions in related areas of the brain. With less high energy trauma memory scars in the throat, neck and brain, the mind becomes less emotional and easier to control. Over 28 years of exercises, feelings of distinct trauma scar releases have been exciting, and have felt reasonable such that the author has continued exercises and written about trauma scar changes and migrations over the years. High energy trauma scars are like cancers in the brain sporadically firing and causing the overall energy of the brain to remain at high levels to overcome these cancerous effects. Initial awareness of trauma release sensations began when manic in 1993. The author felt compelled to exercise his neck to release trauma energy. After 28 years of conflicting neck exercises, trauma release sensations have been mostly released with smoother sensations remaining. We learn the most about our minds at limits. Athletes extend minds and bodies to limits to be all they can be.

Adding to healing he began facial meditation in the last five years to reduce mental energy. Facial meditation with a relaxed face caused subconscious facial and facial skin muscle tensing around the sides of the temples and on the sides of the scalp. While practicing conflicting neck exercises and facial meditation, the author has not been depressed or manic for 28 years – *One Bipolar Cure*.

BELIEF AND SPIRITUAL

In the author's first severe manic episode in 1977, he had a pressing need to learn of God's origin. The *Nothing before Time* chapter is an imaginary model to explain God's origin. While feverishly working to complete his first *healing* book: *Emotional Mind Modeling*, in 1994, he received a high intensity inner voice: *"Don't Leave God Out"* seemingly from all directions. He was shocked that God selected him to write a spiritual book. He had received unusual spiritual messages earlier but never thought he could or should write spiritually about his disorder and beliefs. His first and later books became spiritual. The author integrated his science and Christian backgrounds and his spiritual messages received to write spiritually. Jesus and God became an important part in his healing. They gave the author guidance and patience to complete a long healing and spiritual journey. The author made models for understanding God's omniscience, omnipresence, and omnipotence abilities. With faith we accomplish unexpected and unusual goals.

INTRODUCTION SECTION

Chapter 1

INTRODUCTION

"Imagination can guide us into an exciting future. With conflicting exercises given here we may learn to go beyond our mental limits to be all we can be."

H Fulcher

"The manic mind is excited, energic, and creative toward imaginary and sometimes realistic goals until it reaches emotional or survival limits and goes out of control."

Hugh Fulcher

"Success is a journey not a destination."

Ben Sweetland

"We learn the most about our minds when they are extended to emotional limits. Athletes extend minds and bodies to limits to excel. One writes to understand and communicate unusual experiences believing they will be beneficial to readers."

H Fulcher

Ingrain - firmly fix or establish a habit, belief, or attitude in a person

Note 1: To simplify writing, the capitalized word, "Light," refers to the entire electromagnetic spectrum. The italicized word *"Light"* refers to all Light in the universe and heaven - God.

Note 2: Definitions of specialized words are given at the beginning of chapters.

Welcome to my trials and tribulations in this mind and spiritual rendering of an unusual life. When lost and needing to be creative, the mind surrenders to the pen to write unusual stories.

After 17 years of severe sporadic manic episodes, with medications, the author has been free of episodes for 28 years with his conflicting psychiatric exercises at emotional limits and with his meditation, while continuing medications. Early episodes occurred frequently beginning in 1977 ending in hospitalizations. Episodes after 1992 while practicing conflicting psychiatric neck exercises at emotional limits did not require hospitalizations.

Early chapters in the Life Section give truthful aspects of normal and challenged life. Reasoning about normal thinking in some depth is presented since later emotional models of the brain and mind include manic imagination and creativity to promote psychiatric healing. Models in the Belief and Spiritual Section include manic imagination and creativity for psychiatric healing and for integration of science and Christianity for promoting spiritual thinking and beliefs.

My first mild depression began in 1966 from a severe army boot-camp knee injury. It lasted only for a short time. In 1977, I became overstressed, depressed, and bipolar, due to childhood bullying but mostly due to a deceitful, degrading wife. She was an adult child of a deranged alcoholic mother who had a compulsion and talent for criticizing and destroying those close to her. I never felt loved by my former wife only controlled. My physics and engineering career made sense but my wife's behavior was perplexing and destructive.

I experienced *freedoms* of dying in my 1977 depression, followed by my first manic episode at survival limits a few days later. I have experienced several bipolar episodes and felt compelled to write my story.

I am proud to have had and been healed of bipolar disorder. My mental reconstruction exercises and experiments have been exciting and effective in healing my disorder. Inner feedback sensations from psychiatric exercises have guided my healing processes. Meditation practices and spiritual models have also been exciting for healing and have cultured beliefs.

Prescribed medications had not prevented sporadic manic episodes for 17 years. To make uncertainties, certain, I meditated and pondered my thoughts and activities for understanding my inner bipolar feedback sensations.

After suffering seventeen years of sporadic manic episodes, I developed a psychiatric, physics based, non-drug exercise solution for my disorder. The amazing thing about my psychiatric exercises is that healing sensations have changed so much within the upper back of the neck, back of the throat, and within the brainstem over twenty-eight years while practicing the same exercises and processes. The brain and mind are complex and heal slowly from baby, and later, emotional trauma effects.

By briefly stressing my mind to limits with neck exercises and reasoning about inner feedback sensations, I have *healed* my bipolar disorder. I do not use drugs or medications to extend my mind to limits. I use conflicting physical exercising of muscles closest to the brain at emotional limits to heal my brain and mind. Extending my brain and mind to limits with conflicting neck exercises have had the greatest healing effects on my brain and mind. Neck and facial muscles are the closest muscles to the brain. Meditation restores the mind back to normal after exercises. Psychiatric and spiritual models have guided healing for a consistent sanity.

There are no *final* psychiatric *cures* for stress disorders. Anyone can again become overstressed by further traumas, persistent severe abuse, pains, and extensive uncertainties.

As a nuclear reactor engineer, I used my reactor modeling

experience to model the brain, mind, and God for self-healing and nurturing spiritual beliefs. My spiritual journey began early with Christianity as a child, and later from bipolar disorder and inner spiritual messages received. Philosophy and science expanded spiritual beliefs. Healing and spiritual models do not need to be overly detailed or completely correct to promote inner healing and spiritual renewal.

Early emotionally *limiting* experiences are important to mental health and reasoning abilities throughout life. Children are taught, and sometimes brainwashed, by parents, religions, traumas, and unnecessary restrictions, to lesser or greater extents. Childhood bullying limits thinking, desires, behaviors, and too often devastates lives. Re-experiencing significant emotional life changing events relieves early ingrained learning restrictions.

From years of experience, my psychiatric conflicting and non-conflicting neck exercises purge emotional energy from the brain ingrained by baby, childhood, and later traumas. We have had their effects for so long we are unaware of their restrictions on thinking and on desires for new adventures and excitement.

Early *Life* chapters reflect normal and challenging activities in some depth. Philosophical models of daily activities increase life options. Mind healing is mental and spiritual. Creative mind and spiritual models are basic for healing the mind and nurturing beliefs.

The brainwashed and shallow are so sure of themselves. Science oriented and inquiring minds have so many doubts to reason about and resolve. Intelligent parents teach options and encourage freedom of thought. They teach their children how to think and not just what to think.

To prevent sporadic manic episodes, I continued medications, conflicting healing exercises, meditation, spiritual modelling, and mental experimentation. I have paid careful attention to sensation feedback from psychiatric exercises. Never continue exercises or processes that are painful.

I initially wrote to document my work for *curing* my disorder.

Later I broadened my scope to help heal readers, support care givers, and hopefully influence mental health providers.

My philosophical models and processes may help heal other bipolar suffers and assist researchers in developing new healing methods for disorders such as PTSD. Integration of neuron activated Light within the brain creates consciousness and cognition. Spiritual models give insight into the soul and spiritual dimensions.

After receiving a dramatic spiritual message, I prayed, reasoned, and wrote to understand and praise God with hopes of receiving His blessings for healing and spiritual insight. At times, we should carefully *experience emotional limits* to expand our physical, mental, and spiritual technologies. Imagination soars.

In nurturing others, we consider their weaknesses and strengths and build upon them. We guide and lead to benefit those who trust in us. Controllers use superior positions for their own benefits, with less concern for victims' well-being.

I have kept my work separate from healthcare and religious authorities. It is so different they would have discouraged my efforts. We learn the most about our minds and bodies when they are carefully extended to emotional limits. Minds are forced to be inventive to escape or expand limits and then return to confident thinking. We more easily remember extremely good and bad feelings, ideas, and times.

My mind became my laboratory. I have journeyed through an inner odyssey of dismay, discovery, hope, healing, and spiritual belief. After my first manic episode, I questioned my thinking, interactions, and beliefs. Unintentionally, a philosopher was born. Spiritual feelings and thoughts have also guided my healing practices, writing, and life. Activities of the brain create the mind, and, recursively, the mind controls the brain, nerves, and body.

I have modeled neuron activations in the brain to understand and improve thinking. Integrated Light within the brain exists on borders between physical, mental, and spiritual dimensions. The brain is physical; the mind is spiritual. Neuron emitted, reflected, and integrated Light transmits information throughout the brain creating the mind.

Healing practices are similar to vaccinations. Briefly extending the mind to limits prepares it for greater stresses later on. All creative and spiritual discoveries are controversial in the near term until studied, experienced, and accepted by authorities and others. Hopefully by sharing information, mental patients will be less stigmatized by insensitive societies. When stressed beyond current limits, we either become mentally crushed or creative. It depends upon our approach, attitudes, and reflections toward new adventures.

Traumas cause conflicting, uncertain, and limiting feelings and thoughts. Manic-depressives have been stressed beyond their ability to cope, to their emotional limits, and with *strong* feelings of *no way out*.

When severely stressed beyond limits, life as earlier known ends. Uncertainties erode confidence. Minds and machines go out of control when extended beyond limits. The mind, beyond limits and grasping for control, may end in disaster, or develop exceedingly creative attitudes and limits.

We normally think in complete sentences. In mania, incomplete, often scary, thoughts pervade previously confident minds. Subconscious processes iterate and strive to converge to feelings of *completeness*. Creative thinking extends beyond current limits searching for needed completeness.

If psychiatrists today would have had young Einstein or Steve Jobs as patients, they would have labeled them irrational, unstable, and possibly restrained them. Creative and spiritual ideas are initially difficult to believe but later are recognized as reasonable and feel as if known for a long time. It is uncertain, what new science discoveries will drastically change human futures?

Living beings grow, reproduce, age. Aging is a pervasive stress disorder that should not occur. The brain and mind cleared of trauma effects may restore perfect cell division for renewing the brain and body. People are living longer today. Aging may be cured with bioscience, nutrition, and gene editing. I believe I have had a small success in slowing aging. Some individuals naturally age slower than others.

Healing processes include brain dominance exercises to promote short- and long-distance *focusing* skills. I use a Holusion, defined later, to distinguish between left-brain up-close analytical and right-brain distance and integration thinking.

After twenty years of mental reconstruction exercises, facial meditation has initiated *subconsciously controlled* facial muscle and skin firming for restoring health for a *youthful* face. Facial skin firming from facial meditation strengthens communications between the face and related areas of the brain. Facial meditation promotes neural and glial cell reconstruction in the brain. Smiling relaxes and heals the face, brain, and mind!

When enduring severe trauma or sicknesses, many of us become more spiritual to survive. We must give up who we have been to become who we want and need to become.

In rushing to finish my first healing book in 1995, I received an overwhelming, demanding inner voice from all directions: "Don't leave God out!" It was my spiritual calling. Dreaming and writing became spiritual. Having bipolar disorder, being a Christian, and having a physics background has helped me receive science related spiritual messages beyond those of traditional religions. We usually receive only spiritual information we are able to understand. God is consistent and communicates as strongly today as in traditional religious times. With persistent faith in God, we spiritually *receive*. A goal is to bring science and religion closer together and understandable.

Since 1994, I have received many exciting less dramatic spiritual messages, and have included them in this book. My beliefs are based upon my Christian interpretations, science, inner feedback from limiting experiences, and philosophy.

Healthcare, science, and religious authorities historically have been quick to reject creative ideas to maintain their *unquestioned* authority. The creative must relate new ideas to established ideas in some way to excite authorities and others to accept useful new ideas and truths.

With prescribed medications and creative practices, I have not had a manic episode for the past twenty-eight years and have been blessed with consistent sanity, *my amazing success*!

Without minds, brains and bodies have no purpose. Without God, the universe has no purpose. God is spirit and the universe's *mind*. After receiving spiritual messages, I have made models of God for nurturing spiritual communications and beliefs. Spiritual communications are normally received through our subconscious, inner minds. However, during high emotions in fear of death, God's communications strike like lightening directly into consciousness.

During my first manic episode in 1977, I contemplated God's origin and developed a pseudo-physics and philosophy model to explain God's own *creation* and *transition* from *Nothing before Time*. Primordial time was, and spiritual time is, very different from human experienced physical time. I will never limit God to human sensed time and space. God existed before He created the universe and physical time. He had no beginning and will have no ending in *physical* time. Time at the beginning of the universe was very different than time humans experience today. Spiritual and dreaming time and actions are not limited to physical time and actions.

With different heredities and experiences, human minds are not meant to think and worship alike, or to mimic others. We need a concept of self. Truthful spiritual leaders do not brainwash, *force* their beliefs on, or mentally abuse, followers. They nurture. Religious leaders must be sensitive, as individuals are ready to receive spiritually at different times.

I have pondered how great God must be. With His physical, probability, relativity, integration, and spiritual laws, God keeps-up with our complex speeds and directions on earth as we travel through the universe at:

1. 1.3 million miles/hour – the speed of the center of the Milky Way relative to the very, very distant extra galactic frame of reference,
2. 450,000 miles/hour – speed the sun revolves around the center of the Milky Way,
3. 67,000 miles/hour – speed the earth revolves around the sun,
4. 1,000 miles/hour – speed of the surface of the earth near the equator.

God created or designed, engineered, and constructed relativity and the universe. Scientists experiment to understand God's work in designing His physical laws and truths. In discovering laws of the physical universe, we understand more about God, His work, and purpose. The universe and God are an integrated entity for *His unity and purpose.*

God considers human death differently than from human understanding. He considers the transition of physical and mental life to everlasting spiritual *life* as a purposeful, *continuous* process.

I hope to inspire readers to heal their minds and nurture their beliefs. We must explore our minds to improve interactions, lives, and beliefs. I look forward to new, inner sensations to continue my mental and spiritual advancement. My goal continues to understand physical, inner, and spiritual realities and help readers heal their disorders and discover their own realities.

Healing practices will mostly benefit readers who have suffered traumas, mental disorders, PTSD, insanity, or survived expected imminent death. Mental reconstruction has been worth my considerable, long effort. Sanity is worth all efforts. Progressive inner ideas continue to be exciting. If practicing exercises and reasoning about their feedback, reader's sensations and healing may be different from my own. Minds are different, complex, and heal slowly. Nurturing beliefs gives mental and spiritual confidence and stability.

Neuroscientists have not developed a model to explain consciousness. From my inner experiences, bipolar disorder, and physics background, I have constructed a consciousness model and have also included a creative chapter on the alpha and omega of prayer. The mind and spirit can be renewed. I am thankful for all my direct ancestors without them I would not exist.

I have spent thirty years developing this work and have presented exercises and processes truthfully and work to integrate my mental and spiritual realities. With faith, *manic* imagination, and inner research we can do wonders for our health, those who believe in us, and for God to some extent. I present a science and Christian perspective. An infinite God resides within each quantum of the infinite vacuum of space. God is omnipresent. Atoms are physical not spiritual. The Belief and Spiritual Section may enhance spiritual views.

If I deceive readers, I am *nothing*. All truths are God's; all errors are mine.

MODELING SECTION

Chapter 2
MODELING

❧❧❧

Model: A word or schematic description of a system, theory, or phenomenon that accounts for its known or inferred properties and may be used for further study of its characteristics and use. Manmade models only have human perceptions of reality.

Resonance: a fundamental vibration within a sound, mechanical, nuclear, electrical, or mental system with the same or nearly the same frequency as the natural frequency or frequencies of that system. (A guitar string *resonates* back and forth with its fundamental or harmonic resonances.)

Humans do not know or experience true reality but make models of their bodies and *sensed realities* using their limited senses and minds. Only God knows *true reality*. With their limited abilities, humans navigate environments, nurture relationships, and influence loved ones, customers, voters, and others. I experiment until models of the brain, mind, and God give inner feelings of completeness for predicting and controlling my future.

There are many types of models. For example, Walmart has a successful business model for purchasing, organizing, communicating, distributing, storing, and marketing food and other needed products. Walmart is a large successful retailer.

We make models of useful products, buildings, and cars before building or manufacturing them. We model atoms and even our brains and minds for understanding to advance the quality of our lives. Through our religion we make models for communication with Jesus and God and for spiritual understanding and everlasting life.

We do not know reality but make mental models of reality by integrating sensed data with genetic and memory information for developing reasoning. Mental models do not need to be completely correct to be useful. We sometimes perform research and develop theories to refine our models when thinking about reality. If our mental models have some level of reality, we learn about ourselves and interactions with environments to accomplish goals.

Parents' behaviors and teachings develop critical role models for developing their children's emotions and skills. Dolls build caring skills. Toys build work skills. Without our mental models, we can do nothing.

Carmakers make computer models of components, their connectivity, and interactions before developing assembly lines. Spaceship models must include sufficient thrust, guidance, and aerodynamics to achieve complex space missions. Scientists make models and perform experiments to understand, and benefit from, the earths and universe's resources.

Religions build models and develop dogma for worshipping their spiritual leaders and God for believers' and possibly God's benefits. Religious leaders give their believers spiritual purpose. Spiritual models are important for peace of mind, health, and for believing in and worshiping, God.

Nuclear engineers mathematically model neutron characteristics, interactions, and percentages absorbed in uranium for calculating uranium fissions for *consistent*, safe control of nuclear power plants. After designing models of complex nuclear reactors, modeling the brain, mind, and God seemed reasonable for healing my bipolar disorder, and hopefully helping heal readers' disorders such as bipolar and Post Traumatic Syndrome Disorders.

Brain and mind models advance understanding of subconscious processes and *conscious*ness. Spiritual models consider and question religious dogma for strengthening personal beliefs in God within a complex world. Many of us have received spiritual messages that have guided and deepened our beliefs. God listens to and *learns* from our prayers and is the continuing definition of infinite wisdom, presence, love, and power.

Humans strive to create mind models that give feelings of completion while experiencing activities, and developing sentences and thoughts. Thinking completeness is corrupted by ingrained trauma memory activations with sensed energy releases. Humans will achieve their highest mental potentials when all childhood, and later, excess trauma energy is purged from the brain and we learn our emotional limits.

Neuroscience models help us understand our brains for inner healing. Subconscious processes develop multi-level long lasting resonances to construct consciousness and define who we are. Subconscious processes need *conscious reflection* to heal and refine mental protocols.

A basic mind model is that low-energy thinking is high-level thinking, and high-energy thinking is low-level thinking. Anger increases emotional energy. We can think of only a few aggressive options. With low-energy thinking, we can take our time and think of many creative options. Briefly stimulating the mind to its emotional high-energy limits with conflicting neck exercises followed by calming back down promotes healing, and broadens mental and emotional limits. We develop greater reasoning for the things we think and do.

Forced memorization suppresses openness and creativity and creates rigid, limited brain structures and thinking. Governments and religions control citizens and worshipers by promoting memorization. Governments and religions do not encourage creativity to maintain their control. Creativity and mental freedoms expand minds and souls.

Some mind models are:

- Subconscious processes are much faster and more complex than conscious thoughts. Subconscious processes continually compare sensed data with memories to construct conscious potentials for actions and reactions with environments. Competing subconscious resonances iterate, converge, and integrate to gain energy for constructing conscious awareness, thought, and reason. After purging inner trauma distortions, thinking becomes more efficient and confident.
- We should never feel or act above or below anyone. Be cautious of *friends* who act superior to you. Maintain a humble spiritual attitude.
- Be good to everyone independent of gender, race, wealth, and social status. Cherish those who are good to you. Feel free to avoid, dislike, and if possible correct those who abuse you. Persistent abuse destroys health and lives.
- Humans exist near equilibriums. Our bodies absorb and give off relatively equal amounts of radiation, or we would freeze or burn up. We also need emotional equilibriums most of the time to live healthy lives. We need both challenges and successes. Good parents give confidence to and empower their children. Good managers empower employees.
- Electromagnetic radiation from neuron activations is reflected by, and absorbed within, its own and other three-dimensional brain cell membranes. EMR resonances that synchronize and integrate to become strong enough and last long enough create relatively slower human consciousness.
- The physical, mental, and spiritual are a continuum of one existence. God does not consider death as an ending as humans do but as a continuation and refinement of a spiritual awareness and life without the need for *slow* physical bodies.

Subconscious models:

- Sigmund Freud developed a mind model consisting of unconscious and dream processes to understand consciousness. Today we use the word "subconscious" instead of "unconscious." Of course, the mind is more complex than this simple model. Simple models can help us think about and heal our brains and minds. Psychologists have developed complex models for understanding and healing overstressed and distorted minds.
- Mental difficulties occur when the conscious mind denies reality and does not reflect truth to subconscious processes. Using psychiatric models, psychiatrists provide feedback for elevating subconscious trauma effects and feelings into consciousness for repressed emotions and distortions to be understood, resolved, and healed.
- When awake, fast subconscious processes iterate and usually converge to rational, complete conscious thoughts by using heredity, sense, memory, and inner cognition processes. If subconscious processes do not converge, thinking becomes irrational, reactive, and out of control.

We subconsciously and consciously construct mental models of people we meet by analyzing their faces, body languages, words, and actions. Should we like or dislike, trust or distrust, persons we meet? As we get to know people, we usually can predict they will either support or degrade us. We enjoy spending time with those who support us and feel we can also add to their lives. With time and experience, we develop more detailed models of our relationships. The better our models become, the better our relationships and the better we can give and take.

Many of us remain in destructive relationships too long. Our mental health and self-worth decline or plummet. Abusers and bullies usually do not change unless the abused or others force changes. We should work to develop positive, loving relationships with those we meet.

Social scientists develop models to improve human interactions, stability, and happiness. Creative minds are less predictable and are often beyond normal social models.

If mind models predict future activities, we can either benefit from or avoid them. We must teach our children how to think and not just what to think for predicting and experiencing, or avoiding, future interactions. Great discoveries are made and organizations built by those who have learned how to think. They have nurtured detailed, critical thinking.

The universe is intricately constructed. God must have made spiritual and physical models before creating or engineering and constructing the physical universe. Light (electromagnetic radiation, EMR) and gravity are part of God's deep structure language for constructing and evolving the universe in a rather controlled and somewhat *predictable* manner. Physics, chemistry, biology, and other science laws allow humans to grow and control or accept physical changes and human interactions. Probability laws in nature give the universe uncertainties and humans mental skills and freedoms for control of or accepting future activities. Without uncertainties, the future is entirely predictable. We would have nothing to look forward to. Mental, social, science, and spiritual models are our foundations for living our lives and predicting our futures.

L. Ron Hubbard made a creative mind model in his book *Dianetics the Modern Science of Mental Health* that has helped Scientologists *heal* their minds. Mind models help readers think about how the mind works for healing. As in my work, he claims releasing *engrams*, or trauma scars, from the brain allows the mind to heal and be more creative and productive. I believe my mind models will also help heal the mind. Using his mind technology, *auditing*, he founded the Church of Scientology. I do not believe healing the mind should be a religion and do not wish to start a religion with my mind healing technology. I use conflicting exercises rather the *auditing* to release trauma energy from, and heal, the mind.

LIFE SECTION

Chapter 3

EARLY LIFE

"Don't just teach children to read. Teach them to question what they read."

George Cartin

"You have to live your story before being able to write your story."

Amy Shearn

LIFE: 1. the condition that distinguishes humans, animals, and plants from inorganic matter, including the capacity for growth, reproduction, functional activity, and continual change preceding death.

2. the period between the birth and death of a living thing, especially a human being.

During my first manic episode in 1977, I received a strong feeling that babies are born spiritual and without sin. William Wordsworth, an English poet, (1770–1850) also believed this. Life is a miracle.

Emotional thoughts and actions we have before an egg is fertilized affect his/her DNA, RNA, and future descendants. Parents' genetics *integrate* to conceive their baby with God's "Spark of Life." A fertilized egg consists of both parents' DNA architecture. Life is a miracle. God is great!

God and His infinite wisdom are present everywhere. Challenges and traumas in early life eclipse recall of God's perfect wisdom we received upon conception. In life, we must continue, or return to, spiritual thinking and works to recall God's wisdom and our spiritual purpose in life.

Young babies *view* images holistically as equally important. As they grow, they learn which images and sounds build their confidence, or scare them. Young babies innately yearn to feel completeness for gaining confidence. Babies initially think without words but have a genetic ability to mimic parents' speech and understand words.

Babies' brains initially have an abundance of neurons. Their neural networks and brains become specialized reacting to environments. Neuron connections become stronger and faster with repeated use. Unused connections atrophy or become disconnected. In chapter33, conflicting psychiatric exercises strengthen the most used neuron connections and break rigid overstressed connections. Psychiatric exercises release small distinct energy from traumatized neural networks with small distinct sensations.

Authorities argue over genetics and environmental influences on young brains and minds. *Inner* mental *wars* select left- or right-brain dominance for developing baby's reactive thinking protocols. With early right-brain dominance and with less detailed left-brain dominance, we are unable to recall our baby experiences. Integrated or holistic right-brain thinking and dreams usually have less energy and are more difficult to recall. Similar low-energy, semi-conscious memories integrate to construct feelings and memories. Babies' left-brain dominance becomes active later on for interacting with and managing up-close environments, as mental and physical abilities mature.

Baby ingrained traumas eclipse memory and other cognitive functions. Normal holistic right-brain, long-distant functions use less energy as they do not need to initiate and control quick physical responses. Early stresses develop uncertainties and emotionally restrictive thinking limits.

As young children respond to challenges, up-close reacting left-brain dominance develops quick recall and reasoning for reactions. In growing up, children react to demanding environments and lose recall of refined low-energy spiritual memories and purpose. Worldly challenges force the detailed left-brain to store and recall the higher energy physically related memories. Traumas ingrain high-energy, disruptive and reactive *cancers* in the brain that do not interact with normal brain functions.

Young babies' right-brains imprint their parents, *their gods*, activities with awe and little understanding. As words and actions become understood, a child's mind associates early images, activities, feelings, and emotions with related words. Parents must be careful what they say and do around young babies and children. They are powerful role models. Their words and actions mold their children's early and later emotions, decision making, and actions.

Babies and young children react emotionally to fast actions and traumas. If activities exceed genetic, emotional, and learned limits, little minds go out of control. When their minds go out of control, babies are small, weak, and not overly disruptive to parents. Adults losing control are damaging to themselves and disruptive to those around them.

Young babies and children are genetically prepared to reason about environments. Their young minds yearn for new experiences for increased confidence and completeness. From genetics, babies act and react like little humans with their basic needs and securities. They do not react and act like kittens. With little experience and ability, much of early life is frightful. There are few memories to compare with new sensed activities. Young children observe and accept environments and parents' behaviors *as the way things should be.* Good, consistent parents build strong, confident young minds. Alcoholic self-centered parent behaviors are ingrained in babies' brains and minds that may affect their entire lives.

Normally low energy, fast subconscious thinking processes iterate toward conscious completeness. If subconscious iterations fail to converge, thinking becomes and feels incomplete.

Baby's high energy subconscious iterations do not converge to complete, conscious thoughts. Trauma scars are incurred in specific areas of the brain. Babies and young children's continued reactions to activities and traumas build emotional reasoning limits that influence lifetime thinking and activities. Baby thinking is more rational with low mental energy. Speak softly to your babies.

Prayer and spiritual thinking are more effective when surrendering free will to God. Prayer is similar to returning to childhood and surrendering to parents. With humbleness and dedication, we can improve our prayer technology.

Youth are often brainwashed by parents, societies, and religions. Some *religions* even brainwash their children to hate other societies, races, and believers of other faiths. Demented children grow up wanting to destroy anyone different from themselves. The brainwashed, with repressed free will, may believe they are self-reliant and superior to *weak* spiritual believers. The severely abused believe others are not truly happy since they have never experienced confident feelings of happiness.

Bullying attitudes and hatred often continue over generations. Misguided parents brainwash and destroy their children's creativity and spiritual potentials. Integrated world religions, psychology, and mental reconstruction are needed to unite all minds in peace and with love. Jesus' loving and caring spirit is fundamental to nurturing my beliefs. New technologies may improve in-depth thinking and more rewarding future lives if we remain *humble* children of God.

We should make judgements to determine if we have been brainwashed. If parents, religious leaders, or others who have *controlled* our young lives, were strict, and forced us to surrender to their *perfect* ways, we have been brainwashed. We were taught to think and act as we were told. Later in life we will feel that others must say and do things our *perfect way or* our *perfect spiritual way.* If we think we and our ways are *perfect*, we have been brain washed.

At times, we should attempt to think beyond our mental limits. Reading extends our minds. We must listen to others and be quick to agree and slow to disagree. Others' ideas may have merit. Calming the mind and body activates right-brain dominance for building integrated holistic and spiritual thinking structures.

Bright children were usually not brainwashed by parents, teachers, or religions and were taught how to think. They have free wills!

Most brilliant people have had reasonable, nurturing parents with little forced brainwashing and trauma effects. However, some of the most brilliant people have experienced severe difficulties beyond emotional limits and have experienced mental reconstruction on their own. Their minds have rebelled against and purged brainwashed, trauma restrictions. Free will and creative thinking have been regained, and mental limits have expanded with greater mental freedoms. This work is directed toward replacing early disorganized childhood emotional and trauma limits with broader, more organized, rational emotional mental limits.

Spiritual goals are to learn from and survive environments, lessen ingrained trauma effects, and recover babyhood spiritual wisdom and purpose. It is difficult to be self-centered when one truly loves others and an all-powerful God. Parents should not underestimate importance of baby and childhood nurturing, discipline, and teaching of spiritual values.

Childhood rhymes are important as they give young minds quick, supportive feelings of understanding and completion. Best childhood rhymes are pleasant, have repetitious sounds, include meaning, and may even be funny.

One spiritual model is that an infinite God created spiritual babies with free wills for them to learn and reflect knowledge and praises back to Him. God needs praises and positive feedback from humans. We have a purpose. Parents also need positive feedback from their children. With free wills, we may choose to live our lives for ourselves or for others and spiritual purposes.

Chapter 4

SMILE AND FROWN

"God has given you one face, and you make yourself another."

William Shakespeare

Early on, babies observe differences in behaviors when mothers are smiling or frowning. Faces show caring or angry moods. Faces and facial muscles are connected to specialized neural networks with inner feelings and thoughts. The mind subconsciously, and at times consciously, controls the face. Facial expressions normally reflect current thoughts and moods in youth, and over time reflect persistent, long-term moods in older persons' faces. Is your face normally pleasant?

When smiling, faces and brains relax, broaden, and use less energy. Smiling faces show openness to pleasant, interesting ideas and activities. Muscle feedback from smiling faces increases pleasant moods and is conducive to mental reconstruction improvement. Each of us needs to purge our ingrained, limiting trauma restrictions and dysfunctions. Some faces reveal being easily persuaded, independent and reasoning, or aggressive and bullying.

Ingrained repressed trauma energy is more easily released with relaxed faces and brains. Smiling reflects feeling comfortable with ourselves. We judge faces of those we meet, and should also consider how our faces affect ourselves, and those we meet.

Most of us spend our young lives learning to be what parents and teachers wanted us to be. Later, we should ponder our inner thoughts and skills to remold our lives and faces into who we want to be and how we wish to be observed. We must develop inner-confidence to give emotionally to ourselves and others. When comfortable with whom we are, appearances improve and relationships grow.

We recognize that broadened, smiling faces usually indicate outgoing, caring people. Brain processes are more outward and efficient when the face is relaxed and broadened. Thinking is less self-centered and protective of self and develops refined intellectual abilities. We are drawn to people we believe would be interesting to us, and would care for us.

Smiling promotes right-brain dominance for holistic thinking and sharing. Frowning promotes left-brain dominance for up-close reactive thinking and actions, and eclipses open-minded, holistic and spiritual approaches to situations. *Practicing* smiling promotes holistic right-brain dominance.

We should practice broadening the face. Massaging the forehead and cheeks with gentle outward motions, using both hands, increases blood flow to, and naturally broadens, the face. Pleasant facial skin firming sensations are often felt with meditation and repeated gentle massaging of the face. Meditation and facial exercises help us understand who we are. When the face looks and feels good, the brain and mind *feel* good.

Skill is needed in broadening the face. Rubbing horizontally between the eyebrows and on the bridge of the nose releases muscle tensions throughout the face, brain, and body. If rubbing horizontally between the eyebrows and these muscles feel knotted, the face and brain are tense. We are usually unaware of these tensions since they have existed for a long time. We are also unaware of high blood pressure. Rubbing horizontally on these two areas releases tensions. Repeating these exercises frequently keeps facial, and glial muscles in the brain, relaxed for maintaining a versatile brain and mind.

Practice briefly tensing then massaging and relaxing the face until discovering the most relaxed feelings. After a few months of practice, facial firming occurs when meditating on the face, even without the above massaging. Facial exercises and positive attitudes renew facial youth and appearance. With continued exercises, facial skin feels and looks firmer. Advertisers sell all kinds of facial lotions when all that is needed are facial exercises and meditation on the face to firm facial and facial skin muscles.

During meditation and facial exercises, the heartbeat is sometimes sensed within the brain. Subconscious brain processes slow down and synchronize with *slow* heartbeat rhythms. Resonances in the brain synchronize with *heartbeat resonances*. There are synchronized electromagnetic waves between the face, heart, and brain at times during facial meditation. When this occurs, the face usually feels a little flushed.

When receptive to ideas, we open our eyes wide, raise our foreheads, and broaden our faces. Receptive faces and brains synchronize and broaden. Facial and brain reactions are related. We seldom think of their relationship unless we play poker.

Some hide emotions and intent with false poker faces that are meant to confuse and deceive. For our own well-being, we must recognize, and defend ourselves from, the quick and deceptive.

A basic physics principle is that for every action, there is an equal and opposite reaction. This holds true for the face and brain. With pleasant thoughts, it is natural to smile with a broadened face. Smiling rubbing exercises can free the mind of depressing thoughts. Look in the mirror and enjoy your smile.

I frequently smile when meeting people on the street and briefly care for them more than my general caring for people I do not know. I think of their faces and their reactions to my smile. Smiling people are caring people.

We work to maintain self-control in trying circumstances. However, laughter allows us to relax and temporarily not need to have control. Excessive laughter reveals insecurities that may be degrading to observers.

The basics of humor are building up someone or something as important, followed by a rather quick, unexpected uncertainty, nonsense, or failure. Anticipating uncertainty and disconnects adds to humor. Humor easily follows with continued related humor. When laughing, we temporarily forget our troubles. Laughter is the best medicine for a long life.

Humor should always be so far out that everyone involved recognizes the nonsense. I abhor false humor or put-downs that make listeners question themselves. Controlling perpetrators believe their *degrading humor* makes them superior.

When severely depressed, I would look in a mirror and try to smile. My depressed brain and mind could not make my smile muscles work. I was a sad person without a smile and a lost ego. To help heal depression, psychiatrists could ask patients to practice smiling in the mirror.

After mental reconstruction and glancing in a mirror, I realized I was smiling inside and out. My depression was healed. Pleasant thoughts flowed more easily and seemed to fly at times.

A positive attitude has helped my mental reconstruction be successful. Being humble before God has guided inner learning and inspired spiritual beliefs. I appreciate the small things in life more. A smile is never wasted. Even if not returned, we have been spiritual and should feel good about ourselves. Caring is spiritual.

Frowning hides who we are, and *shouts out* that our minds are self-centered, tense and unreceptive. Focus is on inner uncertainties, concerns, or on degrading others. Listening skills are lessened. Extreme frowning by others may ingrain trauma effects or cause us to flee. When frowning and speaking, we are usually not saying what we really think. We are protecting ourselves and hiding who we are. Deep forehead wrinkles reveal long term self-deception and doubting the truthfulness of others.

Persistent frowning, and circular thinking without finding real solutions, degrade confidence and mental health. Localized trauma scars are ingrained by high energy reactions near, or at, emotional limits. Thinking becomes erratic and faces show uncertainty. Severely sunken upper cheeks usually result from extreme abuse and repressed anger. Overstressed minds often remain tense with survival thinking. The severely abused dare anyone to make eye contact. They seem to threaten anyone who might uncover their emotional insecurities.

Graciously accept, or reject, another's ideas. Be your own person. Love all who are good to you, and those needing caring. Respect those who disagree with you. Sometimes, it is difficult to judge who is and is not being good to us. A major criterion is who is giving us confidence. We do not need to like those who mistreat and degrade us. God gave us many emotions to use wisely. Evaluate and forgive wisely. We are not free without mental freedom.

I love to see smiles. They make me happy. This work is meant to help readers understand their inner minds, improve social interactions, and be happy. Blessed are the ties that bind us with love.

Chapter 5

LOVE AND SHARING

"Love one another but make not a bond of love."

Kahlil Gibran, *The Prophet*, 1994

"Love grows by giving. The love we give away is the only love we keep . . ."

Elbert Hubbard

"By all means, marry. If you get a good wife, you'll become happy; if you get a bad one, you'll become a philosopher."

Socrates

"Love is important in marriage. Building confidence in one another is more important for long healthy spiritual lives."

H. Fulcher

Love is an internal subjective state of unselfish loyal and benevolent concern for the good of, and need to be with, another: Perfect love is complete concern for and giving to one another. Perfect parental love is nurturing a newborn baby only expecting some reflection of their lives. Sadly, some never experience feelings of being loved.

The first skill in lasting love and friendship is listening to each other. In one of her shows, Oprah gives her opinion: "True friendship is about kindness and reciprocity, support, and authentic love." She gives traits that make true friends:

Real friends:

- delight in your happiness;
- care about what's happening to you;
- don't try to live your life for you;
- will tell you if you're in dangerous territory;
- and like just being with you, without needing you to entertain them.

We are vulnerable when we love and should review even close relationships, at times. If we love, who and why do we love? If we share, why do we share? What do we expect of ourselves and others when sharing? What do others expect and how do they react when we share with them? It causes an emotional disorder deeply loving someone who does not return our love? Love is learning about our inner selves and the inner selves of those we love.

Before engaging in close and intimate relationships, as in marriage, we must ask ourselves if we are willing and able to please and elevate the person we wish to care for and love. We must also question if our love interest is willing and able to please and elevate us. We should discuss our needs to be happy and to feel complete. During relationships, we need communication models for discussing emotional successes and challenges. Without doing so, there are greater chances of lost happiness, health, wealth, and of divorce. Counseling may help.

Beware of spouses who frequently repeat they need high levels of security. They are takers at our expense. Good relationships are honest and spiritual. Unfortunately, when young, I was taught to love everyone, even those who bullied me. It was not good for my mental health. We must frequently make judgments on who we should or should not continue loving or we may lose our health.

Love and caring are learned by observing loving and caring parents when we were young. Heredity plays a role in loving and in many aspects of life. Loving parents increase love for each other through their baby's reflections of themselves. True love needs reflections of self and trust in loved ones, but grants encouragement and freedoms for loved ones lives to soar. True love surrenders to loved ones in need. Loving husbands and wives reflect each other's lives, grow together, and look more alike over the years. They share the same concerns and laughs that make faces grow alike.

Women seek security in marriage. Arrogant, confident, and financially secure men *are attractive* to women. Women often want security more than love. Men are often attracted to beautiful self-centered women and too often get only illusions of love. False husbands and wives send good spouses to early graves.

I believed an intelligent, attractive women would be a loving wife. I was shocked to find a cold distant stranger and only an illusion of a wife. Basic emotions and truthfulness are nurtured and established in childhood by parents. We hope potential spouses will be loving and truthful in marriage. "Love" means different things depending upon parents and childhoods. Some spouses are truthful to everyone but their spouses. My former, deceased wife was the adult child of two deranged alcoholics. It may be true that, "Men are from Mars, and women are from Venus."

If we meet a marriage prospect, we think is of a higher status than ourselves, will we continue to help him/her be the best he/she can be, or will we work to bring him/her down to our very low-class level? In close relationships and in marriage we should praise and complement each other daily. We both will *grow* and become our best with shared love.

Some Christians believe they must love Jesus more than their spouses and children. They will then be able to love their spouses and children even more.

Can we love too much? If we love too much, some spouses and *friends* will feel superior, and abuse us. True love must be returned. We must share positive activities to maintain and increase our self-worth. We do not need to love or respect those who degrade us. Some bullies degrade their spouses to the point of making them *feel* worthless. They then *dump* their *worthless* spouses to destroy the next victim.

Pre-marital counseling should include role playing of expected pleasant and stressful interactions. Role playing gives prospective husbands and wives models for evaluating later difficulties. They will have models to discuss and reason about their hopes and difficulties. It only takes one to devastate a marriage and a spouse. My former wife and I had no marriage counseling by our minister who was my former wife's friend.

We should evaluate close relationships. Can they become better? If you are controlling and degrading your spouse, get psychiatric help immediately. You are the problem. Controlling people do not love those they control until they lose them. Love is nurturing and spiritual, not controlling.

Controllers may treat some individuals and their own family well but control and degrade others. Controllers only *love* control over their victims.

It may seem natural to distrust people who look and talk differently until interactions build similar, truthful reflections. With world-wide communications today, we may develop greater understanding and sharing with *world-wide* peoples.

Truthful sexual sharing builds warm emotions and feelings of being wanted, cared for, and a willingness to surrender to one another. It is spiritual when sex partners communicate and share needs, likes, dislikes, love, and caring. Love grows with sharing and caring. Sharing sex is an important time for reflecting love and importance to partners and building closeness with eagerness, and patience at times. Sharing love on earth unites souls forever in heaven. Unfortunately, some never feel or give true love and sharing from the heart. Do divorcees collide latter in heaven, or is love restored? Life is, and death maybe, complex.

Anger increases mental energy when defending oneself with lost feelings of completeness. True love usually develops slowly with low mental energy and greater feelings of completeness. For some, love occurs at first sight with hopes of mutual feelings of completeness. Babies give feelings of completeness to parents. Sex may or may not give feelings of emotional completeness.

With greater opportunities in complex lifestyles today, love can be difficult. Spouses may seldom see one another. Separations, over time and distance, challenge marriages.

Successful leaders inspire, and share successes with, their followers and teams. They nurture and anticipate truthful responses and successful completions. Successful leaders and coaches love those they mentor and build successful team confidence. Subordinates should be nurtured to respect and love one another. Loving parents mentoring their children give them increasing freedoms as they grow.

I met a lady, on an airplane, who managed 4000 employees. She told me, "Success in management is sharing the joy of employees' successes." Good managers and leaders need high levels of confidence, love, and caring. It is easier to feel joy in one's own, and one's children's, successes.

At some point in life, each of us will experience personal, family, or work crises. Will our principles and values be strong enough for us to remain true to ourselves, our families, coworkers, and God? Under crises who are we? Can we learn to love our spouses who we have treated well but who have shown little love and concern for us?

I lived eighteen years of marriage without feeling love or sharing being returned. Without returned spiritual love and sharing, we wither away into hopelessness.

Over the years, I loved my wife less and loved my children and God more. In depression, the only reason I did not commit suicide was I could not bear the thought of my two young children not having a father. My parents', young children's and God's, love saved my life in 1977.

Mass murderers do not value their own lives, or the lives of innocent children and adults. They do not feel loved by anyone. Authorities and responsible adults need to identify hateful preparations, and murderous intent on faces and by their actions. After years of being abused or neglected, evil intent shows on faces. Societies should value and improve psychiatry and encourage or *force* troubled children, teenagers, and adults to receive care early on. Psychiatry can change moods and behaviors. Nip hateful and murderous *thinking* in the bud before mass murder becomes a reality. Does the NRA and their paid off Senate and Congress members share responsibility for mass murders in allowing potential murderers to buy automatic weapons? Should they and responsible psychiatrists feel guilty for lost innocent lives?

Chapter 6

PREDICTING

"Science is not about making predictions or performing experiments. Science is about explaining."

Bill Gaede

"All great deeds and all great thoughts have a ridiculous beginning."

Albert Camus

C hildren yearn to increase control of their lives. They know parents are in control of most of their activities. Good parents strive to give their children appropriate levels of control. We like to be in control of our lives and see those we love in control of their lives. When in control we are able to predict more of our futures.

We are inspired by seeing our favorite athletes gain control of their games. We like to predict our heroes and teams will win their goals or games. We are inspired by dancers in synch and in mutual control in their amazing performances.

Our diplomats and generals study our country's needs and positions with other countries and predict our negotiations and military will be successful for our own and allied countries' needs. America strives to support other countries in building up and predicting peaceful and humanitarian leaders. Disappointedly, Russia's goal is to dominate other countries with military threats, force, and wars. This is obviously the case in Russia's attacking Ukraine.

Our minds become more integrated when we are in control of our lives. We learn to reason through and predict situations and opportunities. After aging we can tell who has been in control of their lives by their faces. It is easy to see if one spouse has been controlled in marriage.

We predict we can accomplish routine and challenging tasks we begin. I have spent twenty-eight years renewing my mind and healing my bipolar disorder. I predicted I could discover and develop *my own cure.*

We like people who are predictable to us. We usually know what to expect from our friends. It is heartwarming when someone does something for us better than expected or predicted. Scientists develop theories of nature's laws to be helpful to mankind.

Scientists predict routine and astounding discoveries. They use current knowledge and intelligent guesses to discover physical laws and predict future benefits. Routine and daily predictions are mostly subconscious. Here are some predictions we make:

Routine predictions:

1. Our legs will support walking for routine activities.
2. We will be able to balance on and ride our bicycles.
3. We will recognize and enjoy our friends.

Difficult predictions:

1. Completing tasks requiring stamina – such as running long distances.
2. Completing complex tasks that required developing mental and physical skills.

3. Before manufacturing products, companies predict that their customers will need and buy their products. Steve Jobs, of Apple, predicted people would benefit from and buy Iphones and Ipads.

Limiting predictions:

1. Stretching out and catching a football beyond *current* limits ignoring possible injury.
2. Predicting that conflicting neck exercises will release localized neck, throat, and brainstem trauma energy, with sensations, positively affecting traumatized neural networks.
3. In designing complex nuclear reactor cores, nuclear engineers must predict and control neutron behaviors to produce consistent, safe nuclear power for a city of one million people.

Predicting routine, long-range, and complex outcomes depends upon our experiences, cognitive skills, and educated guesses. Sometimes we make decisions using inner feelings or instincts we cannot easily explain. Creative people learn that if a first prediction does not workout, others might. Without making predictions, we can do nothing. I predict I can think.

Chapter 7

EVALUATIONS

"A stroke of genius is evaluation of vague and difficult things and making them simple for others to understand."

H Fulcher

SCOPE OF EVALUATIONS

For success, we must evaluate ourselves, our children, spouses, work, interactions, engineered devices, and God's influence on our lives. We must evaluate our everyday and challenging thoughts and environments, with respect to our hereditary, reasoning, social, and survival limits. We make evaluations by considering activities and parameters important to our needs. Everyday evaluations are made mostly subconsciously. Marriage evaluations are highly important to our successes and health.

MARRIAGE

Marriage can and should be spiritual. Many have not spiritually evaluated this very personal relationship. Some continue in abusive marriages for years, simply hoping spouses would change and marriages would improve. We should not expect emotional relationships to improve if we continue to accept abuse. *Why have we stayed in abusive relationships so long?* Good marriages extend lives; poor marriages shorten lives.

Abusive spouses scheme to gain power and control over love-based spouses. A husband or wife may be good to others but abuse their spouses. Dominating spousal bullies need to continually "prove" their *false* superiority.

Abused spouses are often too embarrassed or ashamed to admit making poor marriage decisions. They surrender and accept slow emotional murders. Controllers, and the controlled, often lie about their dysfunctional relationships to themselves and to others.

Some spouses are fortunate. Their parents have taught them to think about and evaluate personal relationships while they were growing up. They have learned to evaluate others and their activities. Reacting to conflicting behaviors is difficult for love-based spouses. Before trusting those who we wish to, or must have close relationships with, we must evaluate our likes, dislikes, and security needs, and the truthfulness and intent of prospective friends and lovers.

SOCIAL

We must evaluate our needs and objectives before entering into close relationships. We must communicate to determine if we and they can and will meet mutual expectations. Spouses and friends must evaluate mutual core values, principles, and significant emotional issues to better support one another.

We must be versatile to continue to be healthy and happy. Spouses grow and change over time. An important principle for nurturing relationships is listening carefully and patiently to understand each-others' needs and expectations.

We must evaluate if, and how, difficulties can be resolved. Marriage counseling may help. Reducing value of poor relationships saves emotional pain and suffering. Value your own life as much as you value others' lives. Continuing to give to a taker is dangerous to health and may be slow murder.

CAREER

Most people desire to earn their own security, importance, and achievements. Some believe they are entitled to be dependent on others or on the government. Some spouses, who do not work, develop attitudes of entitlement, and focus on controlling working spouses as their *career.*

Employees are often evaluated unfairly. Some employees intimidate, degrade, and take credit for others' work. Most employees work hard to please the boss, help others, and promote workplace ethics and success. Creativity, hard work, helpfulness, and honesty are traits for career success. Management should praise and reward employees who are productive, dependable, and truthful. Brief humor, at times, helps working relationships. A pleasant atmosphere reduces worry and increases efficiency.

SPIRITUAL

Christian songs espouse beliefs that God is Holy and communicates with believers through prayer in a *complete* way. Believers can learn and improve their mental and prayer technology to be receptive of God's guidance. Through God, our *simple* prayers become holistic and affect the entire universe and heaven to some very, very small extent. God is holistic and Holy. He normally only reflects spiritual information to us we are able to understand. Often, we must lower mental energy to become sensitive to God's ever-present wisdom. At times, others may help us interpret our dreams.

We can only interpret God's perfect communications and truths, with fragile, imprecise *human made words.* We should frequently evaluate our beliefs to practice and improve spiritual lives. We receive spiritual guidance, when surrendering our free wills to God at times. He does not tell us why He chooses us to bear His burdens, but if we follow His guidance, we receive His blessings.

I received an astounding message from God: *"Don't Leave God Out!"* when attempting to finish my first *healing* book in 1995. It seemed to have come from all inner directions. This inner message was so demanding that I immediately accepted it as true and from God. It has inspired my spiritual writing for over twenty-eight years. God inspires us to work spiritually for Him and gives us freedom in meeting His requests. *God learns from our free wills, within our human confinements.* One of God's purposes seems to be to give humans free wills for Him to learn from their lives and prayers. God learns and is the continuing definition of infinite. Humans do not know what *infinite* means.

Jesus predicted He would arise from death to save souls of those who believed in Him. His spiritual teachings have inspired Christians to evaluate Him as Savior and King of Kings.

Chapter 8

ADVENTURE

"We love because it's the only true adventure."

Nikki Giovanni

"It is confidence in our bodies, minds and spirits that allows us to keep looking for new adventures, new directions to grow in and new lessons to learn."

Oprah Winfrey

Adventure: an enthusiastic undertaking with uncertainties and unknown risks, while searching for and expecting a positive outcome.

We should treat our everyday challenges as adventures in searching for family, social, career, and spiritual enrichment. Begin adventures by saying or doing something that adds to another's day or, possibly, life. Everyone's time is valuable; use a brief, gentle approach in assisting others. Listening is essential. We should always be considerate when communicating with others for supporting their and our needs.

Spiritual needs are different at different times. Spiritual leaders and churches provide spiritual adventures when the time is right.

New communications are adventures. Spiritual adventures may nurture discovery of God's Truths. Believers *have abilities to* assist God in His heavenly work. God listens to our prayers otherwise we would be wasting our time praying.

Most humans feel incomplete without social and spiritual support. We must search for heavenly adventures to discover who we are spiritually. After refining spiritual writings, we should share our spiritual adventures with others, when appropriate.

I have lived my healing and spiritual adventure for over twenty-eight years. From mental exercises, inner sensations have felt increasingly pleasant and spiritual. Experienced sensations reflect inner healing. Healing exercises and processes are given in later chapters. Writing can be an integral part of healing and spiritual adventures.

Mental reconstruction has lasted a long time. It has become a way of life for me. The brain, with its inner stresses and conflicts, is complex. I never dreamed my healing and spiritual adventure would be so exciting and last so long. It continues as my amazing adventure. I do not know final destinations but have gladly accepted my long journey.

We need to purge repressed, disruptive influences from our brains and minds to be all we can be. Adventures have short- and long-term goals. Improving and healing the mind is a long-term, profound adventure. We guide our adventures more easily when we think with lowered energy. Adventures can make uncertainties certain.

Chapter 9

CREATIVE THINKING

"An essential aspect of creativity is not being afraid to fail."

Edwin Land

"Creativity requires the courage to let go of certainties."

Erich Fromm

"Great minds discuss ideas. Average minds discuss events. Small minds discuss people."

Henry Thomas Buckle

"Creativity takes courage."

Henri Matisse

The brain and mind are complex. We must think creatively for healing our mental disorders and for improving spiritual communication technologies. Being creative is thinking of new ideas or making things that we have never dreamed of before. Our minds can construct images and ideas we have never seen or heard of before. We must think beyond things we have seen, read, or experienced to be creative. Creative thinking integrates and extrapolates ideas in unusual, and sometimes in usable, ways.

Thinking has three modes:

1. Concentration on use or avoidance of material things encountered every day for pleasure, needs, and survival.
2. Concentration on thinking beyond material things is spiritual. Creative thinking can be devoted to kindness and building confidence within others. Concentrating on feelings, relationships, and ideas without thinking of physical attributes and gains is spiritual thinking. Light acquires physical attributes when interacting with matter. God's *Light and Spiritual Waves* synchronize with, and influence, brain cell activations and brain waves. Our truthful spiritual prayers interact with and influence God. Humans can think and communicate spiritually. Very fast *spiritual waves*, defined latter, must interact with, or be part of, God to create His omniscience and omnipresence. We think and have ability to be spiritual.
3. Continued concentration on and permeating evil for material or psychological gain forfeits acceptance by God. A lost soul becomes so closely connected to the physical that it is buried with the dead body.

What happens if this or that would occur? We must increase abilities to handle expected and unexpected occurrences. Repeating the same old slogans, ideas, and activities builds confidence in restricted thinking and lives.

Brains are like muscles. They do only what they have been doing with some small additional ability for emergencies. Muscles and brains increase in ability when briefly and rationally stressed to limits. Achieving academic and athletic challenges expand abilities to new limits. Likewise, my psychiatric exercises at limits continue to expand mental and spiritual abilities. Individuals staying in their comfort zones lose creative ability.

Dreaming is an important creativity function within the brain and mind. Dreaming processes are mostly subconscious but become conscious upon awakening, at times. Dreams include three-dimensional perspectives of animated dream characters and background scenarios. Dreams include waking experiences, integrations of waking experiences, integrations of waking realities and fabrications, and creative fabrications.

Dreaming minds subconsciously compare and integrate images and their relationships as three-dimensional holographic memory scenarios. Through heredity and subconscious processes, brains have constructed intricate comparison criteria for connecting dreaming activities with waking memories. Heredity has given brains and minds imaginative reasoning structures. Often, unexpected creative ideas emerge without conscious intent. Subconscious processes develop structures for conscious thought.

Perhaps, thousands or more of subconscious hologram picture thinking processes gain energy and integrate to compete for conscious thought. Electromagnetic spikes from subsets of 100 billion neuron activations, synchronize, integrate, and focus to develop a continuous stream of thoughts - the miracle of life!

If a bullet flies across our line of vision, its image passes too quickly for us to see it but is real. Humans see and experience very little of *reality*. If we look at a tree long enough, our eyes and brains develop a mental image of that tree. God *sees* and *processes* information trillions of times faster than humans do to keep up with a very big universe.

After a while, new creative science and spiritual ideas, feel as if known for a long time! We must write-down creative dream and spiritual ideas quickly as they have very low energy and vanish quickly from memory.

Authorities have always been slow to acknowledge highly creative ideas and work. Over a century ago Louis Pasteur was mocked when he discovered that microbes cause human diseases.

Computers and smart phones are opening minds with shared new ideas. Parents and teachers are no longer children's *educational* authorities. The human race is in a new information age. Children talk to their parents less today. They have their heads buried in their cell phones, ipads, and computers. Cell phones and ipads seem to be more interesting than parents. Children become excited to control games on their ipads and cell phones.

Creative exercises may improve memory. We may visualize images of a new acquaintance with images of two people we know, one with the same first name and the other with the same last name. Learning new names can use image integration skills. Often, it is easier to recall images than it is to recall names.

Broadened faces and open minds increase creative ideas. Studying in selected fields, briefly elevating emotions, and then calming back down, promote creativity. Healed, reconstructed minds are more creative than earlier. Remaining at emotional limits very long is not healthy or wise.

Persons who have experienced little uncertainty in their lives are rarely creative. Overcoming uncertainty develops creativity. Writers dreaming up new ideas are creative. Writers must decide to write either this or that word. Once mental creative processes are developed, creative thinking continues more easily.

Young children are awestruck when seeing exciting new things. Eyes and minds are wide open. Experience has taught adults not to be in awe of new situations or things but either accept or ignore them. Many adults have lost childhood creativity and remain in their limited, *confident thinking zones*. However, scientists and inquiring minds continue to be awestruck and creative.

Chapter 10

MIRACLES

"Every moment of light and dark is a miracle."

Walt Whitman

"The miracles on earth are the laws of heaven."

Jean Paul

"To love someone is to see a miracle invisible to others."

François Mauriac

My first recognized miracle occurred when about twelve years old. I first took communion at Ivy Hill United Methodist Church, in Amherst, Virginia. I felt emotionally high for two weeks. I asked my mother several times if Ivy Hill communion used real wine. She always said no. I have wondered about this amazingly pleasant, important feeling over the years.

In 1966, my second miracle was being saved from *expected imminent death* in a near car crash by a *Flash* of emotional memories. See "The Flash," Chapter 22.

In 1977, I experienced another miracle when deeply depressed, suicidal, and standing in my carport. I was deeply depressed and felt more dead than alive and smelled of death. Unusually dark, smoky clouds drifted toward me from all directions. I sensed an unnatural dimension. Soon, I would not be able to breathe. My vision became only in shades of gray.

As shadows darkened and drifted closer, I felt in a dimension of hopelessness within nothingness. I had lost all hope of life. But unexpectedly felt a strange relief. The dark shadows slowly receded. I again became aware of my frail body being present. I had been a shadow of nothingness. A depressed mind began recovering with a faint hope of life. I believe God gave me this near-death vision to inspire me write to spiritually.

During severely depressed times, I could not recall a single word, or speak. I had surrendered, needing death to set me free from a painful mind, body, and life.

Later in 1977 during my first out of control manic episode, my first psychiatrist prescribed Haldol. Within a week, all muscles in my body began cramping. I could not swallow. While lying on a gurney in Lynchburg General Hospital, feeling uncertain of life, I sensed the world around me continuing, without my being present. Spiritual reality was more important than physical reality.

I was admitted into the hospital. In an emergency room; I *envisioned* my beloved parents, aunts, and uncles, looking down over me with great concern. This *vision* was very clear. Some were living and some had passed on. They came together, spiritually, to save my life. My saints *observed* my body, as my feeble mind began to evaporate into my soul and spiritual dimensions. My Uncle Hugh, a neurosurgeon, guided my soul to reconnect with my fragile mind. My beloved parents, aunts, and uncles supported my Uncle Hugh by placing their hands on his shoulders. I can still picture this vision. I could feel their concern and love.

They were aware my soul was leaving my body and were praying for its return to my fragile mind. My Guardian Angels' faiths were strong. With their faith, love, and concern, they and God returned my soul for me to live and write another day. *This spiritual dream miracle* saved my life.

When working on an earlier book in 2008, I attended services at Timberlake United Methodist Church near Lynchburg, Virginia. I was listening to an interesting sermon and the most beautiful *spiritual flash* filled my mind and soul with spiritual wisdom. My mouth dropped open. Instantly, I *knew* my spiritual purpose and my relationship with God.

I again looked toward the minister. My beautiful spiritual wisdom vanished in a flash, as a forgotten dream. I had had a glimpse of *Heaven.* Thoughts seemed so light they flew like angels and traveled as fast and as meaningful as light. I have worked to recall this wonderful spiritual miracle with little success. With humbleness, we sometimes receive spiritual miracles. One day I hope to recall this miracle to live a more joyful, purposeful life.

I have had so many unexpected creative, spiritual ideas while writing this and earlier books. Creative ideas seem new and exciting, but after some time seem to have been known for a long time. So many ideas I have had are more creative than I could have dreamed of without God's assistance.

I thank God daily for creative ideas and miracles He has given me. Spiritual seeds are like *diamonds in the rough.* God gives us freedom to refine His *diamonds in the rough* into human recognized *sparkling, spiritual diamonds.* Humans can only use fragile manmade words to describe God's perfect spiritual waves and wisdom. Often, I cannot think of words to fit creative, spiritual ideas. However, words must be selected and defined.

Answered prayers are miracles. After *expecting imminent death,* each day is a miracle.

Chapter 11

CONFLICT

"You can't solve problems until you understand the other side."

Jeffrey Manber

"Sometimes, God doesn't send you into a battle to win it; He sends you to end it."

Shannon L. Alder

"That's what peace is, right? Postponing the conflict until the thing you were fighting over doesn't matter."

James S.A. Corey

Traumas cause inner conflict, uncertainty, and guilt, even without fault. Nothing occurs within the brain or the universe without conflict. We must decide to do this or that. From physics, for every action, there is an equal and opposite reaction. We must think of, or do, something or nothing. We have a genetic security code that recognizes and reacts quickly to threats. We become more versatile in resolving conflicts with practice, determination, and increased confidence.

Conflicts arise when there are competitive or opposing thoughts or actions, with divergent interests, activities, and goals. Conflicts include struggles for internal and external needs and expectations.

Persistent conflicts cause stress and a myriad of physical and mental dysfunctions. Conflict and stress can be caused by poor health, destructive relationships, unexpected events, and believing one's life is out of control with little hope of it getting better.

It is advantageous to address and resolve personal conflicts early on for mental health and mutual goals. We remain healthier when experiencing brief periods of uncertainty and conflict rather than having low level stress fester for long periods of time.

After experiencing and resolving conflicts from difficult issues, we enjoy life more than ever. Creative thinking is cultivated by resolving difficult conflicts at emotional limits. Diving and catching a football at limits expand physical and mental abilities and builds confidence. Passing a difficult test after months of study increases mental abilities and builds confidence. We have conflicts on options in preparing for and taking difficult tests. What should we spend time on?

Conflicts from traumas and failures limit thinking, actions, and even ability to love. With mental reconstruction practices, we may regain inner confidence and extend mental abilities to genetic limits. Successful emotional decisions made by our ancestors have ingrained genetic mental limits for our thinking, actions, and lives. We think and act like humans not like cats.

Manic-depressives have greater inner conflicts than most people. They have conflicts in integrating their high-energy ideas, moods, and sensed information with related *normal* memories. In mania, minds become overactive and reason becomes distorted as in dreams. The mind has conflicts in judging truthfulness of highly excited manic ideas. The mind is in survival mode.

I briefly experienced conflict and inadequacy when God ask me not to leave Him out of my first book, *Emotional Mind Modeling*, in 1995. Who am I to write spiritually? Possibly because I had experienced near death on more than one occasion. God asked me to write for him but did not tell me how or what to write. I could only write with the skills and knowledge I had and could learn. I have prayed for God's guidance in my writing.

I have written truthfully; however, my work is so different and unusual that readers may have conflicts in believing my mental reconstruction practices and my mental and spiritual discoveries. Many things in life are difficult to believe unless experienced. Unusual experiences and beliefs are continued in later chapters.

I am grateful for having received spiritual blessings and having been *cured of* my bipolar disorder. I have had conflicts in writing about my experiences and responsibilities to readers. Anyone can become overstressed. So many in our military have been traumatized in wars and have stress disorders.

Some spouses and other perpetrators use conflicting body and verbal language to confuse and control the innocent. Without understanding the conflict between body and verbal languages, the innocent suffers uncertainties and trauma scars. Emotional uncertainty occurs in not recognizing the conflict between the two languages. Body language is processed with the right-brain and verbal language is processed with the left-brain. Conflicts between the two brains cause uncertainty, confusion, and stress.

Conflict from the two languages might be that a perpetrator begins saying something that seems to be important while then turning and walking away. If observing someone perpetrating mixed messages, point out the conflict early on. Perpetrators may recognize their confusing actions and stop, or know we understand differences in their two languages, and stop.

Conflicts become ingrained if we emotionally internalize them without resolution. Resolving conflict and releasing inner tensions develops strong, healthy brains and minds. One way in resolving conflicting languages is to describe to the perpetrator that we recognize the conflict in his or her verbal and body messages. Judge if he or she is meaning to be confusing. If the perpetrator is close to you seek joint counseling to keep misleading communications from continuing your anxiety and health issues.

The opposite of conflicting body and verbal languages is nurturing with both words and body language. Without observing nurturing parents, children become self-centered, power-based adults. Caring parents should introduce children to appropriate levels of challenges early on for teaching them to resolve conflicts. Activities observed may be threatening to some but challenging to others.

Chapter 12

BULLYING

Bullying: Seek to harm, intimidate, or coerce someone perceived as vulnerable.

SERENITY PRAYER

"God, grant me the serenity to accept the things I cannot change, courage to change the things I can, and wisdom to know the difference."

Reinhold Niebuhr, Theologian

"It is up to all of us to change the norms around bullying. Adults need to make sure they are positive role models."

Unknown

"Sin is disobeying any of the Ten Commandments."

Billy Graham

"A child who is allowed to be disrespectful to his parents will not have true respect for anyone."

Billy Graham

"The only thing necessary for the triumph of evil is for good men to do nothing."

Edmund Burke

"Childhood bullying *confines* minds for life unless brains and minds are reconstructed."

H. Fulcher

"Evil bullies do not stop unless circumstances change or someone does something to make them stop."

H. Fulcher

"Having to accept early bullying engrained an attitude of accepting bullying. Worst evils came from a wife with alcoholic parents. Bullying is evil."

H. Fulcher

"Love, hate, read, write, live, and die, I see heaven in the sky!"

H. Fulcher

Bullying the weak and innocent is a scourge on all societies and offensive to God. I have spent twenty-eight years mentally reconstructing and healing from severe childhood bullying, spousal abuse, and bipolar disorder. Repeated abuse ingrains emotional limits in young minds that slow and distort learning throughout life. Severe bullies are constantly on victim's minds. Those bullied have been made to believe they can't do important things. Others' thoughts and actions are more important than their own thoughts and actions. What will our bullies do next?

Persistent mental and emotional abuse can be more lasting and damaging than physical abuse. Through mental reconstruction practices, the abused can reclaim overstressed minds and restore confidence in learning and in being themselves.

Parents are normally the most significant role models and either build children's self-confidence and skills or ingrain restrictive emotional behavior thoughts and limits. Bullied children often misbehave because they feel insignificant and nothing else has ever worked. We must build confidence and hope in our *abused* children, or their highest successes may never be attempted, and lost forever.

Morals must be taught early in life. Young bullies abuse those weaker than themselves for *false* superior feelings. Bullies often continue without consequences. Unfortunately, adult bullies often brag to their children about their bullying with pride. Bullying stupidity often continues over generations. Bullies take pride in making victims feel less than human.

Psychology and psychiatry may release children's ingrained, emotional restrictions and increase their creative potentials. Parents and teachers must recognize the long-term damage of bullying and encourage victims and observers to report bullying to authorities. A police officer's warning may stop bullying early on. Preventing bullying is important to America's future. Bullying should be designated as a crime with significant levels of punishment. Societies must work together for health and harmony for all.

In addition to the abused, bullies must also receive psychiatric unlearning or, if necessary, harsh punishment. By preventing bullying early on, parents, psychologists, and psychiatrists will improve both victims' and *bullies'* lives. They may prevent bullies, and the abused, from criminal activities and incarceration later on.

Bullies revel in making victims feel uncertain and inferior. They believe bullying makes them smarter than their victims. Frequently abused victims become less adventurous and less capable. However, since nothing has worked for them, they may turn to aggressive less-thought-out behaviors. *Something has to change.*

Without being able to counter abuse, victims may become subservient. Young victims waste so much time and ability trying to understand and avoid abuse. They have persistent fear of the next abuse. The bullied have difficulty thinking and reading around others, especially the bully, whose thinking and actions have become more important than their own.

Most bullies have had poor parenting and need psychiatric

redirection. They only engage in activities they feel they can be superior to their victims.

It is more difficult to correct bullied attitudes later in life. Behaviors have become ingrained. A possible bold *solution* to childhood bullying is for parents to be aware of and stop childhood bullying, and alert teachers, and parents of bullies, to help prevent bullying. Praise children that stop bullying. Say they are being wonderful. Let teachers, and parents of bullies, know how destructive bullying can be over entire lives.

Persistent bullying often brainwashes victims until they are unable to cope and feel there is no way out. Victims may eventually believe bullies' negative words and actions are justified and become depressed, retreat, and lose purpose. Without hope, counseling, or significant emotional events, victims may become desperate, overact, and become either suicidal or criminals. Too many parents, teachers, and authorities *have allowed* childhood and teenage bullying.

If parents allow sibling or other bullying, they are mostly responsible for their younger children's degraded health and learning disabilities. They must fight for their children's learning and safety. Siblings have similar genetics and should have similar abilities. There needs to be life-changing events or punishment for school and playground bullies.

Wake up parents! Protect your younger children. They have the same DNA as older children to be as successful. Environment matters.

Good parents and role models make young and older children feel comfortable and important. Everyone learns better that way.

A fundamental cause of mental dysfunctions is that victims lie to themselves and accept degrading behaviors, when knowing deep down bullying is not truthful and is harmful. The bullied avoid confrontations with vague hopes of things getting better. We know deep down that continued submissive behaviors are detrimental to the mental health of the abused. We lie to ourselves *to* avoid arguments and confrontations, and sometimes due to fears of harm or divorce. Divorce was looked down on in my family.

Childhood and adult victims have become accustomed to

accepting bullying behaviors, without being able to effectively confront offenders. In marriage, bullied spouses accept bullying behavior to avoid divorce. We are reluctant to admit we were deceived and made horrible marriage decisions. I became depressed, bipolar, and suicidal. *Everything is lost; nothing has worked!* Some bullied victims lose faith in society *and become mass murders.*

For outsiders, it may be difficult to determine who is bullying who. It begins by a bully thinking he/she is superior or inferior in some way. Bullies have a need to make their targets become and feel inferior. The rich and immoral have sinful needs to be or feel superior.

Victims' immune systems are lessened due to persistent uncertainties, worry, and stress. The severely bullied are more susceptible to colds and flus. Confidence and health are affected by bullies over lifetimes.

God gave us appropriate emotions for various circumstances. We should not deny our own well-being and express truthful feelings. However, if negative feelings are unreasonably spread to others who have not harmed us, we need counseling. We must focus our negative feelings only on those who have harmed us.

When bullied at early ages, the mind continues to worry about the next abuse. The poor bullied has less opportunity and freedom to experiment and learn. Abilities are lessened. Parents must be aware that if they do not prevent bullying, they are limiting their younger child's mental ability. As a grown-up, my older brother has been a good brother.

Being bullied early in life lead me to accept my former wife's degrading behavior. I did not counter her alcoholic-like behavior she learned from her alcoholic mother and father when she was young. Her mother was a vicious expert at degrading her husbands and even her daughters. She loved to criticize. My former wife was an *adult child* of two alcoholic parents.

My former wife acted reasonably when we were with others but was degrading when we were alone. She continually avoided intimacy. I felt rejected and unloved in the marriage. Her behavior caused my depression and bipolar disorder. I became angry at myself for accepting and not countering her degrading behavior. I did not know to get counseling until I had become bipolar and needed a psychiatrist.

For my health, we should have divorced early in the marriage. However, I am fortunate since I have two wonderful children, and their families.

SCIENCE
SECTION

Chapter 13

NEUROSCIENCE

"Wisdom begins in wonder."

Socrates

"What we think we become."

Buddha

The brain is neither predetermined or unchanging, but rather is an organ of adaptation.

Schore, 1994: Siegel, 1999

Neuroscience: Any of the sciences, such as neuroanatomy and neurobiology that study, research, and deal with the nervous system.

Mental hologram: subconscious and conscious higher dimensional *picture* living electromagnetic resonances in the brain that create the mind.

This neuroscience model is an introduction to the brain for assisting healing of mental disorders. Models do not need to be detailed or complete to assist in healing.

Babies are born with genetic preparedness to think about self and environments. Babies' brains have more connections than adult brains. As babies' thinking abilities become specialized to interact with and survive *their* environments, their brains grow and neurons make strong connections. Over time, weak neuron connections do not grow but atrophy or become disconnected. The strongest neuron connections have reacted to severe environments for survival. My mental reconstruction practices, given later, break both weak, and rigid overstressed, neural networks for healing mental disorders and developing strong, specialized subconscious and conscious abilities.

We must free our brains of ingrained afflictions by briefly extending our minds to limits, at times. Some understanding of the brain's architecture and its limits is useful for mental reconstruction and psychiatric healing. Having bipolar disorder, being healed of the disorder, and practicing mental reconstruction, one *senses* approaching emotional limits. Mental limits were originally framed by genetics and ingrained by baby and later traumas and possibly by exciting high-level successes which have extended brains and minds above current limits. The mind either goes out of control or extends emotional limits and abilities depending on approaches to limits.

Neuroscientists study neuron activation frequencies, locations, spike profiles, neurotransmitters, and neural connectivity to understand and improve thinking and *gauge* emotions for appropriate reactions and responses. Neuroscientists and physicians use electroencephalograms to measure charge patterns on the scalp for analyzing brain activities. The brain creates the mind, and the subconscious mind can be carefully extended to limits for healing the brain and mind.

The brain's surface charge contours vary with perception and analytical activities. Each glance produces a symphony of changing neuron activations for creating a flowing awareness and cognition.

This Neuroscience Chapter is based mostly upon CD lectures, *Understanding the Brain,* by Professor Jeanette Norden, of Vanderbilt University School of Medicine, and The Teaching Company, 2007. I present neuroscience at elementary levels to assist healing my and reader's mental disorders.

Neuron chemical activations accelerate electrons to make electromagnetic radiation, Light, which is transmitted to and affects other neurons and their membranes as it filters through various areas and compositions of the brain.

Light from neuron activations integrate to create electromagnetic resonances within the brain or within limited areas of the brain. This Light stimulates other neurons with similar resonances to initiate further activations in the brain. Transmitted neurochemicals through axons to dendrites influence activations of connected neurons. Resonating, synchronized electromagnetic radiation is the brain's fundamental tool for producing consciousness and cognition.

There are levels of uncertainty in the timing of neuron activations. Synchronized EMR from thousands or even millions of neurons integrate to create *relatively slow changing* resonances for awareness and cognition.

Relatively slow conscious resonances are created by integration of *thousands* of fast subconscious resonances and their harmonics. Subconscious processes need consistent conscious feedback to maintain supportive harmonic conscious resonances. Dysfunctions occur when the conscious mind denies reality and does not provide truthful feedback to very fast subconscious harmonic processes.

Psychiatrists and my mental reconstruction processes provide feedback to the subconscious *mind* for it to recognize and heal non-converging *subconscious* processes that do not support conscious *completeness.*

Neurons consist of a cell body, one axon, and up to 7,000 dendrites. Neurons are connected with other neurons by harmonic EMR resonances, axons, synapses, and dendrites. Electromagnetic wave information travels much faster than axon to dendrite information transmissions.

Pre-synaptic neurons influence post-synaptic neurons by sending neurotransmitters along their axons and through mutual synapses to dendrites of numerous other neurons. Neurotransmitters are chemicals that are transferred between neurons to influence one another. Neurotransmitters from pre-synaptic neurons promote or suppress activations of post–synaptic neurons.

Nuclei are groupings of neuron networks with specialized purposes. Neuron connections and communications are more complex than those of the internet.

Plasticity is the property of neurons and synapses to change their internal parameters or functions over activation histories. Neural networks, neurons, and neural membranes increase in structure and detail as they store lifetime memories. Memory is stored by electromagnetic radiation reflecting by, filtering through, and being absorbed by neural membranes.

The brainstem, located at the top of the spinal cord, receives signals from nerves throughout the body, and transfers signals to various brain components. The brainstem is composed of several groupings of nerve cells. The reticular formation extends along the length of the brainstem and is most active during sleep. The aminergic cluster is concentrated in the dorsal raphe nucleus near the top of the brainstem and is most active during waking. These two areas of the brainstem compete to suppress each other's activations for either sleeping or waking dominance.

The limbic system surrounds the brainstem, is an older component of the brain, and includes the brain's fast response system. When stimuli are too strong or fast, neural networks in the brainstem activate the hippocampus and the brain's fast response system. The limbic system produces fast, emotional fight or flight responses. Reacting to normal stimuli, the limbic system passes information to the higher reasoning cerebral hemispheres.

If stimuli are too energetic, occur too quickly, and are above higher mental reasoning energy limits, the fast response limbic system restricts or limits high-energy emotional stimuli from adversely affecting the fragile slower reacting, higher reasoning upper brain.

The cerebral hemispheres surround the limbic system and are the newest part of the brain. Dark grayish matter is a small distance below the surface of the cerebrum. It is composed mostly of neuron cell bodies and is associated with cognition.

White matter consists of glial support cells and nerve fibers below the cortex, the outer layer of the cerebrum. The cortex transmits signals between cerebral regions, modulates neuron activation potentials, supports learning, and may be involved in mental dysfunctions.

Nearly 24,000 genes comprise the blueprint of 100 trillion cells in the human body. There are approximately 100 billion neurons and 600 trillion synapse connections within the human brain. Neurons are connected to communicate information and work together. Humans have a lot to think with and about.

The brain is complex and takes a long time to heal. It is amazing that activities of so many complex brain structures can integrate to focus on one idea or image!

Sight neurons are thought to activate the fastest. Stimulated neurons normally activate 20 to 30 times each second. Under the most stimulated conditions, neurons do not activate faster than 100 times per second. A typical neuron electromagnetic spike lasts about one thousandth of a second. Stimulated neurons spend about ninety-seven percent of their time chemically charging and three percent of their time firing or discharging. Negative impulses from pre-synaptic neurons slow spike rates of post-synaptic neurons.

Neurons rapidly fully discharge and recharge relatively slowly. My theory is that after firing, overstressed traumatized neurons again overcharge and remain overstressed and *rigid*. Recall therapy and mental reconstruction briefly stress traumatized neural networks beyond limits for releasing ingrained, repressed energy. If activated beyond high-energy limits by conflicting psychiatric exercises, traumatized overstressed neural networks return to more normal energy processing levels and reconnect with normal brain functions.

When any neuron activates, its EMR, Light, expands outward within the brain at the speed of light. All neurons are different. They have unique shapes, chemical characteristics, and spike profiles. Synchronization and coordination of neural activations are fundamental to consciousness and cognition.

EMR from activating neurons imprint *mental picture* energy information on their own membranes and then on numerous other neuron membranes. Neuron activations do not completely overlap, creating continuous EMR resonances and, when waking, continuous consciousness. Synchronized neuron spikes cultivate mental hologram details on brain cell membranes. After *numerous* neural membrane reflections and absorptions, EMR finally splits into "strings" affecting individual membrane molecules. While alive, neuron activated EMR continually filters throughout our brains. As a reminder, *Brain cells* refer to both neuron and glia support cells.

EMR is reflected and diffracted many times within the brain as it deposits its refined details on and within numerous neuron membranes until its energy is absorbed in, or escapes, the brain. Subsequent EMR adds definition to brain cell membranes by overlaying Light harmonics onto earlier absorbed, or *reference,* EMR imprints on brain cell membranes. Depending upon spike energy and profiles, some neuron Light is absorbed by distant brain cell membranes with similar resonances.

Neuron integrated resonances must change slow enough and last long enough for creating awareness and consciousness. Humans sense environments with their eyes, ears, taste, touch, and smell to develop *limited human reality.* Consciousness is created by symphonies of *long-lasting* electromagnetic resonances filtering through brain cell components and membranes. Light is reflected, absorbed by, and passes through brain cell membranes and brain surfaces.

Adaptive and synchronized electromagnetic neuron activations are stimulated by sense and from memory data each fraction of a second. Similar memory and sense produced EMR frequencies synchronize and integrate to increase in energy competing for consciousness. Integrated sense and memory electromagnetic resonances produce relatively longer lasting conscious resonances. Longer lasting conscious resonances are created by *greater membrane reflective surfaces.* Dream and subconscious waking mental holograms imprint short- and long-range memories on various brain cell membranes.

The sharpest, most energetic, neuron EMR spikes travel to more distant neuron membranes for wider influence before being absorbed. Two radios, at different distances from a radio station, tuned to the same frequency receive the same music. Each neuron is a mental radio station and a mental radio.

A tuned radio receives and absorbs energy from only one specific EMR frequency. Energy and information from other radio frequencies pass through this radio and are not absorbed. We want our radio to absorb energy, information, and music from only our selected station frequency. Activating neurons are mental radio stations and brain membranes are mental radios.

I am unaware of researchers studying neuron and glia membrane fabric for determining their reflective and absorption properties. Brain cell membrane fabric must have capabilities beyond that of photo film for humans to store and recall lifetime three-dimensional experiences. Remembered dream scenarios are proof that higher-dimensional mental holograms are fundamental to mental processes and cognition.

Genetics, and traumatic experiences, construct resonating EMR mental limits for analyzing and gauging sensed information for reactions and security responses. Reasonable decisions and behaviors depend upon an individual's history of mental, spiritual, social and physical successes and failures. Emotional thoughts and decisions produce physiological change or plasticity to neurons and their membranes.

The pre-frontal cortex processes emotions and is active in moral decisions. Morals are influenced by heredity, learning, reason, and survival reactions.

Cocaine and heroin activate the brain's pleasure reward system creating an internal subjective sense of joy, *for doing nothing.* They create false minds. Anticipating and achieving success with excitement develops true joy.

Glial cells provide the brain's structure. In young brains, they also guide axons to connect with specific neuron networks in more distant areas of the brain. Brain growth is rather preplanned. In a healthy baby, there is little randomness in his trillions of neuron connections. My brain model does not need to be one hundred percent correct to assist mental reconstruction

There are 150 different types of neurons in the human brain. Healthy brain growth is guided by heredity, physics and biochemical processes, and experiences. Brains with 100 billion neurons functioning together are miracles of life. Integrations of Light, EMR, throughout the brain create spiritual awareness.

Eyes have approximately 120 million rods and 6 to 7 million cones as photoreceptors. Sight neuron activations in the brain integrate individual EMR nerve signals to create smooth *continuous, meaningful vision*. Rod and cone EMR resonances must last beyond threshold time limits to create vision. Rods and cones develop unique resonances, and when energetic and lasting long enough, produce their specks of vision. Subconscious resonances synchronize and integrate to create longer lasting conscious resonances. If an object crosses our line of sight too fast, vision is not created.

The more neuroscientists learn about brain activities and inter-communications, the better healing, reasoning, and managing pain will become. Models of the brain do not need to be so detailed, to promote inner healing. We only need a feeling that we can reason about our brains and minds. A goal is to develop readers' confidence in healing their afflictions. Truly confident people experience inner peace, and do not harm others or cause wars. Jesus was spiritually confident, healed the sick, and changed the world.

Neurobiologists research animal brain behaviors to find solutions to human illnesses and disorders. In animal experiments, activating specific genes enhances memory. Deactivating certain genes blocks emotional memories. The goal is to alter animal brains and minds to discover healing events and medications for humans. Difficult experiments and assumptions must be made to determine whether human brains and minds will be affected similarly. Goals are to heal and prevent human disorders.

Stem cells are versatile and transform into all other brain and body cell types, depending upon influences and resonances of nearby cells. After being transformed, stem cells maintain their structure and function over lifetimes. All cells in the body and brain have the same DNA. Some genes have greater influence on growth and other functions than other genes. Cultivated injected molecules attach to specific genes and cause similar molecules to attach to similar genes.

Some genes have dominant influence on early growth. Thousands of regulatory genes have greater influence on behaviors. There are debates over gene and environmental influences on early brain growth, mental development, memory, and behaviors.

Each person has a library of information within their genes. For long term memory, molecules attach to and change DNA functions, but do not change gene sequencing structures. Experimental molecule infusions promote resonances for bonding with specific gene molecules. Injected neuro-catalysts influence and change gene expression.

Neurobiology experimentation is currently performed only on animals. For future human benefit, assumptions must be made as to whether animal brain experiments will have similar influences on human brains. Neurosurgeons and neurobiologists must have regulatory permission to perform new gene editing and other types of experiments and surgeries on human brains. Decisions must be made between benefits and risks. Doctors and researchers must do no harm to human patients. My neuroscience model does not need to be absolutely correct to promote mental reconstruction healing.

Chapter 14

PHYSICS OF THE BRAIN

"We are all now connected by the Internet, like neurons in a giant brain."

Stephen Hawking

"Whoever it was who searched the heavens with a telescope and found no God would not have found the human mind if he had searched the brain with a microscope."

George Santayana

"The human brain may be God's most implausible experiment. Scientists explore to understand and benefit from God's creations."

H. Fulcher

Physics: The branch of science concerned with the nature and properties of matter and energy. The study of physics, distinguished from that of chemistry and biology, includes mechanics, heat, light, radiation, sound, electricity, magnetism, and the structure of atoms.

Diffraction: The process by which a beam of light or other system of waves is spread out as a result of passing through a narrow aperture or across an edge, typically accompanied by interference between the wave forms produced. (Depending upon frequencies and phases, Light waves either amplify or negate each other when interacting with a narrow aperture or edge of a structure.)

Refraction - The fact or phenomenon of light, radio waves, etc., being deflected in passing obliquely through the interface between one medium and another or through a medium of varying density. Refraction is the change in direction of propagation and speed of any electro-magnetic wave as a result of traveling through different media along its wave front.

Notes:

1. To simplify language, the capitalized word, "Light," refers to the entire neuron produced electromagnetic, EMR, spectrum.
2. Italicized *"Light"* refers to my spiritual model of *All integrated Light* traveling throughout the universe and heaven creating God's existence, power, and spiritual abilities. Model: God is all *Integrated Light and Spiritual Waves* traveling throughout the universe and heaven.
3. *"Brain cells"* refer to neurons and glial support cells.
4. "Nuclei," refers to groups of *related neurons* with specific purposes. Note: "Nuclei" also refers to centers of atoms.
5. *Assumption:* Fluid brain matter has less influence in interacting with Light and constructing memories than more structured brain cell membranes.
6. Theory: Mental and dream holograms are the working media for constructing dreams, memory, and cognition.

Definitions were given above as this chapter is a creative model and more technical than earlier chapters. The definition of *resonance* was given in the Modeling Chapter 2. Diffraction and refraction are physics terms that define Light interface characteristics between different surfaces, including surfaces within the brain. There are many brain textures that affect Light reflection, diffraction, and refraction.

If models contain some level of reality, readers may also experience unusual, pleasant inner brain sensations resulting from psychiatric exercises. Trauma scar sensations are released from my throat, neck, and brainstem when practicing psychiatric exercises. This may also be true for readers, especially bipolar suffers. After years of exercises and meditation, emotional wide-spread energy releases were sensed within the brain. One should not continue activities that cause pain over a few seconds.

This chapter emphasizes electromagnetic radiation (EMR) activities within the brain. Little effort is focused on chemistry of the brain. Studying physics of the brain stimulates inner awareness, mental healing, and more control over emotional and stressful thinking. We must fight for our freedom of thought, actions, and beliefs, or others will dictate our thoughts, actions, and beliefs.

Light, EMR, from one neuron activation does not create an idea. *Integrated EMR* from billions of neuron activations creates the mind and supports *spiritual awareness. Integration* is an important concept in modeling and understanding the brain, mind, and God.

Light from neuron activations passing through its own cell membrane, splits into *coherent beams.* Less reflected split EMR act as reference beams for greater reflected coherent sister beams, when both are absorbed within the same neural membrane. EMR from one neuron is transmitted, reflected, diffracted, and refracted many times before being completely absorbed and *integrated* within other neuron membranes for creating mental holograms. Mental holograms include information in more dimensions than that of photographic holograms. Mental hologram dimensions include emotions, levels of belief, and speeds of changes.

If a *thin* photographic film can absorb light energy to create and store three-dimensional holographic images, complex three-dimensional neural membrane *photo film* can create higher dimensional memory hologram scenarios that are always present and ready to *view* quicker than family photos. EMR from one firing neuron with its distinct properties and filtering through the brain may influence memory holograms within neural membranes in one neural network or one component of the brain.

Neuron spikes are very fast, around *one thousandth* of a second, creating very fast waves and resonances. Resonances must integrate and last long enough to create slowly varying images at conscious speeds. Reflections, diffractions, and refractions create changing EMR resonances on brain membranes. With slow mental resonances, we think; therefore, we exist.

Our minds imagine three-dimensional images when viewing two-dimensional photographs or television screens. Our subconscious minds continually search for meaning and *reality*. EMR resonances within the brain construct four and higher dimensional mental holograms by *writing to* and *reading from* complex arrays of *three-dimensional* brain cell membrane *photo film*. Mental processes are much more complex than writing to and reading from computer CDs. Memories contain emotions and speed of change.

Integrated Light affecting neuron membrane holograms create consciousness. EMR passing through *millions* of somewhat different, randomly oriented neuron membranes are diffracted and absorbed at various angles. To more completely model the brain, we must include membrane locations, orientations, thicknesses, and chemical compositions. Related small membrane *molecule areas* with the same orientation *create one mental hologram*. Coherent neuron Light waves become more detailed as they are transmitted through complex oriented neuron molecules.

Human memories and dreams consist of three-dimensional image and background scenarios. Overall or holistic scenario color shading might represent emotions and speeds of changes. Changing mental hologram content is the foundations of memory and cognition. All hologram memory content is subconscious unless recalled when awake or when awakening as dreams slow down to conscious speeds.

Coherent Light resonances constructing mental holograms having the same frequencies and phase angles are absorbed within membrane molecules sensitive to those resonances. Coherent Light has wave highs and lows in the same phases. EMR frequencies, profiles, and resonances, from similar neuron activations integrate to form unique *memory* hologram images within neuron membranes sensitive to those resonances. Neuron membrane resonances change relatively slowly over time with continued absorbed Light energy forming new memory information. Conscious mental images are created by Light affecting thousands or *millions* of complex three-dimensional membrane resonances. Resonating Light, electromagnetic radiation is absorbed by neural membranes sensitive to those resonances.

Mental hologram variations, comparisons, and integrations form inner mental language processes that develop consciousness when energetic enough and lasting long enough. Weaker integrated semiconscious resonances construct feelings, emotions, and uncertain thoughts. Pondering persistent thoughts over time develop specialized neural networks for constructing and recalling frequent ideas easier, faster, and with confidence.

Verbal and picture languages are our everyday communication tools. They are converted or translated to electromagnetic resonances within the brain.

EMR imprints on and within brain cell membrane molecules are overlapped by later coherent EMR for creating similar memories. Coherent EMR striking brain cell membranes at wider angles have greater influence than direct non-coherent EMR for constructing refined, high-definition mental holograms for consciousness.

EMR from neuron and nuclei activations and absorbed by brain cell membranes are similar to specific waves from radio stations absorbed by radios. Radio stations have specific frequencies that radio listeners choose to select. Radios at different distances from radio stations receive the same radio waves and information. Dissipation over distance loses clarity. The same neuron frequencies are absorbed by near and far brain cell membranes sensitive to those frequencies.

Radios not completely tuned to radio stations receive distorted reception. This is also true with brain cell membrane sensitivities. Integrated neuron EMR *waves* slightly different from neural membrane sensitivities are absorbed less with levels of distortion. Distortions degrade thought confidence and clarity.

Spikes from neurons have distinct energy and profile characteristics. Neuron EMR, transmitted through its own irregular membrane, is not symmetric but contains irregular profiles or waveforms exploding outward in three-dimensions.

Neurotransmitters sent along axons to dendrites of other neurons also have unique characteristics. Neuron spike and neurotransmitter *footprints* are absorbed by many braincell bodies and membranes.

Light within the brain is traveling information energy with the potential to share that information with similar membrane resonances within the brain. Light within the brain begins when calcium, sodium, potassium, and chloride *explode* within neurons creating distinct Light, or electromagnetic, waves. Each neuron activation *flash* creates its own unique expanding Light energy and information profile. Neuron Light energy and information exploding outward in all directions influences and is influenced by its own and other brain cell membranes as it travels within the brain. Neuron membranes have been cultured by neuron Light throughout lifetimes. Each neuron membrane segment uniquely influences Light that passes through it or is absorbed by it. Light ingrains information structures on membranes as it is reflected or absorbed.

There is no perfect reflection. Light is cultured by both reflection by and transmission though membranes and other matter. Absorbed Light is converted to physical and chemical energy information. Coherent neuron Light waves add chemical energy information to membranes of one neuron or nuclei for a specific memory.

Light energy and information traveling throughout the brain becomes integrated and greater than the sum of its sources, developing integrated memories. Complex, integrated Light creates the human mind. Information from sense nerves influences, and synchronizes neuron information throughout the brain developing consciousness. Light traveling at the *speed of light* experiences a very different time and space than that of human sensed *physical* time and space. On a much higher scale, God is the integration of all Light and Spiritual Wave potentials and information within the universe and Heaven.

My "Brain String Theory" describes Light from one neuron activation exploding outward in all directions at *the speed of light* gaining complex details. Light travels slower in brain textures. Light (EMR) emitted by a neuron activation is:

1. Reflected by its inner membrane surface;
2. Transmitted through its inner membrane surface;
3. Absorbed within its own membrane;
4. Reflected by its outer membrane surface;
5. Repeatedly reflected and resonated between its own inner and outer membrane surfaces, imprinting energy and information in its own membrane;
6. Transmitted through its outer membrane surface;
7. Absorbed and slowed to some lesser extent by non-cell matter in the brain, or transmitted to the surface of another neuron or glia cell;
8. Reflected by another cell's outer membrane surface with loss of energy;
9. Transmitted through another cell's outer membrane surface at widening angles and longer wavelengths from diffraction and refraction. Light slows when diffracted by denser media;
10. Absorbed by another cell's membrane;
11. Reflected by another membrane's inner surface;
12. Repeatedly reflected between inner and outer membrane surfaces of other brain cells imprinting energy and information;
13. Similar activities continue possibly throughout *thousands or millions* of brain cells creating mental holograms and consciousness.
14. Neuron emitted Light is reflected, diffracted, and refracted, many times before being completely absorbed, adding energy and information to many neuron membranes.

The above EMR activities are repeated billions of times throughout the brain creating complex, integrated three-dimensional subconscious processes for creating human memory and minds. Resonances that converge, become slow enough, and last long enough create conscious resonances. Integration of subconscious processes and retrieved memory from brain cell membranes occurs at *the speed of light* in mass. When resonances last long enough, relatively slower conscious resonances are constructed. Conscious reactions and thoughts are much, much slower than the speed of light.

Sight consists of millions of resonances from rods and cones, which are integrated in the brain to construct flowing conscious images. Human sight and brains are amazing.

Resonating electromagnetic waves die out as their energy is absorbed within or escapes the brain. Awareness of one moment dies out as energy dissipates and is reborn by resonating EMR from the next partially overlapping generation of neuron activations and resonances. Neuron information is disseminated throughout the brain at the speed of light, and much slower through axon and dendrite neurotransmitters for coordinating neuron activations, thoughts, responses, and moods.

My theory is that specific Neuron EMR is absorbed mostly by membrane nuclei membranes sensitive to its frequency. Nuclei membrane molecules with differing resonances reflect or transmit different EMR frequencies.

Light passing through multiple membranes is refracted into widening angles with lower frequencies and longer wavelengths. Successive membrane refractions imprint increasingly widening EMR waves for wider, detailed holograms. EMR waves travel through membranes until strings become only individual quanta of Light energy deposited within one atom or molecule. This is my "Brain String Theory."

Individuals who think of, and react to, many different challenges will have diverse, detailed brain cell membrane structures supporting greater detailed mental hologram scenarios and thoughts. Subconscious Light processes compare and integrate sensed information with membrane memories to create subconscious and conscious mental abilities. Hereditary resonances and current long-lasting emotional Light resonances integrate as memory and reasoning skills on neuron membranes.

Complex subconscious processes iterate, converge, and integrate Light to form simpler conscious processes for thinking. Two individuals sharing the same idea will have very different subconscious processes for developing that idea. Subconscious processes iterate at *nearly* one *million* times faster than conscious thinking. Inner processes are cultivated by genetics and personal histories.

Subconscious iterative processes for thinking converge to various levels of completion. Researchers should study neuron spike shapes and membrane properties for understanding integration and development of mental hologram scenarios and consciousness. They should study neuron EMR transmissions, reflections, diffractions, refractions, and absorption properties of neuron membranes and other brain matter to understand brain characteristics and functions. They might generally determine numbers of reflections before complete absorptions. As an experiment, artificial neuron Light might be focused onto *living external neuron membranes* to measure their properties.

What could be more logical for understanding the brain and mind than constructing *physics models* of the brain? Scientists work to discover God's logic in designing, constructing, and evolving the universe and also to understand human brains and minds. *Integration of Light* is fundamental to my elementary models of human conscious and God's infinite abilities. At each point in space God has infinite spiritual resonances and infinite perspectives of spiritual resonances. God is omniscient and omnipresent.

In *Psychiatric Exercises* (CH. 33) and *Mental Reconstruction* (Ch. 34,) brief emotionally limiting psychiatric exercises connect muscle and nerve activities to brain activities and responsibilities. Stimulating and releasing excess trauma and emotional energy from overstressed brain cells resynchronizes them with normal brain cell activities. The brain and mind become less emotional and more rational with less energy.

Models and theories need to be realistic enough to assist readers and brain researchers to understand importance of releasing trauma energy for healing disorders and other mental afflictions. Mental dysfunctions are difficult to recognize since most have been ingrained since childhood. Readers following practices in this book may or may not receive similar benefits to those I have experienced. If readers have experienced severe challenges and fought back death, they may learn the unlearnable and survive the un-survivable. Healed minds overcome uncertainties and become creative!

As a thought example, Light images are focused and absorbed by video cameras and converted to electromagnetic wave energy information that is converted to television screen images. Television images are transmitted to our eyes through light and then again converted to electromagnetic radiation for mental awareness promoting human thoughts and memories.

Light, EMR, in the brain, absorbs information from its related nerve origins. EMR experiences brain cell reflections, diffractions, refractions, and transmissions and is finally chemically absorbed. During transmissions and absorptions, Light gives chemical energy and information to brain membrane molecules. Light and information from one neuron integrate with that of many other neurons to create integrated *subconscious* information that if energetic enough and resonating for about one tenth of a second create consciousness. Light, imparting energy and information to brain molecules, creates memories, consciousness, and other brain functions. Light and its information, within the brain creates a sense of being, touch, hearing, and sight. Thinking is complex.

In daily lives if light is reflected by a person, our eyes are able to receive light information about that person. We see.

Chapter 15
PHILOSOPHY OF PERFECT

"The true work of art is but a shadow of the divine perfection."

Michelangelo

"There is no limit to how good you can get in pursuit of perfection."

Sachin Kumar Puli

"The perfection of Christian character depends wholly upon the grace and strength found alone in God."

Ellen G. White

"Perfection spawns doctrines, dictators and totalitarian ideas."

Antonio Tabucchi

"Perfection is defined as God's current *infinite* state. He learns from prayers and evolves perfectly."

H Fulcher

Perfection - condition, state, or quality of being free or as free as possible from all flaws and defects

Philosophers reason about the present and future. They make theories to explain physical laws and spiritual beliefs. Proven theories help us reason about and advance our lives. Human theories, ideas, and actions are never perfect.

God communicates through His perfect spiritual waves and resonances. We communicate with God subconsciously and consciously. Wisdom within His perfect spiritual waves can only be translated into fragile, imperfect manmade words and language. Writers and translators of traditional spiritual books, including the Bible, were amazing but not perfect. Humans strive for spiritual certainty but have mental and spiritual limits. Humans have limited concept of God's infinite perfection.

Spiritual writers and translators must strive to be as truthful as possible. Humans do not understand the purpose of every atom and every ray of light. Humans are biased toward their own thoughts and toward those they know and love. Individuals speaking or writing about an involved event give different shades of meaning. Writers never remember completely or write identically about observed or experienced events. Perfection to one may be lacking to another. Some writers are better than others. The same words may be inspiring to some and overwhelming to others.

God's exceedingly fast perfect spiritual waves travel throughout heaven and the universe with perfect complete spiritual wisdom. He does not usually speak in imperfect manmade words. God chooses spiritual leaders to translate His perfect spiritual waves into *earlier defined*, *truthful* human words.

Spiritual books contain ambiguous word translations of God's perfect spiritual waves. However, *the Word of God* is a good traditional shortcut for translations of God's perfect spiritual waves. Very fast spiritual waves are consistent and perfect in the sense that Light and gravity laws are consistent and perfect. Scientists do not know all the characteristics of God's perfect *Light* and *gravity* laws in the universe, especially, in black holes.

"Perfect" is frequently used to intimidate and control. Fundamental Christian leaders refer to the Bible as God's Perfect

Word. They preach that the Bible cannot be questioned, added to, or subtracted from. Humans, with their weaknesses, uncertainties, and fears are attracted to the word *perfect*, and *an all knowing, all powerful, perfect God.* Christians and believers of other faiths have pride and gain power in memorizing and repeating *God's Perfect Word.* Christian scientists strive to understand God's perfect constant physical and *spiritual* laws to benefit mankind.

Jesus set the standard for living a spiritual life. However, He did not teach advanced science to improve followers' lives. Spiritual achievement seemed to be independent of science and technology. Jesus' miracles must have included physical and spiritual technologies. Would Jesus have been "more" perfect if He shared His miracle technologies more fully? Today, medical researchers and physicians share their healing technologies.

If someone or something is perfect one day, can he or it become more perfect later? Must perfect be constant for all times? Christians believe Jesus' life, miracles, and crucifixion defined perfection and His spirit continues to save Christians' souls, forever.

Creation of the universe and human life are miracles to humans but understandable to God. We may understand some things that others consider miracles. Others may understand things we consider miracles.

To be spiritual and know God, we must reconstruct our brains and minds to be cleared of trauma effects. Clear minds will feel God deep within their souls.

Questioning religions for understanding may deepen personal spiritual beliefs? Most of us believe God is perfect beyond human understanding. The word *perfect* is awe inspiring. Most of us would feel inferior to, or feel *conned* by, someone described to us as perfect.

Calling a young child a genius may ruin his life. The word, *genius*, is related to *perfect.* The poor child must continually *act* like a genius. Personalities become distorted.

God's spiritual waves perfectly define God, heaven, and His universe. Near death and mental disorder experiences have given me incentive to *discover* spiritual wisdom. God knows everything in heaven and the universe but normally only gives humans spiritual information we can understand. He does not confuse us with more than we need or can understand.

However, if we learn more about God's universe, we learn more about Him. God, heaven, and the universe are closely related and may well be one entity. God may give us more spiritual wisdom later that we can understand through science and technology. We will not ever understand perfection.

Chapter 16

THE HEISENBERG UNCERTAINTY PRINCIPLE

"Scientists are only discovering how God created the universe. Though science we learn about God."

H. Fulcher

Quantum: The smallest amount of a physical quantity that can exist independently, especially a discrete quantity of electromagnetic radiation. A quantum represents a very small discrete packet of energy or matter.

Heisenberg Uncertainty Principle: a quantum mechanics principle: It is impossible to discern simultaneously and with high accuracy both the position and the momentum of a particle (such as an electron.)

Note: If this imaginative manic model to explain God's omnipresence and omniscience is difficult, it can be bypassed with little loss to later models. Readers only have to believe God's abilities are very, very fast to be omniscient of a very big universe. Something very traumatic had to happen for God to create the universe. Later models are simpler.

This manic model may not be entirely consistent. It is meant to make readers think.

Note: In early manic episodes I felt a need to explain God's omnipresence and omniscience. My philosophical approach for understanding the brain, mind, and God has avoided being highly technical. The Heisenberg Uncertainty Principle and Einstein's equation $E=mc^2$ are the only equations I have used to develop a pseudo-science or philosophical explanation of God's omnipresence and omniscience. Information must travel very, very fast for God to be omniscient of the universe and heaven.

I n a manic episode I felt compelled to calculate how fast God's awareness must be for Him to be omniscient. I have used the Heisenberg Uncertainty Principle for developing my imaginative model of "Nothing before Time" transitioning to a model of His creation of the universe, including creation of physical space and time. Dreaming of this model gave me *purpose* and assisted manic healing.

Manic episodes extend the mind beyond normal thinking. Bipolar sufferers have a need to be creative. I emotionally needed to dream back before organized time into God's creation from a very different primordial time and existence. *Primordial space* had less dimensions and freedoms. Primordial time was random and inconsistent. In my model, primordial existence randomly iterated from a primordial point to one or two infinite primordial spatial dimensions. Primordial space was not well defined without recorded history. After creation, God records complete histories of the universe and heaven.

The Heisenberg Uncertainty Principle is a basic physics principle stating that energy transitions occur only in small, or multiples of, quantum increments. No transition can occur with less than a small fixed quantum of energy. I build models for understanding God, and His properties throughout a great big universe and heaven. He must have communication abilities much, much faster than the speed of light, to be aware of all things in physical and spiritual space and time.

Atoms and physical things cannot travel faster than the speed of light, unless possibly falling into a black hole. Space and time are different near and in black holes.

I have developed an imaginative *model* to estimate the speed of God's *spiritual communication* waves in spiritual dimensions throughout the universe and heaven by applying the *Reverse* Heisenberg Uncertainty Principle. God integrates knowledge of all things in physical and spiritual space and time into spiritual unity and perfection.

In my early manic episodes, spiritual messages and dreams continued during my uncertain times as I pondered "Nothing before Time," God's existence, and how He created the universe. Philosophers construct models and theories and reason about where they might lead.

God and spiritual existence transitioned from a random, uncertain primordial existence to be completely organized existence with absolute certainty. After indeterminant spiritual time, God had a need to create, and created, the universe. At the very beginning of the Big Bang and physical time, the universe was completely organized. Entropy was zero. It was certain a universe existed.

Theories often lead to further research and discovery. I have modeled the uncertainty of the primordial moment immediately before it became a completely organized and certain spiritual existence.

The Heisenberg Uncertainty Principle proves that there will always be uncertainty in measurements of atoms and subatomic particles. Here are the Heisenberg Uncertainty equations:

1. $\Delta E \Delta t \geq h/(2\pi)$
2. $\Delta p \Delta x \geq h/(2\pi)$

This principle defines the precise lower limits scientists can measure atom and elementary particle properties:

In equation 1) the change in energy of an elementary particle multiplied by the time for that change to occur must be equal to $h/(2\pi)$ or some exact multiple, n, of that value. The above product cannot be less than $h/(2\pi)$. Characteristics and activities of very small elementary particles are very different from everyday activities and things humans observe and understand.

From equation 2) the change in momentum of an elementary particle multiplied by the distance for that momentum change to take place must be equal to $h/(2\pi)$ or some exact multiple of that small value.

h̲ is Planks Constant, 6.626076×10^{-34} joules-seconds. When divided by (2π), it is the exact lowest quantum value of orbital angular momentum of any elementary particle. Elementary particles can have exact multiples of this orbital angular momentum value. Values $nh/(2\pi)$ are integer multiples, n, of this *fundamental* physics constant and part of God's *deep structure language.*

Scientists make assumptions in everything we do. In science research, we make assumptions and work to prove or disprove our hypotheses. Before *physical time,* I have assumed primordial quantum existence vibrated between the point of the future Big Bang and an evenly distributed infinite primordial existence. This is my *simple* quantum model of "Nothing before Time" that had potential to create God and then He created the universe. The freedoms of space we now experience did not exist. Uncertainty existed between the primordial point of *nothing* and the infinitely smooth homogeneous *nothing.*

I hypothesized, that before the Big Bang, any *primordial* quantum energy change, ΔE, and time change, Δt, between primordial iterations, when multiplied together were always u̲n̲d̲e̲r̲ less than $h/(2\pi)$. In my model before time, I assumed the r̲e̲v̲e̲r̲s̲e̲ Heisenberg Uncertainty equations held true in primordial existence. There had to be a huge difference in existence for the Big Bang to occur. It was uncertain if "nothing" existed before time and if God and the Big Bang would occur.

Randomly the primordial point and its infinite primordial existence fused and transitioned or exploded into God and spiritual existence. God had the exactness of the point existence and the freedom of infinite *spiritual* space. Primordial and spiritual space and time did not include atoms, matter, or physical space, and was very different from physical space and time we experience today. Without physical time, God existed for zero or infinite spiritual time before creating the universe.

Later, within the universe in physical time, spiritual leaders correctly concluded that God had no physical beginning and will have no physical end. The primordial existence to spiritual existence transition was *less* than that of the Reverse Heisenberg Uncertainty Equations, $h/(2\pi,)$.

Existence before the universe was created was very different from current human reality. Strange things happened back then. At the beginning of the universe cosmologists have concluded that the unified field force, including gravity, was initially repulsive, rather than attractive, propelling the Big Bang explosion *singularity to explode outward as physical space was created.*

This must be true for the universe to explode outward with such force. Primordial point energy and infinite existence fused to create God. There was no measurable or mathematical difference between a spiritual point and spiritual infinity. After zero or infinite spiritual time, God created space, energy, and physical time. Confined quantum energy, or elementary particles, were created in discrete locations in space and later became atoms *immediately* after the beginning of the Big Bang. Space and time were created allowing movement of atoms in an expanding universe. Randomly, at the moment of the Big Bang, the primordial energy and primordial time transition, $\Delta E \times \Delta t$, became greater than $h/(2\pi)$ and a new universe began. I believe God created heaven before physical time and before He *created the universe.*

Einstein proved that mass and energy are interchangeable with His equation, $E = mc^2$. Primordial vibrations or frequencies fused to create spiritual existence. Successive iterations or vibrations randomly and exponentially increased in energy to become the Big

Bang – similar to a nuclear bomb but initially as a highly compressed *point*. Space and Light energy exploded outward at the speed of Light.

Primordial dimensions were more closely related to spiritual rather than physical dimensions. Resonating primordial waves lasted long enough to create spiritual waves and the first awareness, God. Later, He then designed, engineered, and manufactured the universe, with *exploding infinite* awareness. Spiritual reflections occurred between the point of the Big Bang and the expanding boundaries of spiritual existence and physical space.

Primordial waves had higher frequencies creating *infinite* spiritual energy and knowledge, God. He created heaven in spiritual time. Spiritual time is very different from physical time. It may be random and can repeat itself. We can add to or multiply infinity and still get infinity. God has *infinite* energy and wisdom, from a human viewpoint. Everything in heaven is relative.

The transition from uncertain primordial to *infinite* spiritual time violated the Reverse Heisenberg Uncertainty Principle forcing "Nothing before Time" to explode and become spiritual waves with infinite energy throughout existence. The moment God created the universe, space and time were created allowing physical changes and movement. Before physical time, primordial and spiritual changes affected all spiritual existence equally. No history was recorded until spiritual time existed. There is uncertainty as to whether *nothing* ever existed.

Discrete potentials were created in the Big Bang that promoted change. Gravity has potentials. Otherwise, everything would stay the same. God created an expanding universe with potentials for increasingly diverse activities, and with increasing spiritual awareness to record increasing changes in the universe and heaven. Humans have some godlike qualities and can imagine "Nothing before Time" transitioning into God and then His creation of an evolving universe with reality of existence.

Spiritual integration dimensions must exist if God is omniscient and omnipresent. His awareness of all information throughout the universe must be integrated and shared within each point in the universe very rapidly for God to be up to date, omnipresent, and omniscient.

Light, electromagnetic radiation, is the medium between physical and spiritual dimensions. Transition of physical existence from spiritual existence created *Light*. Spiritual dimensions are intertwined with the physical universe. God is constantly aware of the entire universe, which is now 28 billion light years in diameter. Spiritual awareness of a great big universe requires communication speeds much, much faster than the speed of light defined here as the speed of *spiritual waves* known as the Holy Spirit in the Bible.

God and heaven were created before physical time. God was the first Awareness of all of existence in spiritual time and space - heaven. God created physical time and space, and in 10^{-35} seconds later created about 10^{82} hydrogen atoms (the simplest mass.) God, as Virgin Light and spiritual waves in the vacuum of spiritual space, *existed* before the Big Bang.

God was the infinite symmetric reflection of random "Nothing before Time." He then created the universe as an asymmetric and symmetric physical system with matter and physical space and time. Gravity is the residual effect of God emotionally desiring to return the universe and Himself back to its perfect original order at the moment of Creation.

I developed a *creative* model for the speed of the primordial and universal transition. Here I assume God created the universe in zero spiritual time. This philosophical and physics model is a *beginning* explanation for God's omnipresent and omniscient properties. It is a thought experiment!

The energy of the universe can be roughly calculated as the rest masses of all hydrogen atoms in the universe:

$$E = n \times mc^2$$

E = energy of the universe
n = estimated number of hydrogen atoms in the universe – 10^{82}
m = mass of one hydrogen atom - 1.7×10^{-27} kg

c = the speed of light – 3×10^8 m/sec

$E = 10^{82} \times 1.7 \times 10^{-27} \times 3 \times 10^8 \times 3 \times 10^8 = 1.5 \times 10^{72}$ kg-m^2/s^2
   $= 1.5 \times 10^{72}$ joules

There was uncertainty of the moment the universe was created. From the Heisenberg Uncertainty equation:

$\Delta E \Delta T = h/ (2\pi)$

ΔE is the change in energy from zero to all initial hydrogen atoms in the universe.

The estimated final primordial or spiritual time that created the physical energy of the universe is estimated as:

$\Delta T = h/ (2\pi \Delta E)$
   $= 6.626076E\text{-}34/ (2 \times 3.14 \times 1.5E72) =$ roughly 10^{-106}. (seconds)

This value is a rough estimate of the spiritual time of one transition vibration from primordial to spiritual and later to physical existence. Spiritual time is independent of physical time and travels across the universe 10^{106} times per second. This is essentially infinite speed giving God omnipresence and omniscience.

In this imaginary model, God transcended from "Nothing before Time." He then created the universe approximately 14 billion years ago. I have used known equations and assumptions to develop an imaginative philosophical model of transcending from *Nothing before Time* to a new universe. All physics and cosmology models have assumptions.

From relativity, the beginning of a very dense universe had, and black holes have, very different space and time characteristics. Light does not normally escape black holes. God, *Light*, did not escape, but expanded Himself and the universe into heaven.

The mass of the universe was much, much bigger than black

holes. Light does not escape from black holes. The universe and Light expanded at the speed of light. Light did escape the universe.

From expected death, manic, and spiritual experiences, I needed to think of God while modeling "Nothing before Time." This imaginative model added understanding to my manic uncertainties. Manic depressives think beyond normal boundaries. Discoveries begin with dreams and assumptions to form beliefs. This creative *Nothing before Time* model supports later spiritual models.

Sometimes we make guesses to see what dreams might follow. Thinking about *Nothing before Time* helped me make models of God and His Wonders. Readers are free to improve models.

BRAIN SECTION

Chapter 17

BRAIN

"I wish I had a brain!"

Strawman, Wizard of Oz

"The human brain is an incredible pattern-matching machine."

Bezos

"The emotional brain responds to an event more quickly than the thinking brain."

Daniel Goleman

"This is my simple religion. There is no need for temples; no need for complicated philosophy. Our own brain, our own heart is our temple; the philosophy is kindness."

Dalai Lama

Brain: an organ of soft nervous tissue contained in the skull of vertebrates, functioning as the coordinating center of sensation and intellectual and nervous activity.

An elementary anatomy of the brain was given earlier in the Neuroscience Chapter. Integration of activities within the brain creates the mind. Without brains, we are "straw people." Two pressing goals for American medicine are to prevent and *cure* mental disorders and cancer. The brain and mind are an integrated entity for analyzing sensed information from nerves, comparing it to similar memories, and developing consciousness for life's daily purposes. It takes patience and inner awareness to reconstruct, heal, and renew subconscious protocols for improving decision making and emotional thinking.

Nerves transmit signals from eyes, skin, muscles, and organs for the brain and mind to monitor and analyze their statuses for needed or desired reactions. The brain and mind reflect activation potentials and pass control back to muscles, including eye muscles for focusing attention. When we activate muscles, we have activated corresponding areas of the brain.

The mind integrates brain activities and becomes greater than the sum of all its sensed input and memory information. A great painting is greater than the sum of its parts. Integration is a strong concept in my theories of the brain, mind, and God.

The brain and mind *are one* recursive system. Activities within our brains create our minds. Our minds then stimulate and control our brains that then control our muscles. The brain is physical and like muscles grows with use, or atrophies from disuse.

Recursive relationships between the brain and mind are important for consciousness, thinking, and body control. To increase understanding of brain-mind recursion, I exercise an arm or a leg and think of brain activities controlling that arm or leg.

Historically, small children adhered to basic lessons from and principles of their parents, with little questioning. Fundamentals of the brain, mind, and religion have changed, slowly over the years. Technology and the internet are accelerating the rates of learning and new beliefs. This may or may not be good for humanity.

Ponce de Leon traveled to Florida in search of the Fountain of Youth when all he needed was to stimulate his longevity genes. New science using CRISPR will affect DNA and RNA for life longevity. Researchers have discovered longevity genes in yeast and are searching for master regulator longevity genes, in humans, for activating natural defense mechanisms against stress and aging as part of the Longevity Genes Project at Albert Einstein College of Medicine. My work on facial meditation and aging is presented in Chapter 36.

Persistent severe stress and traumas overwhelm the brain and degrade the body's immune system. Bullied and neglected children have more allergies and colds.

Practicing conflicting psychiatric exercises promotes limiting levels of stress, releases inner stresses from the brain and brain cells, and prepares the brain for higher levels of stress later on. Effects are similar to immunizations.

Briefly stressing the brain and mind to emotional limits is much like working out with weights. Afterward, once difficult thinking feels and becomes easier.

Subconscious processes are *aware* of every active nerve and muscle in the body. The mind and brain send signals to nerves to control muscles. Nerve and muscle cell coordination has been primarily organized by genetics and baby and childhood experimentation. Coordination of all muscles for moving an arm was integrated early on and is mostly subconscious in later life.

Writing develops mental organization and precision, refines understanding, and reduces uncertainties. Writing is an integral part of mental healing.

Thinking does not need to be in words. Thinking in pictures can be easier and more efficient, at times. We construct visions of the road ahead as we navigate our destinations. A picture is worth a thousand words, in many circumstances.

Long-term thinking and attitudes effect our faces. Older faces *tell* who has:

- had a hard or easy life;
- loved or hated;
- been abused or abusive;

- has had faith in self or has had persistent uncertainties;
- and has been nurturing or deceitful.

Nerves and brain cells respond to internal and external stimuli. Morals, decisions, and behaviors are influenced by heredity, successes, and failures.

The brain's learning structures include limbic, prefrontal cortex, and hippocampus systems. The prefrontal cortex is important in learning and unlearning memories. Desensitizing Therapy is important for reducing uncertainties and fears from military dramas as evidenced by those with Post Traumatic Syndrome.

Humans have greater ability to configure their brains than I originally thought. Brains and bodies become rigid when we are tense and stressed. After long-lasting or severe stresses, our brains and faces remain tense unless we consciously learn to relax them. Relaxed, supple neural networks support a versatile, creative mind. For many of us, our brains have remained tense for so long we do not recognize the inner tensions until we experience headaches. Frowning restricts blood flow to, and tenses, the brain. Practice smiling and laughing to relax the face and brain. Look for things that are enjoyable and funny.

In need, children surrender to parents with broadened, questioning faces, and open minds. To be listened to nurtures mental health and gives feelings of importance. When relaxed, the right-brain dominates with pleasant moods and spiritual ideas. Surrendering to God relaxes the brain and opens minds.

Relaxing the brain and body briefly and frequently is good for health and creativity. Broadening the face and brain becomes easier with practice. When relaxing, increased blood flow to the brain may cause the face and scalp to feel pleasantly flush. The heartbeat may be sensed within the brain. These sensations have occurred after years of mental reconstruction practices. Certain rhythms and resonances in the brain relax and slow down to heartbeat levels. A less tense brain and body lowers blood pressure and may prevent heart attacks.

When someone is stressed, he is concerned with his own wellbeing, and is not as open to nurturing others. When the brain is stressed, brain cells are stressed and also more concerned about their own wellbeing and their inner functions. They do not share information as freely for developing integrated and overall thinking purposes. Relaxing the mind allows brain cells to work together as one complete nervous system.

No thought or live action occurs in the universe without absorbing or emitting Light, electromagnetic radiation. A brain, healed of trauma effects, will process with lower energy and longer wavelengths. God's spiritual waves can resonate in the brain to slow down enough and integrate with much slower and longer human *brain* waves.

If experiencing headaches, broaden and relax the face and mind to dissipate local tensions. *This is important.* Frowning and concentrating on local pain intensifies it. Relaxing and thinking holistically and away from the pain reduces tensions and headaches.

Psychiatrists do not acknowledge or consider spiritual sensitivities during manic episodes. From the few manic-depressives I have talked with, spiritual themes are similar. However, different words were used, for expressing spiritual experiences, depending upon life experiences, vocabularies, and language practices. Researching manic thoughts and writings reveal the inner mind, provides resonances for spiritual communications, and may prove God exists.

Manic excitement may assist recall of spiritual wisdom we received upon conception. Our spiritual memories and language are influenced by our limiting experiences.

Consider two mature ideas. Each has constructed its own neural networks for memory and recall. If these two ideas connect with reason in some useful way, their two neural networks integrate and function as one broader, stronger channel with more confident feelings.

Each neuron is enclosed by a thin, complexly shaped membrane. After neuron activations, neuron membranes become porous. Calcium, sodium, potassium, chloride, and trace chemicals enter into neuron bodies after cell activations. Neuron membranes close as a discrete event when a pressure or other limit is met. A neuron becomes charged and ready for the next activation.

Neuron activations are *fast, discrete* occurrences. Neurochemicals from one activating neuron *flow* along its axon affecting timing of numerous neuron activations through synapses and dendrites. The brain is complex.

There must be some communications between neurons and glia cells similar to communications between muscles and nerves. The structure and stiffness of the brain affect neuron activations and thinking. Normally, the brain and brain cells have gently varying pressures. When frightened, muscles and glia cells contract. Brain activities are both discrete and holistic.

Light travels slower in the brain than in vacuum. Brain matter alters Light, EMR, characteristics and information. The reflections, integration, and absorptions of Light by billions of brain molecules, give Light in the brain spiritual qualities.

Space is condensed and Light is curved by matter and gravity. Spiritual waves are independent of physical time, atoms, and gravity. God controls spiritual time. It may not be not constant. Dream time is also independent of physical time and gravity. Sometimes dreams go slow and sometimes they go fast.

Our mental abilities are developed by discrete physical neuron activations and continuous holistic spiritual integration. Our left-brains are activated and controlled by relatively fast discrete Light changes. Our right-brains are activated by relatively slower rhythmic integrated continuous holistic Light. It is mentally healing to be able to consciously switch brain dominance. Brain dominance is controlled by fast or slower holistic thoughts.

Various electromagnetic waves are transmitted, reflected, and absorbed differently by different tissues in the brain and body. EMR waves may be transmitted through brain fluids more readily but be reflected and absorbed more by denser neural and glia membranes. Selected X-rays are transmitted through soft human tissue but are reflected more by denser bone tissue.

Consider the brain of the blind. The blind may *think visually*. They may have the same genetic brain makeup that sighted people have. Their brains and minds compensate for loss of sight. The healthy cerebellum yearns to process sight. Ears and skin of the blind are very sensitive. They sense environmental reflections from their own activities and sounds to navigate repeated daily environments. The blind build *dark spatial visions* for navigating their environments.

My blind friend has a tremendous memory. He learns and remembers benchmarks, distances, and sounds to navigate home and outside environments. He does not count steps.

A blind person may make a *blind* model of their house nearly as precise as a person with normal visual. He only needs reference points. The *blind* brain and mind compensate in amazing ways.

I have learned from my blind friend and his amazing skills. With his machines, he reads typewritten words but not handwritten words. On one occasion, he came to me with six hand written numbers each having eight digits. I read them for him. Without notes, he went back to his desk to enter those numbers into his computer. Few people have such memories. I have assisted him at Federation of the Blind meetings in Washington, D. C.

The brain is adaptive. It learns and remembers amazing things if limits are not approached too quickly or forcefully.

Chapter 18

SUBCONSCIOUS PROCESSES

Our brains integrate Light to converge subconscious *processes,* into conscious ideas.

H Fulcher

Subconscious – concerning activities of the brain of which one is not fully conscious but which influences one's inner activities and feelings. Organized and disorganized mental and spiritual activities and potentials below conscious energy and time levels. Potentials for developing feelings, words, vision, and cognition.

Unconscious – concerning activities of the mind, including dreams, which are inaccessible to the conscious mind but which affect behaviors and emotions. (Activities of the brain that do not last long or strong enough to create conscious energy for thinking.)

Inner peace - concerning a deliberate state of psychological or spiritual calm despite potential presence of stressors. Being "at peace" is considered to be healthy, free of pain, and the opposite of being stressed or anxious. A state where our minds perform at optimal levels with positive feelings and outcomes, independent of others' influences, and having peace with God. Peace of mind is generally associated with bliss, happiness and contentment.

Inner Mind – Current memory and cognitive potentials that may become consciously active - the brain's resource for creating mental and spiritual activities.

The relaxed brain and mind can do awesomely wonderful creative thinking. Meditate to set your mind free of the days' troubles. We normally think of consciousness as *thinking*. Consciousness is supported by many subconscious and unconscious brain and mind activities including dreaming and *dreaming while awake*. Sometimes while awake unexpected creative dreams evolve from *nowhere*. Meditation skills develop our inner and spiritual minds for achieving inner peace to live our *own* lives.

Sigmund Freud modeled the mind as in two parts - subconscious and conscious. Subconscious processes are activated by sense, nerve, and memory potentials. Synchronized neurons activate and integrate their Light, EMR, to develop resonances to create memories. If subconscious resonances break through conscious time and energy thresholds, they develop consciousness.

Activities of one hundred billion neurons and trillions of nerve cell connections synchronize to form our nervous system for cognition, consciousness, and life. *Thousands* of subconscious processes and sub-ideas synchronize and integrate for each conscious idea we have. EMR from one activated neuron does not create an idea.

The brain is as active during sleep as during waking. Some specialized neural networks are more active during waking and others during sleeping. The subconscious brain organizes, prioritizes, integrates, and evaluates short and long-term memories for supporting conscious and security goals. During waking, active neurons create toxins. A vital function during sleeping is clearing neurons and glia cells of toxins.

A rough calculation from my *Flash* experience estimates that subconscious processes occur nearly one million times faster than conscious processes. The brain is electrical and chemical and processes very fast. *The Flash* is given in Chapter 22.

Neural networks, which absorb excessive energy beyond their normal limits during traumas fire sporadically, are disruptive to normal brain functions, and may limit the mind for years, or even life. High-energy trauma neurons activate sporadically and act like cancers in the brain. They do not coordinate with normal neurons.

Normally positively charged sodium, calcium, potassium, and chloride atoms are absorbed through neuron membranes to develop chemical potentials for neuron activations. Membranes become closed to absorptions when there is potential for neuron activation.

As Light energy dissipates from current sense and memory activations, the next generation of Light from the next neuron activations creates the next moment of consciousness. All memory is subconscious unless currently conscious. Recall of memories may be easy, difficult, or impossible. Feelings and emotions are integrations of semi-conscious memories. An old friend may stimulate once *impossible* memories.

We may follow every word on a radio. Radio content becomes semiconscious if we concentrate on something else. Certain words, or an increase in energy or volume, may re-stimulate consciousness of our radio programming.

Dream processes organize and integrate the previous day's memories with related historical memories to form *deeper* memories and reasoning foundations. Energy levels, frequency variations, and time stamps of new activities are compared with memories having similar characteristics to form *deeper* memories with related characteristics and time stamps. Usually, we can determine which memories occurred before others. Newer memories are overlaid onto earlier brain cell membrane imprints. Similar memories are stored with similar recall characteristics.

If we wish to develop a skill, we practice with repetition. When ready to perform, we relax to get conscious thinking out of the way so our subconscious processes can perform our skills faster and better with less energy. With positive attitudes and consistent practices, subconscious processes converge and integrate to *remember,* and semi-consciously execute our best performances, such as piano recitals.

Reconstructing the brain and mind reduces dream distortions and increases dreaming realism. Baby and childhood sporadic attentions and perceptions have constructed inefficient, unorganized emotional subconscious protocols. Subconscious activities, including memory protocols, can become more organized and efficient with experimentation and practice even at near emotional limits. Reasoning and learning improve with practice and mental reconstruction.

Thought and memory are developed with non-linear, iterative subconscious processes. We are unaware or vaguely aware of numerous assumptions and decisions made by integrating subconscious processes for constructing conscious ideas. Meditation to become aware of inner assumptions and activities makes subconscious processes more efficient. Thousands of subconscious processes iterate for one dream or waking awareness. Depending upon childhood experiences and traumas, subconscious processes may be disordered or logical while iterating for consciousness.

Let's develop a simple model to think about subconscious processes and conscious ideas. I represent each sub-idea with a letter.

Suppose a potential conscious thought consists of ten related subconscious resonances or sub-ideas: "abcdefghij-kl." "k" is a conscious – on-off switch. It has an "k-off" beginning value and switches to "K-on" when a conscious thought is achieved. "l" becomes capital "L" when a conscious thought has been ordered and integrated within historical memories and includes its time stamp related to earlier memories.

A current subconscious *hologram as a higher-dimensional picture,* or dream resonance, from senses and inner processes, integrate to gain energy for replacing the previous conscious idea as its energy is dissipated. As a simple model of consciousness, capital letters represent sub-ideas that have enough energy and last above *threshold times* to influence consciousness.

Let's think of a simple example of consciousness. Some related mental hologram or sub-ideas become excited enough to support conscious energy levels and times: "abCdeFghiJ-kl." C, F, and J have energy to meet sub-idea thresholds. However, the total energy of this subconscious model is not strong enough for an idea to become fully conscious. In this simple model, conscious ideas must have a *majority* of sub-idea components, or letters, above conscious thresholds. In building an idea, some letters may fade and new capital letters replace them. Sub-idea energy and time varies during conscious process development depending upon emotions or mental energy.

Upon further iterations, excitement, and subconscious concentration, more sub-ideas meet the sub-idea energy threshold. If the majority of sub-idea hologram resonances are elevated above sub-idea energy thresholds, the subconscious process develops a conscious idea such as: "AbCDeFgHiJ-KL". "K" and "L" become capitalized. When the energy of sub-thoughts, "ACDFHJ", is multiplied together, a conscious thought is created with some certainty of truth.

If half of the synchronized sub-ideas are below and half above conscious limits, we only have feelings about some idea or activity. *I know his name but cannot recall it.*

A highly emotional "Flash" or my spiritual message, "Don't Leave God Out," may have constructed an "ABCDEFGHIJ-KL" idea that is *Immediately Believable* and forces action. Emotional, believable spiritual value is determined by multiplying the energy of capitalized sub-ideas. Simple models aid in understanding confident, truthful ideas.

Awareness begins with senses initiating subconscious sub-ideas and activating related memories. Our subconscious and conscious minds compare current ideas to related memories. The subconscious makes initial evaluations. Current sense and memory resonances support the next converged conscious idea.

After much practice, the very fast control of hands and fingers of concert pianists is mostly subconscious. At times in typing I hesitate to think of spelling a word and realize my hands have already subconsciously typed that word. After experience typing, we only think of the words we want to type. Our subconscious processes and fingers do the details of *thinking* and typing letters. Frequent activities are mostly subconsciously controlled.

Walking straight at the same speed is mostly subconscious. Changing directions or stride requires some conscious attention. Study and concentration make subconscious processes conscious and uncertain things certain.

Einstein must have had many uncertain sub-thoughts and thoughts while working on his famous, complex relativity models that have given scientists a better understanding of the universe. Analyzing *uncertainties* makes them more *certain.* We study in areas of interest to become a more confident and creative in those areas. Creative people are not limited by past errors, activities, and memories. They live in the *now.* Inventive people give up who they are to become who they want to be.

At times when manic and after meditating and then attempting to remember something, I have *felt* sub-ideas converging into conscious thoughts. A goal of meditation is to reduce conscious activities so more sub-thoughts can be integrated to construct *in-depth* thoughts.

Meditation reduces conscious activities, freeing subconscious processes to converge and become more efficient and organized. Meditation gets the conscious mind out of the way freeing inner processes to support sub-idea convergence and integration for stronger memory and consciousness.

We may improve problem solving by carefully considering problems before sleep and waking up with solutions. Genetic and subconscious processes may iterate and converge to solutions during sleep using detailed earlier input. It is the energy efficient thing to do.

All sensed data is uncertain until subconsciously compared to and resolved with historical memories. Genetics, sensations, memories of earlier activities, and other subconscious processes integrate to form awareness and cognition.

Modeling the mind as subconscious and conscious is a simple

model. In reality, there are many mental levels. Skin nerves are mostly subconscious when concentrating on other things. We may be vaguely aware of most of our skin, and very aware of *touched* skin. Posture may be semiconscious until we change position. Organ processes are mostly subconscious until there is pain. In a darkened room, we may be vaguely aware of a dark image. In vision, there is little separation between subconscious and conscious awareness. Our minds focus on separate parts of vision.

Neuron EMR is transmitted through, reflected, and absorbed within the brain at near the speed of light in vacuum. Subconscious processes are very fast and develop *inner* understanding, healing, and versatility.

During waking, breathing is mostly a semiconscious activity. During sleep, breathing is subconscious. We do little exercise during sleep but breathe deeply. Sleep replenishes oxygen to the brain and body. Consciously breathing deeply and yarning at times helps clean toxins in sleep from brain cells.

During twenty-eight years of inner experimentation, inner healing feelings have been pleasant. It takes inner awareness and positive feelings to renew and keep our *subconscious minds* healthy. Inner healing and creative progresses are slow but *recognizable*. I am as excited as ever in practicing and writing about mental reconstruction. Dreams can become conscious for a fascinating reality.

Chapter 19

DISCRETE AND HOLISTIC

"The measure of success is happiness and peace of mind."

Bobby Davro

"The mind has two waking modes of operation: discrete and holistic. Discrete is focusing on one activity or thought. Holistic is the integration of discrete ideas to create a more complete concept. A great painting is greater than its parts."

Hugh Fulcher

Discrete thinking means focusing on something detailed or distinct, near at hand, requiring relatively fast understanding, reaction, or action – like hitting a tennis ball. Discrete thinking is usually left- brained. Holistic thinking is mental and spiritual completeness in preparing for possible future activities. Holistic might mean analyzing and developing a tennis player's entire approach to his game for his tennis future. A long-range view of mountains is holistic right-brain integrated awareness. No immediate action is needed or expected.

Relaxing and lowering mental energy allows the right-brain to become dominant for long range, holistic awareness and futuristic thinking. God's actions and reactions are holistic and complete in spiritual dimensions. God's spiritual decisions affect the entire universe and heaven.

Practicing switching between left- and right-brain dominance integrates mental structures for building confident spiritual skills. At times, we get bogged down with left-brain details when we need to relax, step back, and let our right-brains organize and construct creative long-range plans and solutions.

Dancing appears, and is, awkward when the detailed left-brain is dominant. The left-brain focuses on separate individual body movements. When relaxed with holistic right-brain dominance, the entire body becomes coordinated and flows smoothly with an integrated purpose. The rhythmic right-brain coordinates all body movements. We enjoy organization and coordination in sports, dance, other activities, and prayer.

Discrete thinking may be thought of as one member of a choir singing solo. She makes wonderful vibrations in the air, for us to hear and enjoy. If her voice is on key with rhythm, she may inspire love, faith, and great memories. We may lose ourselves in her voice and *feel* part of her.

Holistic may be thought of as a five-hundred-member choir singing in perfect harmony. Some sing tenor, some sing bass, and others sing in different parts. Members sing differently without standouts for unity of expression and purpose. All voices are equally important and fill the air with beautiful, rich, integrated, and holistic vibrations in the air. Each discrete voice constructs an important part of integrated air vibrations for listeners to enjoy. Holistic always has an integration quality. *Integrated voices* unite hearts, minds, and spirits.

The discrete left-brain integrates Light, electromagnetic radiation, to create consciousness of one or *two* ideas at a time. A subset of billions of synchronized firing neurons can focus on one thing. When relaxed, the holistic right-brain synchronizes and integrates Light from billions of neuron activations to sense and create integrated feelings, thoughts, and music in some similar way to integrated voices of a five-hundred-member choir. Integrated Light creates spiritual feelings. The mind is spiritual. God is *Light and Spiritual Waves* integrated throughout the universe and heaven in the vacuum of space. God is holistic and independent of space. We can pray anywhere. God's depth of awareness and wisdom has some similarity to integrated voices of our five-hundred-member choir.

Loud music activates left-brain dominance for strong emotions inspiring fast actions and reactions. Classical music activates the right-brain with repetitive, flowing, and integrated sounds for calm and moving spiritual feelings. Classical music can promote both left- and right-brain dominance transitions for feelings of uncertainty and certainty. The brain/mind has subconscious protocols for left- and right-brain dominance transitions. Transition protocols change with experience, emotions, concentration, and focus. However, when relaxing and meditating, and near emotional limits, we learn more of our inner mental processes. The mind is complex.

The right-brain analyzes distant and wide views of environments for possible *future* interactions. The left-brain analyzes up-close environments and prepares for reactions and threats relative to visual, emotional, and intellectual limits. Visual memories are *usually* more accurate than future visual predictions. Great minds calculate, imagine, and predict the future. Too often our minds are stuck in hurtful pasts that make the future appear difficult and bleak.

With the elevated mental energy of mania, the right-brain is more dominant. In episodes, manic-depressives tend to concentrate on *big picture* and *spiritual relationships*. They lose detailed left-brain reasoning and generalize that very different activities and results are of *equal* importance. In mania, the right-brain may be either creative or have irrational dream characteristics while awake. Needed control for everyday left-brain reasoning is lessened or lost.

The right-brain is dominant when energy of the brain is below or above normal energy or emotional levels. Emotional thinking can be either depressed or manic, and spiritual.

Psychiatrists prescribe Lithium and other psychiatric drugs to prevent mental energy or mood levels from going too high or too low for stabilizing left-brain dominance for everyday normal reasoning. Some psychiatric drugs or medications slow and distort mental processes to the point of feeling, thinking, and acting like a zombie. The brain and body lose rhythm. Body movements become uncertain and awkward. With some medications, thinking and creative abilities may become a small fraction of once normal brain abilities.

Psychiatrists should monitor and test patients' mental abilities. Will they work for us to recover our thinking back to normal or will they simply keep us from being disruptive or damaging to ourselves or others? Detailed physical and psychiatric exercises given later may lessen need for mind slowing medications.

Most of us mostly use left-brain thinking in our jobs and social life. Practicing switching brain dominance adds right-brain creativity to left-brain skills and adds to mind control. Manic-depressives, when manic, may regain mind control by concentrating on up-close details for promoting left-brain dominance.

Creative people switch brain dominance frequently. Visionaries accept their past and dream of the future. Low-energy depressed and high-energy emotional thinking are beyond normal thinking limits and may not be reasonable at times.

Consider the brain. Electromagnetic spikes from one neuron might relate to one choir member's voice. One activating neuron does not create consciousness. Synchronized firings of billions of neurons create subconscious and conscious activities, relating to music of a very, very large choir. Continued subconscious EMR iterations synchronize and integrate at near the *speed of light* in vacuum to construct our relatively slow integrated consciousness. It is a miracle of life that the brain has the ability to synchronize and coordinate EMR from so many nerve and neuron activations.

Recalled memories, dreams, visions, and words are building blocks for cognition. Upon waking, dream hologram scenarios sometimes become conscious. When resonating Light energy of subconscious and *dream* scenarios become strong enough and last long enough, they create consciousness.

Millions of neural resonances are synchronized at any one-time creating consciousness. Individual rods and cones within the eyes stimulate EMR resonances, within the brain, which integrate to produce the *smooth* vision we see. Our eyes and brains organize and integrate individual rod and cone specks of Light to form *smooth* images and views we recognize.

Millions and possibly billions of neuron activations synchronize and *integrate* to construct subconscious resonances throughout areas of the brain at near the speed of light in vacuum. These resonances may *integrate* with further subconscious focus to create *slower long-lasting* resonances for consciousness. Neurochemicals flowing along axons to dendrites between neurons are much slower than EMR but are fundamental for synchronizing brain EMR resonances for thoughts and moods. The brain has protocols for abruptly changing ideas. Moods are integrations of semi-conscious, related neuron protocols.

If a thin *near two-dimensional photographic film* can store three-dimensional holographic images, spatially complex three-dimensional arrays of *thin* neural membranes can store higher-dimensional information and scenarios. *Loving, humble,* and t*ruthful* mental resonances synchronize and integrate spiritual relationships in spiritual dimensions. The mind can be spiritual.

Memories and dreams often include emotional dimensions. Dream and memory scenarios might include faint holistic red tinting for representing levels of negative emotions. Slight holistic gold tinted memory scenarios might express levels of truth and faith in ideas and beliefs.

We are normally unaware of subconscious assumptions and decision-making processes in constructing conscious thoughts that control our lives. Subconscious energy and algorithms determine what information becomes conscious and what does not. All minds are different. In high-energy manic episodes, subconscious and spiritual processes may become conscious with little normal reasoning.

Babies learn mechanics of walking using heredity and their detailed left-brains. Adult consistent walking is repetitive and no longer needing full conscious attention. The right-brain controls consistent walking, semiconsciously. The left-brain becomes dominant for detailed thinking needed to change stride or direction. Normally left-brain processes learn from right-brain processes and vice-versa.

Words are symbols for expressing discrete, flowing, and holistic ideas. Readers engage the detailed left-brain for interpreting discrete words. Readers' inner thoughts differ, to lesser or greater extents, from writer's inner thoughts. Words never perfectly represent reality. Great writing activates reader's holistic right-brains for imagining flowing thoughts, images, and actions.

We have discussed left- and right-brain dominance. What happens if we need to read distant signs? My model is that the two brains briefly become equally dominant or have very fast dominance changes. With genetic and learned knowledge and abilities, the subconscious mind switches dominance for up-close and long-range security needs.

Chapter 20

DREAMS

"The interpretation of dreams is the royal road to a knowledge of the unconscious activities of the mind."

Sigmund Freud

"Here we are, all by day; by night we're hurled by dreams, each by one, into a several world."

William Browne

"Some men see things as they are and say why. I dream of things that never were, and say why not."

Robert Kennedy

"Life may be scary and dangerous when dreaming while awake."

H. Fulcher

"Once when severely depressed, I felt the joy of death and rebirth, and felt my soul evaporating into God's infinite being."

H. Fulcher

Dream reasoning is less restrictive than waking reasoning. In dreams, we imagine doing things beyond waking abilities. In mania, reasoning is on the border between waking and dreaming. Waking reasoning limits are overridden. Manic-depressives may believe in, and *live*, impossible dreams, and be vulnerable to predators.

We see ourselves in dreams, as others might observe us, or as, we wish to, or wish not to, be observed. Dreams consist of both life-like and bizarre three-dimensional hologram scenarios. Manic-depressives tend to believe in energetic dreams beyond normal waking realities.

From computer programming experience, developing protocols for information and image comparisons are complex with defined levels of precision. Dream-like hologram scenarios integrate sense information with similar memories for manic awareness and manic decision making. Dream hologram comparisons are much more in depth and complex than computer comparisons.

Highly emotional dreams are more easily remembered as they often awaken us. Memories include action potentials in order to be able to be recalled. Manic dreams have energies near or at waking potentials. We confuse dream thinking with reality thinking. Normal dreams have energy levels below conscious energy thresholds. However, abrupt awakening increases dream energy to conscious levels.

The dreaming brain exaggerates and repeats images, emotions, and actions to increase importance of dream content and to strengthen ability to recall *dream* memories. Dream distortions are caused by a few traumatized neural network activations near mental and survival limits. Emotional limits were formed by genetics and ingrained mostly during babyhood and childhood. Dreams include earlier actions and reactions and actions we wished we had or had not experienced. Dreams normally have low mental energy, unless traumatized neural networks are activated that awaken dreamers. Dreaming activities normally occur much faster than waking activities and thoughts.

There are differences between emotional and trauma limits. Emotions excite us or make us sad. Trauma memories exceeding normal mental limits, create fear, and threaten our security and possibly threaten death. Normal mental limits may be either overridden or destroyed giving loss of control, overreaction, or more restrictive thinking and actions. Experiencing a trauma limit, we may cope, retreat, fight, or experience a brief blackout. When experiencing a blackout, our brains and minds become ingrained with a trauma scar and a thinking restriction.

If we cope while experiencing trauma, mental limits may widen and develop a higher *reasoning* limit for processing greater emotional information. However, fear caused by trauma might also restrict thoughts and actions. Traumas create mental and emotional reactions. Mental reconstruction is meant to broaden trauma limits for reasoning at higher emotional levels.

Flying in dreams seems natural since we floated in the womb. In dreams, we *observe ourselves* as characters in a play. We may even sense God observing and caring for us.

Emotional activities during the day are prevalent in dreams the following night, but having exaggerated forms and actions to enhance memory. Subconscious processes interpolate, extrapolate, and integrate mental holograms to develop dream *reasoning* and long-term memories.

Freud claimed he could always determine the meaning of dreams. Dream exaggerations amplify importance of dream relationships and enhance memory.

Freud emphasized that recalling and understanding *repressed* memories frees the mind from their ingrained, adverse effects. As long as trauma memories remain, they sporadically activate disrupting and restricting normal thinking and lives.

Freud refers to remembered dream scenarios as *manifest dreams*. Manifest dreams are the visual images we become aware of at times. Dr. Freud's dream analysis interprets the meaning of dream distortions. Meaning of dream content is revealed by analyzing manifest dreams.

Within the brain, images and words are converted to electromagnetic resonances and neurochemicals for developing memory and cognition. Dream scenario distortions are due to complex processes of encoding and integrating sounds, images, feelings, reactions, and so on, into electromagnetic resonances for ingraining information within brain cell membranes.

Dream encoding of sensed information depends on genetic and learned inner technologies. Subconscious processes encode information on brain membrane molecules. Subconscious processes recall, interpret, and integrate hologram scenarios within encoded neural membranes to develop memories and cognition.

Sometimes we struggle during important dream tasks *seemingly for hours* and awaken to find our effort was nonsense. At times, subconscious processes seem to waste energy, emotions, and time. However, they are preparing our minds for future activities and purpose. Repetition in dreams adds importance to activities and makes them easier to be recalled.

For learning experiments, neuroscientists might expose patients to the same emotional videos, and after a period of brief sleep abruptly awaken them and have them discuss their dreams and dream distortions. Scientists may then compare patient responses to understand differences. This experiment may help scientists understand dream and subconscious encoding.

I have experimented with *Dreaming While Awake* to increase awareness, and control, of dreams. I present two repetitious dream experiments leading to limits in searching for subconscious understanding: *The Dragon Dream*, and *Asleepened*:

THE DRAGON DREAM

With eyes closed, meditating, and lowering the energy of the brain not long after my last manic episode in 1993, I was able to develop a rather consistent image of a scary ole dream dragon. In this experiment, I void my mind of words and meditate on the darkness, and wait. Eventually, I become aware of a big ornery ole dragon coming toward me. He is scary! He gets closer and closer, and the dragon dream disappears. I did not remain calm enough, and the dragon dream was gone in a poof. I did not give up. After much practice, I stayed calm so the dragon did not *poof* away so quickly. I finally mastered this dream experiment. What do you think happened?

One of two scenarios happened when the big, mean, ornery dragon comes to get me. He gets closer; I feel the closeness! I wince a little; *he gets me!* I experienced a brief emotional dream black out. I am a goner for sure! But wait! The next thing I am aware of is sliding down the dragon's throat and laughing as the dream ends.

Why do I laugh? The reason is from genetics and childhood experiences. We have been taught to avoid sharp teeth. Staying calm during the dream attack, tricked the subconscious mind and forced it to continue the dream scenario.

My dreaming mind logically placed me in the dragon's throat. I was no longer afraid since from childhood I only feared sharp teeth and not of being swallowed. It was also funny because, as the dream image dissipated, I became aware, that a dream dragon cannot really eat me. Rapidly releasing of tensions added to the laughter. I was able to take an emotional dream to limits.

That brief dream blackout created an *unconscious trauma scar in my brain*. I created a *dream trauma*. The subconscious mind momentarily did not know what to do. The dream had me sliding down the dragon's throat as I fully awakened. This was the first emotional dream option.

The second dream scenario is simpler. The big mean, ornery ole dragon comes to get me. He gets closer; I feel the closeness! I remain calm. The dream dragon suddenly looks sheepish, quickly turns, and gets smaller as he runs away. I experienced a dream victory in this option. Slight differences in emotions and facial expression may have affected my dragon scenario options.

I used patience, calmness, and imagination to explore subconscious limits when dreaming while awake and suppressing conscious control. Persistence and repetition were needed for this dream experiment. It was meant to prepare inner processes for handling greater traumas and threats. I was able to do these dream scenarios only for a short while at a certain healing level.

ASLEEPENED

The second dream experiment is *Asleepened*. Upon closing my eyes and becoming calm, I eventually produce a kaleidoscope of flowing colors in a similar manner to *The Dragon Dream*. Without thinking in words, I slowly increase the flow of kaleidoscope colors. I then calmly move my eyes from side to side with a slight flutter of my eyelids to imitate Rapid Eye Movement, REM. The right-brain becomes dominant. What do you think happens?

My whole body begins to twitch. I have tricked my subconscious mind, again, and am on a dreaming-waking boundary. My eye movement, fluttering eyelids, and the flowing kaleidoscope of colors, simulated REM dreaming. I experienced a reversal of being abruptly awakened. I was abruptly *asleepened*.

This reversal shows how words are developed for waking and sleeping states. While stimulated for sleeping, I quickly fell asleep. Brief sleep caused muscles to relax and nods awakened me, as I quickly fell asleep again. The quick repeated changes in state caused the twitches. I have experimented to discover limits between waking and dreaming.

From a neurological viewpoint what happened? I'm awake and aminergic neurons within the brainstem are firing as they should. I create activities stimulating REM dreaming. Reticular formation neurons become excited and begin firing for sleep dominance. Nods briefly awakened aminergic dominance and the waking state. In brief sleep, muscles relax and nodding reactivates the aminergic cluster for waking. We have again experienced emotional limits between dreaming and waking. These unusual dream abilities lasted for only a short time as mental reconstruction evolved.

Without an organized, *complete* set of emotional/trauma limits, manic thinking becomes too fast with loss of control. Subconscious iterations lose resonance without converging to complete thoughts and reasonable thinking. When manic, without subconscious convergence to normal consciousness, one may believe any *dream.* Thoughts are no longer compared to, and resolved with, similar historical memories to maintain consistency and sanity.

In my 1990 manic episode, in Phoenix, Arizona, while consumed with inner thoughts, I entered an entertainment arena with dancing. To my amazement, I saw images of fast dancer's *recent* feet and leg images trailing their *current* feet and leg images. Images looked like fast-moving cartoon characters. Recent trailing images lingered in my mind longer than usual.

I worried only briefly, believing that this strange sight was caused by the changing of my inner timing protocols due to mental reconstruction activities. I did not believe reality had changed. This visual *distortion* occurred only once. Normally, visual images dissipate very quickly and we are aware of only the *current* image.

Observing a fast-rotating wheel, we do not see reality. Our eyes and minds are unable to visualize the fast-moving wheel correctly. Our eyes produce an *integrated* or blurred vision. We do not think the material of the wheel melts or deforms because when the wheel slows down or stops it has its original form. We simply conclude that our eyes and minds cannot keep up with fast moving *realities.*

We do not see individual facial atoms but integrations of facial atoms for creating visions of faces, and other things we see. Human sight is limited. God may see all atoms of our faces.

Before sleeping, relax and broaden the forehead and face. Rub horizontally between the eyebrows for awareness of facial symmetry. Symmetry is important in understanding the brain, nature, and spiritual thoughts. Faces that are not symmetric are sad and scary. Symmetry occurs often in nature. A relaxed face sooths body, mind, and soul for relieving stresses of the day. Pleasant dreams may follow and solve our problems.

Waking mental processes continually prepare muscles to act or react. Waking and preparing for activating muscles uses more energetic mental processes than dreaming. Awakening activates higher mental energy and the mind has difficulty recalling low energy dreams. This is good. Otherwise, it would be difficult to distinguish between our waking and dreaming *realities*.

Dream processes normally have less control over muscles. Dreams are much faster, more varied, and *usually* use less energy than waking processes.

With higher manic energies, when dreaming while awake, it is difficult to distinguish between waking and dreaming. Manic inner dream processes demand attention, lessening waking reasoning.

Understanding our inner minds is essential for staying healthy and living longer. The best attitude is to feel comfortable with who we are. With patience, mental reconstruction, and determination, we can become who we want to be.

Subconscious processes iterate and converge for continuous awareness and purposeful thinking. While awake, EMR from neuron activations is reflected and diffracted many times by neural membranes for integrating and converging to *slower, longer lasting* conscious resonances before being totally absorbed.

In healthy lives, the mind searches for completion. We should calm our minds at the end of each day for feelings of completion that last for sleeping. Falling asleep will be easier. When simply awakening or awakening from dreams, give your mind a minute or so of calmness to begin the day with feeling of completion.

When awake, we have semi-awareness of follow-up ideas related to current speaking words. Without semi-conscious follow-up ideas, we would not have confidence to continue speaking. The subconscious mind organizes and prepares for supporting semi-conscious ideas to support continued thinking and speaking.

Dreams had an important role in biblical stories. Pharaoh's dream about an upcoming famine is well known. Joseph interpreted Pharaoh's dream so Egypt could prepare for a seven-year famine. God normally gives us only information we can understand, but Pharaoh needed help from Joseph to interpret his emotional dream.

In biblical times, dreams were often messages from God. Noah received a dream warning of a great flood, in time for him to build an ark and save his family. These two dreams were spiritual miracles that changed history.

Chapter 21

TRAUMA

"Unlike simple stress, trauma changes your view of your life and yourself. It shatters your most basic assumptions about yourself and your world . . ."

Mark Goulston,
Post-Traumatic Stress Disorder for Dummies

"Traumas early in life are the most limiting and most difficult to overcome."

H Fulcher

Trauma: an overwhelming, unpleasant experience that causes mental or emotional dysfunctions, usually lasting a long time; a serious, painful injury to a one's body

Trauma Limits: Thinking limits caused by extreme encounters beyond one's ability to react normally that cause a brief *black* out and a *trauma scar ingraining an emotional thinking limit.* Normal subconscious thinking processes work to avoid activating trauma scars. When activated, trauma brain scars send the mind out of control and sometimes initiate emotional flashbacks. However, when carefully activated, trauma scars release their ingrained excess energy that has sporadically disrupted normal thinking. Depending upon emotional energy of the activating trauma, an individual may feel threatened causing one to retreat, go out of control, or attack.

Traumas can be caused by internal or external events. When very fast or high-energy threating events are sensed, the brain does not have ability to react reasonably. The limbic system restricts highly energetic information from damaging the fragile upper brain. The upper brain experiences an information blackout causing a moment of insanity, of not knowing what to do. Later re-stimulation of trauma scars may re-traumatize the afflicted over lifetimes, unless trauma memories are unlearned, purged, or reduced to more normal mental energy levels with therapy or my mental reconstruction.

Neck and throat nerves and muscles are stressed when reacting to traumas. My psychiatric "conflicting neck" exercises release disruptive tensions from afflicted muscles and related brain areas. Nerves in the neck and throat are communication paths between the brain and body. Neck and facial nerves and muscles are affected by traumas giving a path to heal trauma scars and afflictions.

During trauma, affected neural networks and their glia support cells, become ingrained with high-energy that restrict blood flow to the brain and cause sporadic emotional disruptions. Trauma memories are stored with high-energy in the fast response limbic system. We must reactivate trauma memories slowly at or near incurring energies to dissipate their energy and restore them to more normal activities and memories. Careful conflicting psychiatric neck and throat exercises give an inner sense of approaching emotional limits.

Emotional *reasoning* failures cause embarrassment, stress, and ingrain *failure trauma* scars within the cerebrum. Mentally preparing reasoning processes ahead of time for expected emotional stress reduces the impact of traumas.

Stress from earlier traumas and persistent degradation causes depression, and bipolar disorder. Everyone has a breaking point from severe traumas and persistent stress. Psychiatric feedback and conflicting exercises prepare minds to handle stress, depression, and mania.

Conflicting body and verbal languages from perpetrators ingrain trauma scars in innocent victims. Body language is interpreted by the analog processing right-brain, and words are interpreted by the discrete processing left-brain. Quick conflicting gestures and verbal language confuse. Words may be positive and body language negative. Conflict between left- and right-brain interpretations ingrains reasoning trauma scars.

Perpetrators degrade victims with their false, mixed messages. Some perpetrators may not recognize effects of their degradations but are simply mimicking parents' behaviors. Conflicting languages, when not understood, confuse victims and ingrain uncertainties. Some perpetrators become addicted to their power of confusing and degrading victims. Perpetrators corrupt by exerting power over victims and develop a false, sinful superiority.

One might respond, "Your verbal and body languages give mixed messages. That is a form of lying. I will point out your conflicting verbal and body languages until you make them consistent." Mimicking or exaggerating their verbal and body language may cause perpetrators to stop. In any event, recognizing the conflict and letting the perpetrator know you recognize the conflict is healing for you. If continued over time, mixed messages may be devastating to victims who do not understand the conflicting effects.

Impulsive controllers are as damaging to victim's mental health as are conflicting body and verbal language perpetrators. Conversations and tasks may seem normal. Then, an unexpected, degrading voice demands unsuspecting victims do his or her bidding.

Impulsive commands are more damaging to victims when perpetrated in front of others. They are usually so quick, unexpected, and demeaning that they are difficult to counter. Perpetrators *know* when to pounce to get brief rushes of control and power.

A *prepared* solution is to immediately reject impulsive commands.

"Do not use that tone of voice with me. Why did you say that in such a degrading tone of voice?" Simply walking away does not stop impulsive, controlling abuse. Impulsive perpetrators must be confronted in the act.

Perpetrators are power based and enjoy degrading and embarrassing others. Impulsive controlling addiction may be similar to a heroin addiction to overcome. Victims must reduce importance of their bullies. "I will not be degraded by your abusive tone of voice and conflicting body language."

Trauma scars are similar to cancers in the brain not synchronizing with normal mental processes. We must reduce energy of recalled trauma memories so they will resynchronize with normal mental activities.

Persistent stress and significant losses cause preoccupation and lessen abilities to accomplish daily activities. The brain and individual brain cells become less efficient. Thinking becomes less confident, painful, and with loss of reason.

Correct abusive relationships early on, get counseling, or get away as soon as practical. Persistent mental abuse causes loss of confidence and slow murders. I stayed in an abusive relationship for seventeen years. I was fortunate to get out of my dysfunctional marriage alive. Her mother caused frequent conflicts and degraded those close to her. My sweet mother avoided conflict and made people feel good about themselves.

I may have prevented my bipolar disorder and divorce if I had been assertive early on to my former wife's abusive behaviors. We may have had an *acceptable* marriage. She may have unlearned her deceptive behaviors she learned from her deranged, alcoholic mother when young. Marriage improves quality of life or causes slow death. Men usually die before wives.

My goal is to understand fundamental causes of abuse and prevent my and readers' abuses. There needs to be harmony in life, marriage, and in the world. Think what the world could be like if everyone respected and loved everyone. Resources need not be wasted on armies.

Chapter 22

"THE FLASH"

"Trust in dreams, for in them is hidden the gate to eternity."

Kahlil Gibran

"Death be not proud, though some have called thee Mighty and dreadful, for thou art not so . . ."

John Donne

"During my expected imminent death *Flash*, emotional memories were recalled nearly one million times faster than in my normal awareness. *Flash* awareness was without questioning or decisions. I was simply an observer of my emotional thoughts. Imagine how fast God's awareness and thinking must process in *spiritual time!*"

H Fulcher

My emotional *Flash* during college times was traumatic. It was the night before registration for spring quarter at Virginia Tech, in 1967. At that time, we had to select computer cards for courses we had to or wished to take.

There was a party the night before in Lynchburg, Virginia. I returned to my parents' home after midnight. I did not drink at this party. I needed to wake up at 5:00 A.M. the next morning and travel nearly eighty miles to Virginia Tech to register for classes. The alarm awakened me. I had never felt so tired but left for Blacksburg around 6:00 A.M.

After about an hour, I began nodding while driving. A dangerous thought occurred that I could rest while driving. Several times a nod would awaken me. My irrational thinking and tiredness continued.

It happened! I fell asleep at the wheel! My head nodded down and awakened me. As I recovered consciousness, immediate awareness swept through my being. My foot had relaxed on the accelerator. The speedometer was reading 80 mph and a tractor trailer was only a few yards in front of me going slowly up a hill.

I started for the brake, but immediately knew it was useless. I lost all hope of life continuing. In shock of imminent death, *my emotional history "flashed"* before my mind as I prepared for death. A *dream thought flashed* into my mind to use the center lane to avoid and pass this truck. My arm jerked the steering wheel to the left. Tires screeched. Someone else *seemed to be* driving. I was a concerned bystander in a tragic play. There were two lanes up and one lane down this mountain.

As my car entered the center lane, another tractor trailer was coming down in the opposite direction toward me. My hand jerked the steering wheel to the right. Tires screeched again. With God's help, I went between those two tractor-trailers going 80 miles per hour. The ordeal was over in a flash. Immediately, I was trembling like a leaf. Time awareness flashed back to normal.

I had no difficulty staying alert the rest of the trip. Feelings linger to this day that no racecar driver could have avoided those trucks without God's help. This story never ended. I continued wondering about this high energy, lightning awareness of emotional memories that rifled through my awareness when I had lost all hope of life continuing.

Years later during *high-energy* manic excitement in 1977, I worked mentally to relive, remember, and understand this *high-energy Flash* and its highly *detailed and realistic* scenarios. Highly-emotional manic energy levels must have approached Flash mental energy levels to activate recall of the *Flash* scenarios. I recalled emotional visions. They were recalled quickly, realistically, and profoundly. All emotional events envisioned had successful endings. I had survived the impossible. This dream miracle was an awe-inspiring spiritual awakening.

Vision speeds were astounding. I estimated that in less than one tenth of a second, nearly one hundred vivid *significant emotional scenarios* flashed through my consciousness. It occurred between the time I was aware of the first truck and before my hand jerked the steering wheel to the left. There seemed to be no rush in experiencing dream scenarios.

I estimated the *Apparent Vision Time Spans* (AVTS) of each vision *appearing* to last at least ten minutes. A few visions appeared to last an extremely long time. Other dreams seemed to last for long times. In one vision, I was a young child peering out the window waiting and waiting for dad to come home. I was elated when I saw his car turn into the driveway.

Let's perform a rough estimate of AVTS.

AVTS = 10 minutes x 100 visions x 60 seconds/minute

AVTS = 60,000 seconds of apparent time span of all flash visions

Let's look at the ratio of the apparent time span of all visions and the actual time:

Actual Time (AT) of visions = 0.1 second):

Ratio = AVTS /AT = 60,000/0.1 = 600,000

This rough estimate indicates that my mind semi-consciously processed nearly one million times faster than normal awareness. Thank God, we have capacity to think very fast in *expected imminent death* situations. In fear of and in preparation for imminent death, subconscious processes momentarily became conscious.

The Flash was an unexpected, amazingly rapid awareness of normally subconscious processes recalling life-saving emotional memories for a critical decision. Would it be helpful to become aware of very fast subconscious processes for our benefit, at other times? Could we learn from such fast scenarios?

If God presented *The Flash*, I have little capacity to understand it. If God has given the brain and mind capacity to process so quickly, we may be able to develop some understanding.

Visions appeared as precise memories of truthful emotional events in high definition. There were no dreamlike distortions. No judgments were made during scenarios. Judgments take time. I was simply an observer of my emotional life events. Emotional scenarios evolved without feelings of needing to rush.

Subconscious processes selected and integrated emotional scenario potentials that guided my arm to avoid an *expected imminent death* car crash. I only observed my hand jerking the steering wheel to the left. God seemed to control my hand and save my life that morning.

It seemed odd that highly emotional visions did not relate directly to the immediate need of avoiding a devastating car crash. None of them had anything to do with driving a car. The connection was that high-energy emotional resonances in earlier and later *memory scenarios* had near the same mental energy level I experienced when seeing the truck in front of me. This high normally subconscious energy prompted my *instant* life-saving reaction. From this limiting experience, I believe highly emotional decisions are constructed by *subconsciously recalling* earlier emotional memory scenarios with high emotional or trauma energy. Normal high energy subconscious mental processes became conscious.

So many emotional scenarios flashed through my mind without awareness of any judgment. Living in the moment without conscious judgment is mindfulness.

The timing, flow, and coordination of my recalled *Flash* scenarios were *energy encoded*. From this experience, memories can be recalled *consciously* at very fast *Flash* speeds. *The Flash* is proof for me that God is always present. He was within my mind and soul as *I* survived *certain death*.

Chapter 23

OPERATING THE BRAIN

Operate: control the functioning of a machine, process, or system

Engineers design, build, and operate complex machines. In designing and operating nuclear reactors, I had to understand and control complex parameters. Before getting into the nuts and bolts of operating our brains and minds, let's begin with simpler models.

Before we flip a light switch on, we anticipate a light coming on and being able to see things in a previously dark room. We associate the light switch with light and a lighted room. We seldom think of designing and manufacturing the light switch and light bulb, transmission wires and the electricity generation for the bulb. We benefit from operating things but seldom think in depth about processes that make them work. We drive our cars thinking mostly of its controls, our comfort and safety, traffic concerns, and destinations.

When riding a bicycle, we operate our legs, feet, arms, hands, eyes, backs, bodies, brains, and minds. With experience and repetition, most of these activities become subconscious until we make changes. Our brains are operating with strong, confident, and dominant neural networks.

When performing routine activities, thinking is easy, requiring little conscious attention. Subconscious minds take over operating well-known, repetitive tasks, not needing full conscious attention and control. Difficult tasks are easier after we have practiced them. A concert pianist plays semi- and sub-consciously after much practice and experience. Repetition transfers tasks mostly to subconscious mind control. The subconscious mind is very fast and can be very precise.

Operating the brain includes:

1. Vision is a complex process of subconscious and conscious awareness and control for understanding environments, light sources, relative locations, and limits of control. Control includes eyes, nerves, posture, brain, and mind. Eyes and brains react to brightness, color, movement, speed of changes, and various details. Vision from each eye is processed through different neural paths and areas within the brain. The brain must synchronize and integrate light information from our two-eyed and neural paths for developing integrated three-dimensional vision. The subconscious mind is continually analyzing incoming light for familiar, unfamiliar, and friendly or threatening, images.

2. Protocols for vision are initiated by light activating rods and cones. Each rod and cone promote resonances within the brain. There are millions of resonances in the brain at any one time. As views change, resonances, vision, and consciousness change. Resonances from all rods and cones integrate to form a seemingly smooth *continuous* vision. We are not aware of individual rod and cone activations. Integration is a big part of seeing, thinking, and spiritual life.

3. Our eyes and brains operate with up-close discrete and long-distance holistic protocols for short- or long-range vision. Understanding mental protocols gives us appreciation for, and improves, thinking. Sound travels along different paths within the brain and is coordinated with vision.

4. The brain monitors, controls, and supervises autonomous organs including heart, lungs, digestive track, and other internal organs. Breathing is semi-autonomous. To some extent, we can control breathing.

5. Skin sensitivities are mostly subconscious until skin areas are touched or injured. A touch makes an area of skin conscious. Severe pain within the body or brain dominates awareness. Other awareness lessens. The brain's protocols have priorities to see, hear, feel, and understand important things first.

6. Subconscious operating protocols analyze importance of sensed activities by recalling, and making comparisons to, related memories for reactions or actions. Integration of currently sensed information with genetic and related memories construct consciousness for solving every day and pressing problems.

7. Our souls are our pathways to heaven and Eternal Life. During high energy expected-death or extremely low depressed energy, the mind becomes aware of the soul and heightened spiritual communications. Others and I have received unexpected messages from God and have felt compelled to surrender to His bidding. God gives us free will, but either influences or operates our brains and minds in highly emotional, threatening, and severely depressed, times. God does not view life and death the way humans do. My feelings are that God considers death as a normal transition. He is aware of our lives and our *existence after physical death.*

We have considered senses, brains, and minds performing subconsciously and consciously. Our brains and minds have *engineered* operating protocols for prioritizing and reacting subconsciously and consciously to normal and pressing events. Our brain and mental protocols prepare us to live our lives, and prepare for *spiritual lives* after physical death.

Cognitive priorities are mostly selected by mental resonances and energy levels from senses and memory. High energy threats require fast, forceful reactions. A gentle touch gives feelings of love and closeness with rich, deep feelings.

Current sensations and related memories guide the brain's operation. The upper brain becomes dominant during non-threatening and long-range thinking. True love is normally a long-range integrated process. Worry restricts thinking to the past, uncertain futures, and restricts every-day creative thinking and activities.

Stimuli sensed from an event may be perceived as either pleasant or unpleasant depending upon genetics, experiences, and moods. The same circumstances may be good for some and bad for others. Thinking of and caring for the needs of others develops spiritual operating procedures.

Operating the brain is somewhat similar to operating a car. We feel the pressure on the accelerator with our foot and relate that feel to the acceleration of the car. We turn the steering wheel and feel and see the car turning. We operate our brains and minds to ensure our environments change *safely* in front of us. We develop feelings and feedback from our actions.

A small acorn has the information, structure and potential to control and operate the growth of a huge oak tree. It *knows* how to grow the limbs and leaves for them to respond to water, wind, earth, temperature, and sun. A fertilized egg has the ability to control or operate the growth of a human. Our brains use feedback and develop potentials to grow and operate our changing bodies, and minds.

Human brains and minds continually refine protocols for completing daily and difficult tasks. Operating the brain includes genetic and learned protocols. Successfully operating our brains and minds during challenges builds confidence, joy, and supports restful sleep. The same words, situations, and challenges mean attack to some and flee to others depending upon histories and confidence. A potential lover expressing love to another may be breathtaking to one and frightening to another. It is a matter of perspective.

MIND SECTION

MIND SECTION

Chapter 24

MIND

"The hardest prison to escape is your mind."

Unknown

"The mind is its own place, and in itself can make a Heaven of Hell, or a Hell of Heaven."

John Milton

"The mind is everything. What you think you become."

The Buddha

"We should think of the brain and mind as one entity."

H Fulcher

"Dreams create multi-dimensional mental picture Holograms including emotions and timing of changes."

H Fulcher

"Exercises and models that help thinking positively about healing the brain and mind helps heal the brain and mind."

H Fulcher

Mind: the element of a person that enables him/her to be aware of the world and his/her experiences, the faculty of consciousness and thought.

Spiritual hologram: Man's living higher dimensional mental hologram including spiritual waves when praying or being spiritual.

I have mostly modeled our minds up to this point as normal. To make significant advances we must extend our minds beyond *normal mental or thinking limits.*

Our minds are our most important possession. Without them, we are nothing. The brain creates the mind, and the mind recursively controls the brain, and body. Nerves transmit inner and environmental information for processing by the brain and mind.

Models of the mind do not need to be highly detailed or perfect to help us improve our thinking processes and life. The brain is electrical and chemical. Subconscious processes are very fast.

L. Ron Hubbard made Dianetics models that have helped his readers evaluate and heal their minds. Dianetics models included little brain anatomy. Any *positive* study into the brain and mind may be helpful in healing the brain and mind. However, I have concerns of mind healing models and processes creating a religion that control people's lives. Gaining unchecked power over people creates dictators and ruins lives.

My brain models included elementary anatomy. Coherent electromagnetic radiation from billions of neurons travels in all directions and are reflected many times before being completely absorbed by brain cell membrane molecules, and other brain matter. *Brain cells* refer to neurons and glia support cells. Resonating EMR must last beyond time and energy thresholds to develop consciousness. Consciousness is created by specific integrated, coherent resonating neuron EMR that writes to and reads from brain cell membrane molecules that are sensitive to specific frequencies.

Neuron activated Light (EMR) traveling, reflecting, diffracting, refracting, and integrating throughout the brain that create resonances lasting long enough create consciousness. The brain must have EMR wave and energy equilibriums or it blows up or freezes. Neuron activated Light energy is created and dissipates at similar rates. There are millions, perhaps billions, of slightly different neuron created wave profiles, lengths, and frequencies creating subconscious activities and consciousness. There is subconscious awareness of each *speck* of vision we see.

Brain resonances last longer with greater reflections and slower absorption. Attention changes cause EMR resonance changes.

Light waves interfere and integrate with other Light waves having the same or nearly the same frequencies. There are many resonating waves and resonating supporting waves for each idea we have. Higher frequency harmonic waves ride on longer fundamental waves to create billions of subconscious details for integrated consciousness. Resonances in the brain iterate in many directions with millions of slightly different frequencies to make human *sense*.

Water waves interact similarly to light wave interactions. Water or Light waves meeting from opposite directions create standing or slowly changing waves when they are of the same wavelength. Neuron Light is reflected and absorbed by brain cell membranes. Resonances die out with absorption and are renewed with the next generation of neuron activations with the same or nearly the same frequencies or wavelengths. EMR waves creating consciousness are similar to standing or slowly changing water waves.

Current neuron resonances overlay refined EMR information on membranes with earlier brain cell *hologram* information. Brain cell membranes store higher dimensional information similar to light storage on commercial three-dimensional hologram media. Detailed, refined membranes are more reflective creating longer lasting resonances with greater influence on constructing conscious thought. Thinking is constructed by integrating, comparing, analyzing, and extrapolating information between current and memory holograms. Fast dream and subconscious hologram resonances must be integrated for constructing longer lasting *standing* waves for consciousness. Longer lasting mental resonances give greater confident ideas.

Mental processes and memories are stronger and more confident when constructed by greater numbers of related neuron activations. Normal brains and minds work together as one entity. Severe traumas repress highly emotional memories and even compartmentalize the brain.

Subsets of one hundred billion neurons activate, to synchronize and integrate their Light to construct millions of resonating mental holograms. Subconscious mental holograms during waking are similar to dream holograms. They are influenced by the senses. The brain and subconscious mind coordinate and integrate subconscious holograms as *its* medium for constructing consciousness and thought. The brain and mind operate using genetic and learned protocols. The mind is complex. We learn with attention and practice.

We *see* millions of details in our dreams and vision. The mind processes vision as either up-close and detailed or integrated and holistic. The brain changes left- or right-brain dominance subconsciously as attention and focus change. Coordination and integration of light from millions of rods and cones, and related neuron activations create our continuous, *smooth* vision.

Confident, repetitive ideas construct refined, smoother, reflective neuron and glia membranes for longer lasting resonances. EMR travels *very fast* in the brain but resonates *relatively slower* to develop conscious resonances.

Human mental limits are originally constructed by heredity and later by our emotional failures and successes in completing difficult challenges. Successfully achieving challenges expands emotional limits. Failures usually narrow emotional limits.

Nuclei refer to groups of neurons with specific purposes. Traumas and intense emotions stress nuclei to limits creating survival protocols. Without distinct mental limits, decisions must consider one's entire memory and reactions to environments in order to converge to successful conclusions. A reconstructed mind accepts wider academic and emotional challenges and develops wider logical limit structures for creative, detailed ideas and decisions.

Different nerve intensities activate specific recall and response protocols within the brain. Hitting a finger with a hammer creates high-energy fast resonances in nerves and related areas within the brain. When experiencing high intensity nerve signals, minds temporarily lose awareness of *normal* sensations and thoughts. High energy reactive responses over-power normal thinking. *The mind screams: Get that hand off the hot burner!*

In thinking about thinking, I estimate it takes one thousand times more energy to say a word than it does to think of that word. Similarly, it takes one hundredth less energy for processing a *thought* subconsciously than consciously. We should gather input for difficult problems, and solve them subconsciously while sleeping, and then recall results upon awakening. It is the energy-efficient thing to do!

The purpose of the subconscious mind is to control organs and operate conscious processes. The fast-subconscious mind iterates and integrates to construct much *slower* consciousness. I work to make more of the subconscious mind conscious. This process gives confident feelings and makes dreams more conscious upon awakening to gain more control over our minds.

We take our minds for granted until we experience depression, bipolar, or other disorders. Thinking becomes difficult and uncertain with lessened reason and confidence. Minds are horrible things to waste. We must take care of and protect our most valuable possession. Thinking and love are God's most valuable gifts to us.

Bullying destroys minds. If anyone is bullying or degrading us, we should confront them early on, if possible, mentally reduce their importance, avoid them, or *possibly* suggest counseling together. Allowing abuse and degradation to continue becomes more difficult to confront and correct later on. Persistent degradation is slow murder.

Societies, parents, and teachers should be aware of, and prevent, bullying. No one should make anyone feel inferior. Sibling bullying is often ignored or accepted as normal by parents who have bullied or been bullied. If bullied or mistreated, we should make new friends so no one person or group can dominate, degrade, and isolate us. Do not let a bullying spouse isolate you from your family and friends. With self-centered perspectives, some parents even think it is acceptable and ego building for their child to bully other children. I have seen it.

Bullying imprisons minds, restricts freedoms, and shortens lives. "The hardest prison to escape is your mind," *Unknown*. Bullying builds invisible mental prisons.

Genetics has given our minds greater inner intelligence than we will acquire in our lifetimes. Genetics defines us as humans. We don't look, think, or act like cats.

However, my cat thinks in anything that *matters* to him his thinking and actions are superior to mine. In petting my cat, I feel I am doing something good for him, and that makes me feel good. I try to make him feel wanted and confident. Well-adjusted individuals search for *recursive* relationships in life.

Memories are divided into two parts. The first is short term for up to an hour. The second is long-term memory believed to be embedded in brain cell RNA or ribonucleic acid. My model for long-term memories is that "coded" protein structures are within brain cell membrane DNA that responds to specific Light resonances for creating specific memories. Memories have complex structures. Models help us think about how the brain constructs the mind and how memories interact with senses. God is aware of our prayers and sometimes our thoughts.

One simple mind model is to imagine resonating EMR within the brain as *integrated sounds from billions of resonating micro-guitar strings* sharing and integrating rhythmic vibrations within the brain for creating the mind. We have awareness of music integrated sounds. When emotionally performing fast activities, guitar strings vibrate faster with shorter resonances. Each string is slightly different and creates slightly different sounds. *Integrated sounds* from vibrating slightly different micro-guitar stings integrate to make mental music that resonates throughout the brain creating the mind, and the soul with God's assistance at times.

Confident conscious thoughts are from the more synchronized and integrated EMR. They relate to integrated sounds from many guitar strings. Each strike of a micro-guitar string represents the firing of a neuron. Think of the *sounds* or Light integrating to make subconscious and conscious thoughts.

Rationally organizing helter-skelter baby experiences into organized memories is impossible for young brains and minds. Early memories must be stored within refined energy levels and frequencies. Different EMR resonances have different energy levels and wave profiles. Adult memories are stored by both energy level and relationship criteria. Baby brain processes and their memory protocols must be reconstructed for adult thoughts to be efficiently stored and recalled. After mental reconstruction, recall and reasoning will be faster, more detailed, and feel more confident and complete than earlier visions and thought. However, aging slows the mind in some respects.

Four mental processes are:

1. Normal sense and mental processing for everyday actions and reactions that do not activate *extreme* emotional or trauma limits. Only normal subconscious processes are selected for constructing conscious reactions and decisions.
2. Analytical reasoning by the upper brains iterates to converge to consciousness with memory information for simplifying complex problems and building new skills. It makes the unknown, known.
3. Defensive and survival reactions tense the mind and body and activate emotional and trauma limits. Survival reactions beyond limits, do not converge to reasonable solutions.
4. Reasoning beyond the physical world for receiving spiritual communications and guidance from a higher power gives inner confidence and hope. Earthly thoughts and fears lessen when sharing spiritual communications.

Our eyes and minds fail to perceive images that appear too briefly in our scope of sight, or if stimuli are too weak. Conscious resonance limits are not met.

Subconscious processes and nuclei compete for dominance and

conscience completion. We talk and write in complete sentences. Striving for and meeting daily and long-range goals gives feelings of completion. Meeting long range goals usually gives greater feelings of success and completion. We are more successful if we logically break long range goals into organized and attainable shorter-term goals. While successfully completing related short-term goals we can also focus on long-term goals. If long-term projects are unorganized, uncertainties build without feelings of completion or accomplishment.

We may study and practice for years to become a champion at some intellectual or athletic pursuit. Long range goals build character and are the most satisfying.

We love to share ideas with those who accept and support our ideas and activities, increasingly so, as we get older. There is comfort in repeating and sharing uplifting songs, rhymes, and spiritual hymns with like-minded friends and believers. However, some strive to cause and win arguments.

We should learn from others but also develop our own reasoning protocols. Most of us believe in something greater than ourselves. As young children, we grew up believing our parents were our protectors and were greater than ourselves. As adults, many of us turn to God for feelings of completion from God who is much greater than ourselves. Hopefully dying will give *spiritual* feelings of completion.

Mental holograms, alphabets, and words are building blocks for thoughts and language. Studying inner processes and writing ideas down refines thoughts and language. Our thoughts are constructed by comparing and integrating subconscious mental holograms as our mental picture language. We must translate our subconscious picture thoughts into our best organized words, sentences, and paragraphs to communicate with others.

Mentally reconstructing improves reasoning abilities and confidence. Becoming aware of and analyzing inner thoughts enhances reasoning. Briefly and slowly extending minds to limits builds mental infrastructure, imagination, and spiritual communication skills. We must strive for coordination and cooperation with others but retain thinking independence. Otherwise, arrogant people may control us.

TV, radio, cell phone, and outer space radiation continually bombard our brains and minds. Fortunately, our brains are not very sensitive to outer space EMR wave lengths. They pass through our brains and bodies without depositing significant controlling or disorganizing energy.

Our brains and minds are most sensitive for recognizing words in our own language. We are less sensitive to unknown words in unknown languages. Words in our language integrate awareness and make *sense to us.* The mind strives to make sense and completeness!

After mental reconstruction, with eyes closed, images from memory appear slightly clearer. However, memories of daily events seem to decrease with age. Some words are more difficult to recall. Age takes its toll.

The limbic system is the brain's rough, fast response system. It monitors nerve information and energy levels to protect the fragile upper brain. Normal, less-energetic information is transmitted to the upper brain for higher reasoning analysis.

Light, EMR, resonances imprint information on brain cell membrane micro-segments for constructing memories and actions. Specific micro-membrane molecules absorb their distinct EMR waves and resonances for building specific sub-thoughts for consciousness and control of the mind and environments.

Environmentally activated nerves, integrated information from neuron nuclei, and subconscious memory protocols operate to control the mind. Mental protocols have the continuing tasks of matching sensed information with *subconsciously recalled* memory holograms. Mental holograms formed by sense data match up with recalled memory processes to create thought. Subconscious memory processes search for related memory resonances one million times faster than conscious memory recall. The mind is a subconscious *matching machine.* The Flash was very fast.

The mind and body stimulate one another. Some speakers communicate unemotionally with little body and hand movement. Energetic body and arm motions of an emotional speaker stimulate listeners' brains and minds. Body language accentuates importance to spoken words. The eyes, brain, and mind subconsciously and consciously search for importance from speakers' motions and words. Coordinated gestures influence listeners more than just words.

When awake, senses and the aminergic cluster in the brainstem have activation potentials to create conscious resonances. Specific nuclei resonances are activated for specialized purposes. The mind iterates between subconscious memory and sense information for creating versatile, truthful thoughts. If matching sensed and memory resonances are not found or activated, we have not recalled a conscious memory. We either sense a new experience or feel uncertain with a sense of wonder or failure. Recalled memories often give a sense of usefulness, truth, and completion. It feels good to recall a long-lost memory. As the first order of importance, the subconscious mind is continually comparing sensed information to emotional memories to protect against threats.

We simply press a button to save a computer word file. There are many hidden procedures or algorithms for saving and recalling computer memories. There are greater complex procedures in storing and recalling human memories. Human memories are more easily recalled if emotional or repetitious. Computer memories are recalled perfectly, without emotions. Some people press our *emotional buttons* that distort our memory and reason.

I give a comparison between nuclear reactors and the brain and mind to help understand how the brain and mind work. In operating nuclear reactors, nuclear engineers and nuclear reactor operators cannot control the firing of any one *neutron* but can *statistically* control the firing of *billions* of *neutrons* to safely control nuclear reactors.

We are unaware of the firing of any one *neuron* in the brain, nor can we control the firing of any one *neuron*. One firing *neuron* does not create an idea. However, our *conscious minds* have *awareness* of and can *statistically* control the firing of billions of neurons to produce and control ideas and thoughts. Our thoughts are the awareness of up to *billions* of firing neurons. Our thoughts are similar to the control of *billions of activated neutrons in a reactor*. Senses and the mind statistically control millions or *possibly* billions of neuron activations for our awareness and thoughts.

For every glance we make, our senses and conscious minds control the firing of a statistical set of neurons. There is no sensed control of the firing of any one neuron. Thinking is the sensed control of millions of coordinated neurons. Our conscious thoughts and images are integrated EMR resonances from the firing of related statistical sets of neurons each fraction of a second. Our senses and conscious minds control statistical sets of firing neurons for thoughts.

Brains and minds are matching machines. We recognize people and images we have seen before. The same images we see later activate the same sets of firing neurons in the brain.

Light, EMR, is the medium between physical and spiritual dimensions. Relativity has shown that Light has unusual properties. Our spiritual sensitivities are constructed by our most integrated neuron EMR. The mind integrates Light, EMR, to construct holistic and symmetric structures that are shared in spiritual dimensions. The brain is physical, and the mind is spiritual. The mind's integration abilities create spiritual *completions* that are independent of physical space and time.

Without minds, brains have no purpose. Without God, the universe has no purpose. God is the universe's mind. We learn more about our minds and God when experiencing emotional limits. *Briefly* and slowly extending our minds to emotion limits with conflicting exercises extends our minds spiritually for activating our souls for experiencing God.

The mind extends beyond the physical. Loving God, others, and self is spiritual. Our subconscious minds normally build *models* to support waking needs. We should work toward reasoning limits to discover our inner minds, souls, and God. God has given us free wills and imaginations to think spiritually. If we have established spiritual principles, we will respond spiritually to ourselves, others, and God. Our free wills have abilities for loving and supporting God's Purposes.

We usually do not *see* or *hear* God but *sense His presence and guidance,* at times. It is beneficial for many of us to pray. We make mental models of God using inner feelings and thoughts, or we accept what others want us believe. It is spiritual if leaders teach us truthful spiritual beliefs. Humans feel they need either dependence on, or independence from, religions and God. Emotional, spiritual needs and beliefs may change over time with challenging experiences and age.

Believers pray to and worship God to receive spiritual blessings. Our mental EMR and spiritual resonances synchronize, integrate, and converge to construct our souls that *constantly* communicate with God. Our souls reside in spiritual dimensions that extend throughout the universe and heaven. They remain connected to the mind through personal spiritual waves. Our souls cultivate and integrate our life-time spiritual thoughts and actions into spiritual oneness for God's judgment. Freed of trauma effects, our minds may have perfect spiritual communications with our souls. Mental trauma scars degrade communication with our souls, which have perfect communication with God.

Many of us learn very little about our inner minds and spiritual processes until we endure severe difficulties. If spiritual goals are met upon death, our everlasting spiritual holograms will become more real than our physical lives. It is difficult to prove spiritual abilities or that God exists. Feelings matter. How will our earthly histories affect our spiritual existence and influence God? How will they be influenced by God? If our lives have been spiritual, our souls will be released from our brains and minds to become heavenly spirits with much greater freedoms, upon physical death.

Mental freedoms have spiritual characteristics that extend beyond physical space and time. Minds are designed to think physically and spiritually. We can think of our cat in one moment and a star that is light-years away in the next moment. Light cannot travel as fast as thoughts. God's spiritual waves can travel much faster. In my theory, the Big Bang created very fast spiritual wave reverberations between its origin and expanding boundaries of the universe. Spiritual waves are fast enough to give God His up-to-date omniscience and omnipresence throughout the universe and heaven.

Virgin Light, directly from the Big Bang (not from atoms) expands outward at the speed of light creating the universe's expanding space and spiritual dimensions. As the universe expands, *Nothing* is *lessened*. Spiritual waves, much, much faster than light, are continually reflected at the universe's expanding boundaries by the back side of Virgin Light and focused on the point of the universe's creation to support God's omniscience and omnipresence. Virgin Light appears nearly stationary relative to spiritual waves. God is not restricted to human time and space.

Spiritual waves are referred to in the Bible as *The Holy Spirit*. On a universal and heavenly scale, physical and spiritual dimensions integrate to construct one physical and spiritual purpose. Humans can be an important part of God's reality and purpose.

God maintains constant communication with our souls in spiritual dimensions. Our souls integrate all of our spiritual memories and activities in striving to make us spiritually complete. God judges our thoughts and activities holistically over our entire lives. Our souls may be transformed at the moment of death to have greater freedoms and love that last forever in spiritual dimensions. Spiritual and physical dimensions are intertwined. Upon death, bodies are no longer needed and discarded. Our souls are set free of physical time and space to support, and be supported by, God in spiritual time and space. My models have healed my mind and given me spiritual confidence and hope. Being spiritually saved is *certain* only at the moment of death. It is a sin to boast of being spiritually saved. It is good to feel like oneself will be spiritually saved. We should prepare for our dying process with love in our hearts for others and God.

From my experiences, I would like to further define the human mind:

Human Mind: a living higher-dimensional hologram in the brain created by reflected, integrated, and absorbed neuron electromagnetic radiation spikes and with transmission of neuro chemicals that create cognition and control of the body. Conscious higher-dimensions include memory, language, depth of beliefs, moods, and interactions with *spiritual waves during prayer.*

Chapter 25

PSYCHIATRY

"Life isn't about finding yourself. Life is about creating yourself."

George Bernard Shaw

"Psychiatry is a strange field because, unlike any other field of medicine, you never really finish. Your greatest instrument is you, yourself, and the work of self-understanding is endless. I'm still learning."

Irvin D. Yalom,
The Spinoza Problem

"We must value our own lives to truly value other's lives.

H Fulcher

Psychiatry: a branch of medicine that deals with mental, emotional, or behavioral dysfunctions and disorders.

give a patient's perspective of psychiatry. Prolonged stress too often causes a chemical imbalance in the brain and bipolar disorder. Psychiatrists question patients for feedback and discovery. They prescribe psychiatric medications to resolve chemical balances for controlling patients' moods, quality of thinking, and behaviors. Psychiatric medications are designed to limit the mind from going below and beyond reasoning limits and prevent it from going out of control. Unfortunately, psychiatric medications, such as Haldol, too often limit normal productive thinking. Certain medications may limit reasoning and other mental functions to a *small percent* of earlier abilities. Psychiatrists should be active in giving mental ability tests, and adjusting or changing medications, if patients become and feel mentally limited.

Ministers and psychiatrists must ask their overstressed members and patients questions to help them understand root causes of their disorders and especially give them confidence for mental improvement and healing. Root causes are often suppressed.

When I was depressed in 1977 and then highly manic, no religious leader or psychiatrists asked me reasons for my disorder and episodes. Spiritual leaders and psychiatrists should work to together to discover relationship and other causes of stress disorders. I had repressed my former wife's abusive behaviors for five years before my depression and then mania. I was too embarrassed to admit that early bullying and a dysfunctional marriage caused my disorder.

Freud's psychotherapy of questioning and feedback have assisted patients in recalling trauma memories and releasing their disruptive energy for healing overstressed, erratic minds. My goals were to reduce inner stresses, relieve emotional pain, and expand mental freedoms while culturing positive moods, creative thinking, and adaptive behaviors. We must be fierce in fighting against continued abuse.

In 1977 in my first manic episode, I had my first encounter with a psychiatrist. I was emotional, unsure of my thinking, and reactive. I was skeptical of those I met but expected miracles from this first psychiatrist.

My senses were acute. At a distance, I overheard this first psychiatrist tell my dad he could not do anything with me. In my state of mind, I expected death shortly.

This first psychiatrist prescribed Haldol without requesting to see me again for two weeks. Within one week, muscles all over my body were cramping. In severe mental and physical pain, feelings of death engulfed my mind and soul. In agony, I asked to be taken to the emergency room. My mental and emotional limits were exceeded.

I had had a severe reaction to, and was taken off, Haldol by my second psychiatrist, Dr. Gene Goode. He was encouraging, helpful, and most probably saved my life. I developed confidence in him, and in psychiatry.

Emotional limits, established early in life, remain over lifetimes unless overridden by psychiatric drugs, persistent degradation, a significant life changing event, my mental reconstruction, psychotherapy, expected death, or God's intervention. Minds and machines go out of control when stressed beyond limits. Erratic, fast thinking evolves when mental limits are exceeded and subconscious processes do not converge to reasonable complete thoughts. Complete thoughts are supported by thousands or perhaps millions of resonating subconscious converging neuron iterations.

Loss of health, a loved one, job, and so on, may lower self-esteem and cause depression. Self-image is distorted and lessened. *Inner* communication skills and thinking deteriorate. With prescribed antidepressants, my mind quickly rebounded from depression into fast thinking and bipolar disorder.

When depressed, uncertainties became greater than my mind's ability to cope. The subconscious mind panics. Fast, irrational incomplete spiritual-like thinking erupts. In mania, one is aware thinking is emotional, distorted and incomplete. In my case, I turned to God for him to save me from my mental pain and agony.

As a psychiatric patient on maintenance prescriptions, I have often received strong spiritual messages. Bipolar patients should be told that spiritual thinking is not uncommon, and they are not alone. Spiritual thoughts are exciting but often occur too quickly to be complete or helpful. Patients must work to slow thoughts down. Meditate on simple things. Frequently write and refine ideas until you make sense to yourself first and possibly others later. Read writings over slowly. If possible, ask for feedback from a trusted friend. It takes calmness and patience to make spiritual messages believable to others. Spiritual writing was and is emotional and was essential for my mental healing.

Mental patients must make sense to others to be believed. From my experience, psychiatrists do not and should not comment on patient's spiritual revelations. Psychiatrics cannot easily understand or control spiritual excitement. Psychiatrists should not comment on or dissuade spiritual writing. Patients need to understand themselves. Spiritual understanding and goals are good to strive for.

Brain cell membranes and brain boundaries reflect neuron EMR thousands and maybe millions of times for creating *long lasting* resonances for building conscious thought. Patients need some level of creative and spiritual thinking but be restricted to socially acceptable behaviors. When *established* emotional limits are eclipsed by high-energy mania, the mind goes out of control. If manic energy is not too fast or excessive, mental limits may expand and control rational, creative thinking.

Rigid religious beliefs and practices give followers *perfect spiritual certainty* for *limited* lives and the rejection of other religions and non-believers. Religious leaders and psychiatrists should work together to convert prejudices, hate, false superiority, and desperation into love, peace, and hope.

Unfortunately, some psychiatrists may not believe patients have ability to discover and practice their own mental health solutions. Psychiatrists can make fast improvements with prescription drugs. However, they are not complete cures. The brain and mind become accustomed to, and rely on, prescribed medications for maintaining thinking within emotional limits for sanity. Mental health patients must be careful and notify their psychiatrists if they intend to reduce or stop prescribed medications on their own. Some patients may have the discipline and courage to experiment and work slowly toward controlled non-drug solutions to *help heal* or *heal* their disorders. Drugs are never complete solutions to cure patients of mental disorders. With medications and mental reconstruction efforts, we can heal our mental disorders.

Patients and psychiatrists must work together. Psychiatrists must be alert and smart to know if patients have ability to help heal themselves. Patients have responsibility in healing their minds. Psychiatrists must continue asking patients the right, specific questions to put *them* in charge of their lives. Psychiatry is not an easy profession or an exact science. Patients and psychiatrists are not always logical in healing minds.

Scientists work to discover God's intricate, perfect logic in His creation of the universe. God was perfectly logical in creating perfect constant physics and probably laws of the universe. There are no perfect mental laws.

In a psychiatric ward, manic and tittering on the boundary of insanity, science became my hope to prove and restore my reasoning and sanity. Without notes, I derived complex physics equations. Physics made sense. I could not find reason in my wife's destructive behaviors. In mania, Christianity continued giving me faith in God, however, it did not give me a *quick cure* in my time of great need. However, I learned from manic episodes.

Christian leaders teach spiritual benefits of forgiveness. We must be wise in forgiving. I believe in forgiveness when a perpetrator expresses guilt, remorse, and will no longer repeat evil or degrading offences. I see little purpose in forgiveness when knowing an offender will continue to repeat offences. There are evil people that even hide in churches and their religions. If we must hate someone for severe wrongs against us, hate briefly. God gave us ability to hate for our protection. Let it go quickly to remain mentally healthy. Victims often feel guilt, without fault, when abused. Hopefully, we will find solutions and mentally rebound from evils experienced. When things get tough, search for mental and spiritual help.

Fully recalling repressed, destructive memories reduces their energy and disruptions. If disruptive high-energy memories remain in the brain, disorders continue. With lowered mental energy, we can better reason about what we should and should not do. Psychiatry needs to be involved when there are threats of suicide or harm to others. Psychiatrists must make critical judgments.

Psychiatry may be needed early on to prevent harm to oneself or others. Parents should have their children's mental health evaluated early on to free them from early ingrained trauma effects, and difficulties later on. Most young brains and minds need adjustments to heal from unnecessary restrictions and losses of control.

Children who believe they are free to abuse, or incite others to abuse, those who are weak were not disciplined by socially ignorant or unethical parents. These children learn deep-down immoral behaviors that may become more active in their teen or adult lives when they encounter opportunities. Everyone has levels of mental imbalances and prejudices to lesser or greater extents. We have ingrained prejudices and negative influences from genetics, parents, society, and biased religions.

Parents and others telling young children and teenagers they can't do challenges limit their experimentation and thinking. The affected and bullied restrict their thinking and actions to be *safe, keep the peace*, and accept their *assigned place in life*.

Brainwashed, socially limited victims may eventually reject their *assigned unbearable* social status. Some turn negative against everyone since no one has helped them or given them confidence. A weapon *gives* a dysfunctional victim *quick* confidence. They may become mass murders and *raise* their status by momentarily feeling above those they injure and kill. They do not care about their own lives. Others find a higher status in religion with perfect beliefs in an *absolute perfect, unquestionable spiritual leader*. It is emotional to be part of a *perfect* spiritual family.

Childhood counseling may prevent lifelong suffering and give confidence to do amazing things. Professionals and a concerned society must develop solutions for immoral, destructive thinking and behaviors. We should promote competitions in sports and other activities for all children to have successes, confidence, and creativity. Children learn to be creative and adaptive to win competitions. Minds must learn to adapt. There should be games everyone can win.

Child counseling needs to be a routine part of young lives. Elementary and High schools should have psychiatrists or counselors talk individually to students each year. Bullies need to be identified *cured, or neutralized*. Unfortunately, most parents do not understand or value benefits of, and *fear*, psychiatrists. They are afraid their own training has not been good enough or acceptable. Attitudes on psychiatry need to change. Early psychiatry can help children and teenagers become confident, productive adults. Today, only dysfunctional children and adults receive counseling. Parents should study childhood psychology to nurture and correct their children's behaviors. A gentle nudge, encouragement, and guidance encourages children to be successful in society. If freed from trauma effects, children and adults will be happier, confident, productive, and sociable.

Goals are for children and adults to learn at their own pace without being brainwashed, *forced* into unquestioned beliefs, but to reason through creative options. Brainwashing may lead to false superior beliefs. We must develop solutions for immoral thinking and abusive behaviors.

Giving children appropriate options and praises for good answers and behaviors builds confident reasonable children. If young children abuse others and cannot be corrected, their parents must also have psychiatric training along with that of their child. Societies will benefit.

We should psychologically adjust our thinking to believe in relativity and God. Science and spiritual thinking are different from everyday thinking. Psychiatrists should briefly take patients to limits and then quickly calm them back down with reason and *love*.

Chapter 26

MEMORY

"Memory is a way of telling you what's important to you."

Salman Rushdie

"Memory is a way of holding on to the things you love, the things you are, and the things you never want to lose."

Kevin Arnold

"Literature becomes the living memory of a nation."

Aleksandr Solzhenitsyn

Memories are the essence of who we have been, are, and, to a significant extent, who we will become. They contain inner thoughts and histories of our lives, including who we've helped, and who has helped us. Memory is necessary to do our jobs and remain independent, but, too often, declines with age. Without genetics and memory, we cannot judge importance of new activities and events.

Some memory loss with age is normal and not a sign of dementia. A healthy brain and resilient memory are nurtured by staying physically and mentally active. Walking is a healthy exercise. Reading and writing keep the mind active. Predictions using memory with continued refinements build confidence for future successes. Memory, study, and preparation make the future more successful.

Mental reconstruction may renew subconscious and conscious processes for improving memory and cognition. Right-brain, left-brain dominance exercises synchronize our two brains for having creative right-brain solutions with normal everyday thinking.

If afraid of forgetting an idea, we write a note. We feel sure we will remember to read our note and recognize and understand the letters and words we have written. Note-taking and other mnemonic tools support recalling memories when needed.

After years of mental reconstruction, I have greater ability to recall emotional events. Recalling good memories is pleasant and relaxing. Healthy minds retain all emotional memories but recalling may be difficult, more so with age. Talking with an old friend may stimulate long forgotten memories that could not have been recalled on one's own.

We may improve mental health by briefly recalling negative events and poor decisions, and then reducing their importance. We should consider how they have affected our lives, and what we could have and could not have done better. Analyzing negative memories helps avoid repeating mistakes.

In math, if we integrate a parameter within a function from minus to positive infinity, the resulting function no longer varies with that parameter's influence. If we think through negative influences, they may have less effect. The somewhat *semi-conscious* right brain integrates control of the entire body for dancing to be coordinated and synchronized with the music, and a delight to behold.

It is pleasing to recall rewarding accomplishments. Parents have pleasing memories of their children meeting important milestones. They feel they have some responsibility for their children's accomplishments.

What good is awareness and memory, if we cannot use them for our benefit? Some of us remember life changing spiritual communications. They give deep feelings of importance, completeness, and purpose.

We don't appreciate our minds and memories until we begin to lose them. We can do nothing without memory. It is the foundation of thinking and reasoning. Writing down emotional memories may help us understand their negative and positive effects.

Chapter 27

DEPRESSION

"Depression is being color blind and constantly being told how colorful the world is."

Atticus

Depression: feelings of severe despondency and dejection. "Self-doubt creeps in and that swiftly turns to depression"

The basic purpose of the conscious mind is to evaluate sensed information, recall related memories, integrate information into meaningful, executable data, and prepare for current and future needs and desires. Remembering the past is a current activity.

When depressed and contemplating suicide, the subconscious mind rebels against consciously ending its existence. Subconscious processes slowdown to survival mode. Suicide thoughts are "normally unthinkable." Subconscious and conscious minds are designed for life not death. Suicide thoughts creep in when there is no inner peace or joy, and with no hope of mental pain or life getting better.

During my only depression in 1977, I expected imminent death, but unexpectedly sensed a spiritual presence, just in time. God had not given up on me. Suffering and spiritual sensitivities were intertwined. In depression, mental abilities lessened; but spiritual *abilities* may become lifesaving. God gives us free wills and lets us live our lives independently until we need help, or he chooses us for His spiritual purposes.

Suffering pain of depression awakened spiritual receptiveness. Jesus' suffering death and rebirth created hope of everlasting life for those believing in Him. My suffering became spiritual and saved my life. At *our time*, we will celebrate death of our bodies for our souls to escape and become more real than our lives on earth.

Mental uncertainties and suffering made my inner mind and soul sensitive to God's spiritual waves extending throughout the universe and heaven. Most who have suffered earlier in life tend to be more spiritual and caring.

If someone shows signs of depression, parents, employers, church leaders, and spouses should help him *express* and *correct* fundamental causes. So much pain and suffering can be avoided with understanding of causes for early recovery. Often causes of depression are deeply repressed, and not easily expressed. The depressed may be too embarrassed to admit that *gradual*, emotional degradation has caused depression. Ask if there are changes you or others can make to reduce depression. Show caring. Be persistent. It maybe you who needs to change. Uncertainties from subtly abusive spouses, parents, and bosses may slowly increase depression over time.

I did not receive psychiatric care until I was highly manic and out of control. I never recalled any psychiatrist or minister asking the cause of my depression and mania even though I had severe symptoms. In the worst of depressed and manic times my former wife never expressed love or concern.

Psychiatrists and ministers should be trained to help the depressed understand and express root causes of depression. They only need to gently repeat, "Why are you depressed?" Understanding causes of depression should be the goal after stabilizing patients. The main cause of my depression was frequent deceit, coldness, and degradation by my former wife and to a lesser extent being bullied when young and even into teen years. Because of early abuse, I accepted my former wife's abuse.

Bullying was responsible for my continuing to accept abuse from my former wife. We should have had counseling or divorced early on to save my health and possibly her life. She died of a heart attack when fifty years old. Her deranged mother was persistently degrading to her.

During depression, physically weak, and mentally limited, I sensed a general or holistic spiritual purpose. I continued loving my children and parents. Feeling their love kept me from committing suicide. I never felt love from my former wife, an adult child of two alcoholic parents. With her background, my former wife always seemed to look for things to go wrong.

Experiencing uncertainties and suffering mental pain while locked in a psychiatric ward, I began frantically writing to understand my distraught mind and to save my sanity. While confined in this psychiatric prison, I experienced spiritual feelings that babies receive complete spiritual wisdom from God upon conception. I also sensed an unusual, not unpleasant, movement within my brain. My brain felt different and thinking felt less painful and easier.

Depression may be divided into two categories:

1. **Reactive Depression** is a profound depression. Temperament becomes negative about self and the future. The energy of the brain and mind is lowered. There is lack of attention and responsiveness to others, profound despair, and thoughts of suicide. Reactive depression may slowly return to normal moods and thinking without medication.

2. **Clinical or Unipolar Depression** is a neurological disorder involving an imbalance of neurotransmitters within the brain. Thinking slows down and becomes painful. The clinically depressed may become so preoccupied with hurtful thoughts, failures, or losses that they may appear hopeless and lifeless. Extreme emotional lows with lack of attention to family and others are symptoms of preoccupation on failures, losses, or

pain. The clinically depressed experiences repetitive, circular thinking and persistent worry without effective attempts of solving causes of concerns and problems. Solutions seem impossible. The afflicted gives up on restoring self-esteem and health.

In depression, the mind lingers in negative, and often self-destructive, moods. Depression may be caused by loss of self-esteem, health, a loved one, or exposure to persistent physical or mental abuse. Life becomes confused, hopeless, and dreaded without *any possible* way of the mind returning to normal. Wherever a depressed person happens to be, never seems to be the right place. Mental pain follows everywhere. There is no place to hide your hurting mind. After about two months, my depression erupted into bipolar disorder.

My depression was caused by repressing anger over allowing a stupid lifestyle to continue over such a long period of time. I continued to praise my former wife and she continued to degrade me. Praising was all I knew how to do. Our behaviors were unhealthy for her and me. I repressed inner anger for letting myself live such a stupid life. Over the years, our marriage made less sense with less purpose.

Praising others was all I knew, and needed, to live in my country community. My parents, relatives, and friends were always positive to everyone. I never heard them be negative to anyone.

I had to deal with bullying and abuse. Over time, I regarded him as having low value to me. Continuing to live with someone, early in life, who is degrading you limits mental abilities and life. You are dumb and can't do this or that. Generally, I was happy when I was away from abusive behavior.

I knew my former wife's degradation was untrue and dumb, but persistence took its toll. From the youthful ingraining of her parent's alcoholic behaviors, she felt she had to act and *be* superior. Putting down those close to you is the easiest way to act, and *eventually be*, superior. It happens too often. Such persons are spiritually inferior.

My repressed anger degraded into depression for letting abuse continue in an unhealthy marriage for years. With no sisters, I did not know how to deal with or correct a woman's *degrading behavior.* I hid my stupid married life from everyone. I did not complain. My former wife was an expert in pushing for control and discontinuing if I began to react. Our marriage was a fraud from the beginning. Her coldness showed signs of her having been sexually abused earlier in life.

Janet Geringer Woititz's book, *Adult Children of Alcoholics,* (Expanded Edition) 1983, explained my former wife's behavior accurately. I wish I had read it early in the marriage. With understanding, our marriage could have been better, or maybe even good.

Because of severe abuse as a child, I had learned to accept abuse even as an adult. In the beginning, my former wife's abuse did not seem so unusual. It worsened over the years.

I share some blame for my disorder. I never confronted my former wife early on about her deceptive and degrading behavior. It took me years after the divorce to understand her behavior. I observed her deranged mother severely criticizing and degrading her last former husband. Frequently, this deranged mother severely criticized my former wife, and disrupted our lives. In turn my former wife was aggressive to ensure no one else would *abuse her.* Life for her was abuse or be abused. What a deranged life we lived?

A dysfunctional person may be good to some, and bullying and destructive to others. My former wife was good to our children, neighbors, students, and coworkers.

After our only psychiatrist's session together, my former wife was aware of how she had shocked the psychiatrist and refused to attend further sessions. We should not underestimate the mental damage caused by an abusive childhood.

My former wife was cold and evasive. I wanted a divorce only weeks after our marriage; however, I thought a divorce would greatly disappoint my mother. I did not mention my former wife's degradation to my mother. I had ill-begotten hopes that things would get better. There seemed to be no way out. I was trapped.

In depression "impossible" situations and problems were repeatedly recalled without organized efforts toward solutions. Chemical changes within the brain slowed thinking. In embarrassment, I retreated from the outside world into a hell of recurring negative, painful thoughts. At one point, I had rather have been a fly I saw flying near me. It seemed to have a purpose. Suicide became appealing to escape the mental pain, and embarrassment of feeling and *being less* than human.

In the depths of depression, I could not recall a single word or speak, and could not simile. I had lost control of my smile muscles. The brain and facial muscles are closely related. For a few days, suicide was my only *pleasant* thought.

In my only depression, I was sure I had severe brain damage and would never recover. I had reoccurring thoughts that life is not worth living as a mentally damaged person.

With abnormally low mental energy, left-brain discrete reasoning is overpowered by general, holistic right-brain negative thoughts and emotions. Right-brain rhythm and harmony became erratic but included glimpses of Big Picture and spiritual thinking.

Without anticipating a future, I would walk down a hall and freeze. There was no purpose to think, move, or do anything.

Worry and circular thinking did not allow sleep for releasing inner tensions, renewing the mind, and restoring energy. Without sleeping for weeks, thinking was never conclusive. Hurtful memories flew round and round.

Low and high energy moods promote long-range, holistic right-brain dominance. The depressed have sporadic *big picture* thinking, without left-brain details or rhythm for true solutions. Persistent, right-brain dominance precludes detailed left-brain problem solving. Years later, mental reconstruction rebuilt sharing protocols between detailed and holistic thinking.

To support healing, family and caregivers should give examples of others who have successfully recovered from severe depression. Realistically, describe healing from depression as a slow systematic process including readjustments of self-image and ego. Assure patients that depressed minds can fully recover.

Friends and family should talk about good things the depressed has done in the past and realistic opportunities for the future to rebuild self-worth. Be truthful.

Healing is enhanced by caregivers defining and helping the depressed follow simple step-by-step processes. Encouraging the depressed to do routine chores helps restore needed left-brain thinking and control. Setting the table and folding clothes are simple left-brain tasks. Give the depressed an opportunity to help. Don't push. It may hurt the depressed to think or do anything. Folding clothes may be a challenge.

The depressed need simple successes to return to positive thinking. Show an interest in him. Be alert and careful not to bore or insult a depressed patient's intelligence. With your help, he will recover faster and be *smart* again.

Humor is never advised as the depressed will take humor negatively. Depressed minds are predisposed to negative thinking.

Helping the depressed be active attracts his mind away from painful circular thinking. Never push but leave simple things for the depressed to work on if he chooses to do so. Pushing may add to feelings of failure.

It is important to have counseling together. You may be able to correct simple things that make both lives better. An ideal marriage is for both husband and wife to be confident, caring, and loving enough to sincerely praise each other daily.

Selfish perpetrators will deny responsibility of causing depression and bipolar disorder. Psychiatrists must determine causes of depression and suggest that involved spouses, parents, children, or others be part of counseling sessions. If they will not join, care providers must help patients become emotionally separated from perpetrators. It may be a life-or-death decision. There are too many suicides. I praise the Lord for my parents and Dr. Gene Good, my second psychiatrist, in supporting my recovery. My children were small. I lived for them.

I was mentally tough in solving physics and engineering problems. However, childhood abuse contributed to my not being emotionally assertive in my dysfunctional relationship with my former wife. She seldom told me of her childhood experiences and conflicts with two alcoholic parents. She hid her abuse. I believe her dying of a heart attack was caused by her internalizing her mother's harsh criticisms.

She was rational in most endeavors and usually with me when we were with others. Damaging, degrading, and twisted behaviors occurred when we were alone. Her goal seemed to be to divide and conquer. We had different dysfunctions.

From childhood abuse and feeling emotionally restrained, I did not correct my wife's abuse and remained in a horrible, deceptive marriage. Parents must encourage children to speak up when abused, or they may not speak up when abused later in life.

It's your parents' and then your responsibility to protect your sanity, health, and future. We and those close to us must recognize *effects abuse is having* on us. Abusers become addicted to power over victims. Abuse and bullying seldom stop without intervention.

Chapter 28
BIPOLAR DISORDER

"The unexamined life is not worth living"

Socrates

"Mental illness is nothing to be ashamed of, but stigma and bias shame us all."

Bill Clinton

"People with bipolar disorder have difficulty with boundaries."

Claire Danes

"Bipolar disorder can be a great teacher. It's a challenge, but it can set you up to be able to do almost anything else in your life."

Carrie Fisher

"Psychiatrists and ministers must help patients uncover causes of depression and bipolar disorder to guide inner healing, and not rely solely on medications"

H. Fulcher

Bipolar disorder, also known as manic-depressive illness, is a brain disorder that includes extreme shifts in mood and mental energy levels, lack of thinking control, and loss of ability to carry out routine tasks. Moods range from extremely low energy in *hopeless* depression, to extremely high energy, and uncontrollable energy and elation. Bipolar disorder often follows clinical depression.

If you are bipolar, congratulations, you are in good company with: Ralph Waldo Emerson, Beethoven, Charles Dickens, and Winston Churchill. Think of the creative work they have done and you may also do if you have the will, patience, organization, and courage to heal, be unique, and *control* your manic creativity. Manic-depressives are smart and creative but have difficulties with, and *beyond,* emotional limits, at times.

A manic person is excited, energetic, creative, and often too excited to sleep. Imaginary or realistic goals become exciting and pressing. Anxiety becomes high and expectations often exceed reality. Normal interactions and goals are overridden by high energy creative thinking and goals. A manic person eventually becomes exhausted and goes out of control beyond emotional or survival limits, and may need psychiatric care. Trusting in Jesus helps.

A primary cause of bipolar disorder is persistent stress and feeling there is no way out. Feeling *trapped* in a degrading job or marriage causes stress. When stressed near limits, uncertainties degrade confidence. Thoughts, responses, and actions no longer feel *good enough or complete.* Early childhood developed mental limits become degraded, erratic, and lost. The mind goes out of control.

Healthcare authorities must consider that bipolar disorder is often caused by someone close to their patient, who is abusing or neglecting him or her. Most bipolar persons were originally gentle, loving, and abused by aggressive, uncaring, and self-centered bullies. Bullies will not admit abuse or express remorse. Bipolar disorder is an inner reaction to stress and persistent bullying.

In my case, bipolar disorder was triggered by my lying to myself. My wife was continually degrading me and avoiding closeness. She showed no love, only control. She had learned when young from her deranged, alcoholic mother. I was embarrassed by her behavior but kept her abuse to myself without telling others close to me. Lying to oneself is mentally degrading.

Bipolar disorder often follows clinical depression and amplifies negative, and sometimes spiritual, thoughts. Without hope of *normal* life continuing, spiritual thoughts emerge. After depths of depression, bipolar thinking became distorted and incomplete. *No human could endure such pain and live.* I felt I was either less than human but possibility spiritually gifted.

Psychiatrists should work to discover triggers that initiate patients' reoccurring manic episodes. Later understanding and responding to persistent controllers has increased resistance to manic triggers.

In 1972, I was rather confident at the beginning of our marriage but not prepared for my wife's continued degradations. I did not counter her behaviors early on. After five years of marriage, I became depressed. Depression lasted for only a few months and then erupted into bipolar disorder, dreaming while awake, and frantically grasping for reality. Persistent degradation destroyed a rather confident person.

My mind became overactive and raced in search of completions and sanity. I felt that a *normal* person could not endure so much mental pain and live. The highly manic mind searches for the highest survival limit bypassing normal emotional limits in thoughts and actions. Searching for hope, I briefly *discovered* I was Jesus. But quickly, I knew I did not have Jesus' love, or healing abilities. I returned to being a poor confused, sick person again. I could not trust my own mind.

Initial manic episodes were scary. Thinking felt unusual and inconsistent. As early episodes progressed, the mind became hardened, fearless, and desperate to regain sanity. My mind felt incomplete and yearned for earlier confidence. At times, extreme limiting thinking overrode fear and embarrassment. The mind raced toward unrealistic dreamlike goals. It was a tragedy not knowing if one's thoughts were dreams or reality. What is reality anyway?

During my first manic episode and riding in the backseat of my dad's car, I felt becoming increasingly lighter and feared floating out of my seat. Another time, I felt someone or an evil spirit was reading my thoughts. It was unsettling and scary.

Schizophrenia occurred briefly in only one or two severe episodes. I experienced hallucinations. I *saw* trailing images of dancers' legs as seen in cartoons. This was due to timing adjustments occurring in critical vision areas of my brain. Subconscious processes were converging to consciousness slower than normal. These images lasted only briefly on this one occasion.

Near the end of manic episodes, recalling and reasoning through my abnormal experiences was revealing and healing. It motivated me to expect and *accept* exciting ideas. Feelings were somewhat similar to alcoholic highs. Delusions occur when subconscious processes extend beyond emotional limits and fail to converge to rational thoughts. Drinking too much alcohol might have a similar effect. I did not drink alcohol.

During my last manic episode in 1993, high energy near manic ideas evolved differently from normal ideas. They felt more creative and converged as acceptable and felt unusually good.

Early insane, erratic, and creative, thoughts varied from suicidal to dreams of a Nobel Prize. I easily recalled physics equations during my first manic episode while confined in a psychiatric ward. The manic mind has huge mood swings and expectations.

After mental difficulties, we learn our minds are our most important possession. My mind has been my inner personal experimental laboratory since 1977. Who knows what emerges from a manic mind?

In severe depression, mental limits were breached and no longer provided conclusive neural EMR reflections for convergence to complete conscious ideas and decisions. Beyond limits, minds and machines lose control and may self-destruct.

Persistent stress causes uncertain, distorted subconscious processes that lessen abilities to reason and cope. Without consistent limits, the brain and mind panic and fast thinking begins in hopes of recovering sanity and normalcy. Continued fast thinking overstresses brain cells causing *chemical imbalances.* Abnormal neurotransmitter concentrations cause mood swings and thinking distortions.

Bipolar fast thinking evolves into *big picture, holistic* thinking with little normal left-brain restraint needed for detailed everyday reasoning. While awake, mania includes fast dream characteristics. The manic mind has difficulties distinguishing between waking and dreaming. Dreaming characteristics become as energetic as waking thinking.

Psychiatrists prescribe medications to correct neurotransmitter imbalances and to control mood swings, or energy levels within the brain. My conflicting mental reconstruction exercises and processes purge manic energy from traumatized neural networks, and glial support cells. With lowered energy and less pressure, the brain becomes easier to control for iterating to complete ideas for regaining consistent thinking.

Normal neurons fire and synchronize with related neural networks for developing reasonable, complete thoughts. High-energy, overstressed, and sporadic neural activations interfere with, and override normal brain resonances, processes, and ideas. Normal brain processes must increase energy to overcome high-energy sporadic trauma neuron activations. With high levels of trauma scars, brain energy and stress stay abnormally high. Ability to relax is lessened.

Neural networks, like muscles, re-grow after being briefly stressed to limits. Prolonged stress is damaging to muscles and the brain. When briefly stressed to limits, subconscious processes are forced to be creative for developing new synchronized activation patterns to process within reasoning limits. After the brain and mind have been at limits, one must relax allowing subconscious processes to recover and construct wider, more complete reasoning limits. Operating the brain above emotional limits over a brief time often causes inconsistent thinking and loss of reality.

Mind limiting experiments briefly extend subconscious processes beyond early childhood emotional limits. If the mind is overstressed too long, current emotional limits are destroyed. Any machine will self-destruct with broken limits. Limits can be rebuilt and expanded if approaching limits slowly and carefully. We must work to understand our minds and their limits.

If approaching disorganized trauma limits carefully, subconscious processes construct new, organized kinder, and wider emotional limits. We will no longer panic when old limits are approached. We increase abilities by periodically, briefly, and reasonably stressing our minds to limits, for developing new wider limits.

Broader more logical, less emotional limits replace earlier established high energy trauma limits. New wider subconscious limits improve subconscious convergence to conscious ideas. Genetic mental limits will be *uncovered* with higher thinking processes. Genetic limits are more consistent since they have been established through generations of emotional and life-saving decisions. With practice, the mind becomes more comfortable thinking near limits for accepting and resolving greater challenges.

Curing bipolar disorder requires understanding of its root causes, and its effects on the brain and mind. Manic-depressives are drawn to high-energy emotional ideas and actions. At the edge of a cliff, a normal person may briefly think of the excitement of jumping off and flying. We must consider effects of the things we think about and do. In mania, dangerous ideas linger. High energy ideas often occur too rapidly to converge to reasonable conclusions.

A normal complete idea might be: "I went to school to study physics." A manic incomplete idea might be: "I went to school . . . *and . . . but . . . and . . . but . . . and . . . but . . .?*" Extreme manic ideas feel uncertain and incomplete. It takes a troubled man to sing a troubled song.

A manic person may feel the need to prove his sanity, often unfortunately, at risk to himself, or at the expense of others. Proving sanity requires organized thinking.

Unfortunately, during episodes, manic-depressives may believe any dream or scam. I pray that those preying on the weak, disabled, and manic receive God's justice.

In mania, behaviors are seemingly uncaring and erratic causing observers to stigmatize manic depressives. Some observers feel superior, others see an opportunity to degrade, and some want to understand and help. Once stigmatized, it is difficult for manic-depressives to regain respect and trust. Negative attitudes change slowly. Criminals and deranged bullies take opportunities to degrade the afflicted. Criminal bullies seldom change unless caught. Blessed are the nurturers!

Bipolar patients may have other illnesses and abuses, without being manic. Even some medical doctors are biased against manic-depressives. Being free of manic episodes for over twenty-eight years is my *cure* and monumental success!

At times, new low-energy spiritual ideas synchronize with earlier spiritual ideas to give inner confidence and build strong beliefs. With high-energy, some spiritual messages have exploded into my consciousness that may take a lifetime to recall, interpret and understand. They opened spiritual communication channels.

Spiritual purpose may briefly become focused during manic episodes but also expected imminent death feelings may occur. One might feel weak and uncertain. The Bible expresses comfort when feeling weak in 2 Corinthians 12:9: ". . . My grace is sufficient for you, for my power is made perfect in weakness." I have felt God's guidance when alone, weak, and humble and yearn for further guidance.

Some might consider love a disorder. It begins with over-active emotions similar to bipolar disorder emotions. Bipolar disorder and love make individuals vulnerable. The first time in true love, one feels and thinks irrationally. Love is a disorder if not returned.

True love is to treasure another's happiness as much as one's own. He wants to help her be all she can be. She thinks similarly. They form a unit that is greater than two individuals. One hurts if the other hurts. Blessed are those in true love!

Labels can be helpful or harmful. Being labeled bipolar causes many to expect erratic, irrational, and, sometimes, forceful behaviors. I want society to think of bipolar persons, as loving, creative, and spiritual, and be understanding if their thoughts are erratic. Bipolar disorder can be cured with psychiatry and my mental reconstruction practices.

Childhood traumas and insecurities cause stress and trauma scars within the throat, upper neck, brainstem, and, to a lesser extent, in the limbic system. These overstressed, disorganized neural networks slow and disrupt communications between the body, brain, and mind. The brain has to unravel and translate trauma distorted, sensed nerve signals after they pass through a disorganized nerve system to construct the mind's subconscious and conscious processes. The brain has to make sense of distorted nerve signals in the throat and upper neck caused by trauma. Healing the throat and brainstem of trauma effects makes emotional nerve signals more-straight forward.

This is somewhat like looking through dirty or distorted glasses. If distortion is not too severe, the mind makes sense of distorted objects in environments.

My psychiatric neck exercises release trauma energy from the neck, throat, and affected areas of the brain for constructing organized communication channels between the body and brain. The brain does not have to work as hard to unravel sensed nerve signals. I have paid attention to and learned from inner sensation variations within the neck, throat, and brainstem for over twenty-eight years of psychiatric exercises while practicing mental reconstruction.

I have gained some understanding of the reactive sensations within my neck, throat, and brainstem during my 1994 manic episode. The energy of my brain and mind had become so elevated that the most energetic neural networks exceeded their limits releasing their repressed trauma energy. Neck energy release sensations felt exciting during and after exercises while purging sporadic trauma energy. After releasing trauma energy, previously afflicted neural networks interact more normally with related neurons and nuclei.

Aging is a pervasive stress disorder that may be cured with genetic engineering, psychiatry, and my mental reconstruction exercises and processes. Aging should not occur. Humans are living longer and should mature not age. Gene editing, CHRISPR, is a new and promising field for extending life.

Genetics and the mind control growth and aging. With genetic engineering and advanced nutrition, the brain and mind will slow, *or even stop*, aging. Cells in the body will *perfectly* divide maintaining the brains and body's abilities. The brain will grow and replace non-functioning neuron and glial cells with stem cells.

I began healing processes too late to significantly prevent my own aging. Younger manic-depressives and intelligent others may learn from my and other's processes to significantly slow aging. Some individuals age slower than their classmates. With less trauma effects, fortunate souls age slower. Lives can be beautiful longer. It depends upon how we think as we have lived our lives. Fortunate individuals have less adverse effects in their necks and brainstems.

Healed manic-depressives will develop greater and wider mind control. Practicing psychiatric exercises carefully extends minds to emotional limits for healing. Healed brains and minds have confident control in meditating and calming back down to normal mental energies. With practice, activating high energy emotional and trauma scars initiates creative ideas while returning back down within normal mental energy limits. For understanding, creative ideas will be compared to normal ideas and activities for healing and providing solutions to everyday and academic problems and concerns.

Meditation on, and relaxation of, the face promotes subconscious facial tensing or firming. There is a feeling of renewed youth within the face. Over the last three or four years, *subconsciously* controlled facial skin tensing has occurred during meditation. We must be alert to recognize and study new processes for healing disorders. Mental reconstruction, at early ages, will be shorter, easier, and more efficient in slowing or preventing aging.

With better nutrition, mental reconstruction, and gene editing, future generations will live longer. The brain and mind, cleared of all trauma effects, may promote perfect cell reproduction in the brain and body to maintain a *youthful* life.

This chapter has documented manic thoughts and memories for inner healing. My intention is to help readers heal their disorders to be healthy and happy. Life is a miracle that should be cherished. God does not like *anyone* degrading *anyone*. Mind and spirit can be renewed. If someone needs help, lean way, way down, and lift them way, way up. Amen.

Chapter 29
EPISODES AND INSANITIES

XLIV
One need not be a chamber to be haunted,
One need not be a house;
The brain has corridors surpassing
Material place,
Far safer, of a midnight meeting
External ghost,
Than an interior confronting
That whiter host,
Far safer through an Abbey gallop,
The stones achase,
Than moonless, one's own self encounter
In lonesome place,
Ourself, behind ourself concealed,
Should startle most;
Assassin, hid in our apartment,
Be horror's least
The prudent carries a revolver,
He bolts the door,
O'erlooking a superior specter
More near.

Emily Dickinson

INITIAL MANIC EPISODE

Depressed in 1977 without sleep for weeks, a tortured, slow death was permeating my mind and soul. Thoughts seemed stuck in molasses. Anxiety, stress, and fear of death forced a depressed mind into erratic fast thinking in search of lost hope and sanity. Life seemed frozen as in a tragic play.

My former wife's abuse over our first five years of marriage led me to distrust her. I would not respond to her during my first manic episode. Unbelievably, I stayed in a dysfunctional marriage so long. She showed no love then, or ever. She was degrading and deceitful when we were alone. She was reasonable when we were with others. A healthy person does not become a severe manic-depressive unless deceived, abused, or controlled over a long period of time. I hid her abuse without telling others. I was too ashamed of my marriage decision.

During my first episode, she recruited my parents to get me to the hospital. I trusted my parents. They took me to an emergency room, and I ended up in a psychiatric ward.

In this psychiatric ward, a thought occurred to me. How could any one person endure so much mental pain and live? *I must be Jesus Christ! Hallelujah!* I yelled to mother and dad, "I am Jesus Christ!" To my surprise, mother was not pleased with my revelation. She gently forced her face directly in front of mine and calmly said, "Hugh, you are not Jesus Christ!" For the first time in my life, I did not believe my mother. Excitement and emotions were too strong.

I went out into the hall and proclaimed to a poor elderly lady: "I am Jesus Christ!" She responded with raised hands, a bowering of her head, and a "Praise the Lord." Her response made me feel genuine, for a brief moment.

A not-so-manic thought abruptly occurred. If I am Jesus Christ, I have responsibly to this lady, mother, dad, and my children. With this thought, I knew I was not Jesus Christ and did not have His love or ability. I became a tired, sick, and lost person again and retreated to my hospital room. With some coaxing, I accepted a tranquilizer resigned to give up a hurtful life. The next morning, I felt better and was more reasonable after my first sleep in weeks.

I began emotional writing while locked in my psychiatric cell, fearing insanity, permanent confinement, and death. Writing was the most stabilizing thing I could do. I wrote about physics and injustices to prove my sanity. I could recall physics equations more easily than usual. Equations made sense. My wife's behavior did not. Writing added reason and purpose to my life, and a sense of completeness, at times.

Unfortunately, my first psychiatrists prescribed Haldol. He drugged and numbed me, and sent me home. After a week, Haldol produced horrendous side effects that nearly killed me. I could not swallow and muscles cramped all over my body. I again thought death was imminent.

Severely depressed and manic patients are not able to explain pains, illnesses, and debilitating side effects. I knew I needed and asked for emergency treatment. I was then assigned to Doctor Gene Goode and taken off Haldol. I returned to being a normal manic-depressive, if there is such a condition. Doctor Goode gave me hope and confidence in psychiatry.

After my battle for life, I have felt as if living on borrowed time. Psychiatrists must *frequently* monitor helpless patients for side effects. I never saw, or wanted to see, that first psychiatrist again.

During my episodes, my parents and aunts and uncles were so helpful and encouraging. I trusted my family but distrusted my former wife. Our children were young.

My former wife was a taker and never encouraged me in anything. Before my first manic episode, I had always been encouraging to her. In divorce, she tried to take everything she could. Unexpectedly, years after our divorce, she tried to get back together after causing me so much pain and health issues.

From my experience, adult children of alcoholics have an insatiable need for security. During our marriage, my wife frequently told me she needed a high level of security, *at my expense.*

1990 EPISODE

At work in Phoenix, Arizona, there was an atheist who frequently told me: "It is so stupid to believe in God." Without believing in God, I thought he believed he was the highest intelligence in the universe. Stress from his abuse added to initiating this manic episode.

I became manic and obsessed with drug dealers who ruin innocent lives. Unfortunately, I thought many individuals looked suspicious and were drug dealers. I was put in jail for one night for my protection. I had attempted to save the innocent from drug dealers.

I was confined in a holding cell with about 15 tough looking prisoners. Unfortunately, many of them looked like drug dealers. I was on a mission with no fear, beyond my reasoning limits. I yelled at them for ruining lives. One *fellow* prisoner came up and swung at me. With a reactive mind, I dodged. He looked rather sheepish because he had missed. I had no fear. I beckoned him to come back. Luckily for both of us he walked away. In my normal state of mind, I am not a fighter.

After this overnight jail experience, I was more reasonable. The night had been long with no place to sit or sleep. The next morning, I was too preoccupied to listen to or answer exit questions. I was a protester against drug dealers. My blind friend had protested several causes. I identified with him and signed out of jail with his signature. I could recall *exactly* how he signed his name. Now, I'm free, or am I?

I walked out of jail that morning with absolutely no idea where I was or how to return home. I was too embarrassed to call anyone, so I walked and walked including through rough looking streets in Phoenix all night without fear for my safety. Adrenalin began wearing out. I was very tired the next morning as the sun arose. I noticed street signs enough to find my way home. I had walked for more than a day and night. That was two days without sleep.

Hours of weary walking allowed some sleep. I had been fearless for days. Apparently, a chemical that suppresses fear was running out. Little things began to have unusual importance. People on a nearby balcony were spies. TV programs seemed directed at me. I was uncertain how to react. I became afraid of almost everything. I told my story to the police. They suggested I stay in a nearby Holiday Inn.

I must have slept some, for the next day I was able to be concerned with the outside world. I drove home, remembered I was prescribed Thorazine and lithium, and took my medications. I called my Phoenix psychiatrist and told him of my ordeal. Surprisingly, he did not suggest an appointment.

Things began getting better. I became aware of missing work for a few days. It was difficult explaining why I had missed work and had not notified anyone. I told the truth that I had gotten my nights and days mixed up. Things slowly became more normal. I still have strong memories of this episode. Some things made sense and others did not.

This ordeal was important. I learned I could find my own way back to sanity without a doctor's assistance. However, if I ever have similar difficulties, I will seek a doctor's help early on. This episode was way too risky.

1994 EPISODE

This episode was milder than earlier episodes. I seemed to function normally but became sensitive to unusual sensations when turning my head left and right. I believed my brain became sensitive to magnetic or electric fields such as the earth's magnetic field or electric power wires.

Forceful manic ideas demanded attention and, too often, caused inappropriate actions and reactions. Waking and dreaming became confused. Mania sometimes included schizophrenia, with bizarre dreamlike, and displaced characters. Manic thinking is more difficult to decipher than dreams.

I was vulnerable to bipolar disorder since not being able to confront longtime childhood and later spousal abuse. Victims *must* confront abusers early on when possible. Manic-depressives can recover from their insanities to become better than ever.

INSANITY

In her childhood, my former wife learned that husbands were to be abused, from her deranged, alcoholic mother. From early abuses, we both became imprisoned in emotional time warps.

During our marriage, my former wife's deranged mother was more abusive to my former wife than to me. My former wife was emotionally trapped by ingrained behaviors caused by her mother. She hid her mother's drunken harangues from others. She died of a heart attack in 2000. I still strive to make sense of, write about, and overcome my abuses. So many arrogant people abuse the weak, and so many suffer in silence.

Chapter 30

INNER TRAUMA

❧

"Childhood trauma does not come in one single package."

Asa Don Brown

I experienced two high-energy emotional energy release events in 1989. Energy released from these events was shocking. These inner events were sensed as being widely spread throughout the brain, and very different from tiny distinct localized energy release sensations in the neck, throat, and brainstem.

A reverberating high energy *Inner Metallic Sound* startled my mind and soul when playing tennis in Phoenix, Arizona in 1989. My knees began to buckle. Thankfully, I recovered before falling. The reverberating sound was deafening inside my head, but over quickly. This energy release and mental adjustment must have occurred in primary sound processing areas of my brain.

The number of neuron networks exceeding limits and releasing energy did not need to be great if they were in the most important auditory formations. When auditory neural networks exceeded limits, synchronization was lost. Adjustments, at limits, produced the metallic, reverberating inner sound. The metallic sound occurred a second time a few months later, with significantly less energy released and no real disruption.

In 1990, I experienced a *Mental Nuclear Explosion* awakening me in the middle of the night. Visual neural networks, within the occipital lobe of the cerebral hemisphere, lost synchronization. Networks in visual formations exceeded limits causing the *Mental Nuclear Explosion,* an *Extreme Inner Flash of Bright Yellow Light.*

As I awakened from sleep, my awareness was engulfed in powerful yellow light exploding outward from my brain in all directions. I *knew* I would never survive to see normal vision again. The powerful light subsided after a *very long* two or three seconds, a *dream eternity.* I became conscious of sitting up in my bed and sweating profusely. I was in disbelief I survived.

There was no sound during this inner mental visual explosion. After walking around for about thirty minutes trying to understand what had happened, I was exhausted, went back to bed, slept, and went to work the next morning.

My explanation is that I was overwhelmed by a highly unusual phenomenon. I concluded that traumatized networks lost synchronization between the reticular formation and aminergic cluster in the brainstem. These two areas are important in sleeping or waking dominance.

When the *Light explosion* occurred, both the reticular formation and the aminergic cluster nuclei fired frantically competing for dominance. Earlier manic episodes had reduced communication energy levels between the reticular formation and the aminergic cluster. The Mental Nuclear Explosion was caused by a communication adjustment between the boundaries of these two competing brainstem components. Both components fired simultaneously at full speed vying for dominance. I make models for my understanding.

I had briefly lost hope of life. However later on, I have not recognized any negative or positive effects from these two traumatic events. It is difficult to believe these two events occurred without negative effects.

I did not tell anyone about these two extreme events. Everyone would think I was crazy! Even psychiatrists would not understand or believe such events. I was on my own. I write to make sense of and document my unusual *limiting* events. Hopefully, after reading this book, readers will have less worry if they experience similar traumatic events.

I met Dr. Eben Alexander in Lynchburg, Virginia. He was signing his book: *Heaven: A Neurosurgeon's Journey into the Afterlife.* In a coma and near death, he saw a spiritual image of a young lady he had never met or seen before, who guided him away from *death* and saved his life. Later after recovering, he recognized a picture of that young *dream* lady who was related to him and had died several years earlier. When expecting death or experiencing near death, others and I have had spiritual visions of living and deceased loved ones guiding our souls to return to our bodies and minds saving our lives.

From Dr. Alexander's and my spiritual lifesaving experiences, I know our loved ones in heaven have very active spiritual purposes. I no longer pray for deceased loved ones *to rest in peace.* I frequently pray for *God to give my beloved ones in heaven wonderful spiritual activities and responsibilities in heaven.* It makes me feel good and, I believe, helpful to them. Doing nothing for eternity would be Hell. Spiritual time is very different from earthly time. God controls spiritual time to keep up with the entire universe and sometimes guides human activities by interrupting their free wills to enhance or save their lives. God only abruptly interferes with human free wills if we humbly ask His assistance or if there is an imminent life-threatening occurrence. Also, if we have done something spiritual, God may give us a burden to do for Him. Working for God is ones' greatest honor.

Chapter 31

MENTAL LIMITS

"When you push yourself beyond limits, you discover inner reserves, which you never thought existed earlier."

Manoj Arora, *Dream On*

"You are never too old to set another goal or to dream a new dream."

Aristotle

Limit: point or level beyond which something does not or may not extend beyond. Restriction on what is possible or permissible.

We or others set our boundaries. We have some control over boundaries *we* set. Breaking boundaries has less effect on us than breaking limits. Breaking mental limits has emotional effects and may cause loss of sanity or even death.

Let us consider emotional boundaries and limits. Going beyond emotional limits may cause our minds to go out of control or cause our brains and minds to expand abilities. It depends how fast or carefully we approach limits. In the *Psychiatric Exercises,* Chapter 33, I practice exercises to extend the mind to limits with the goal of expanding mental limits.

In mania the mind goes beyond *normal* mental boundaries and limits. By carefully extending thinking to limits we may learn to control the mind at emotional limits. My mental exercises at limits have prevented manic episodes and bipolar disorder for 28 years. The goal is to control the mind in stressful situations. It is wonderful not worrying about becoming manic and out of control.

When manic, our minds have extended beyond their normal emotional limits. To regain sanity, we must restore rational thinking within current or expanded mental limits. We must carefully discover and understand our emotional limits to expand and strengthen them. We can do this with conflicting psychiatric exercises and meditation that promote fundamental changes within the brain and mind.

Athletes practice extending their minds and bodies to limits to expand mental and physical abilities. We can make that *impossible* football catch.

To assist in understanding EMR resonances and limits within the brain, let's consider a simple physical resonance. A guitar string is elastic and attached at its two ends. It stretches and gains potential energy when struck. When released it vibrates or resonates with its fundamental or harmonic frequencies creating its characteristic sound. Resonating strings lose energy to the air while making sound energy and slowing down.

For one strike of a string, sound lasts for a few seconds or so until the string is struck again. When struck or stretched, energy is in the string's tension. Tension energy of the string becomes motion energy when it is, released, becoming less tense, and traveling back and forth. The greatest part of its characteristic sound is created when the string is traveling its fastest and giving the most energy to the air as sound.

If a player strikes a string too hard and it breaks, the *traumatized* string thrashes in the air out of control with no purpose losing its elastic energy quickly. Music and harmony cease. The string has been stressed beyond its limits.

There is some similarity when trauma activations are too energetic for responding neural networks. Neuron membranes are overstressed, and subconscious vibrations cease. Normal inner communications are corrupted. Distorted trauma energy is rapidly ingrained within traumatized neurons and their neural membranes. This is similar to the broken guitar string losing its tension energy *very quickly* with lost purpose. Traumas do not create normal long-lasting resonances in neural networks. High energy quickly overstresses brain cell membranes, which disrupts normal neural network resonances and inner communications. *Normal thinking processes are* disrupted.

A guitar string is attached at two ends to limit and control string vibration energy. Resonating EMR waves from many neuron activations pass through, are reflected, integrated, and absorbed by many brain cell membranes at various angles, as they affect the brain and mind. EMR resonates and integrates between neuron membranes at many angles. EMR resonates between thousands or perhaps millions of neural membranes in many directions. Similar to radios, EMR wave energy is mostly absorbed by brain cell membranes that are receptive to their frequencies

Let's extend dimensions of our guitar string model to think more about the brain and mind. One vibrating guitar string, the sound it makes, and the information within that sound, may represent one subconscious EMR resonance and the information within it. Suppose the guitar string ends could vibrate in and out, rotate on many axes, and have many different densities and sounds. These imaginary strings would make many different sounds and we can relate it to numerous varied EMR resonances within the brain. Neuron activations relate to the striking of guitar strings. Like our imaginative complex guitar string analogy, there are millions of varied EMR resonances throughout the brain. Models help us think about and heal our disorders for happy, productive lives.

Small fractions, of neuron EMR wave energy, are lost with each brain cell membrane reflection. Reflections are not perfect. Neuron activated EMR resonances have complex frequencies that are reflected and absorbed at complex angles by varied membrane micro-segments with varied characteristics. Each micro-segment has distinct reflective and absorption characteristics. Too high EMR energy disrupts membrane reflective and transmission characteristics.

Neuron membrane micro-segment limits may be exceeded, expanded, and re-grown. Fundamental mental limits usually do not change significantly throughout lifetimes unless significant emotional events or traumas stress brains and minds beyond early developed emotional limits. Failures and trauma limits restrict thinking and reason. Brain cell membranes must reflect neuron EMR long enough for it to converge to much slower conscious resonances. We must focus our minds on our bodies and environments to survive and thrive.

IQ's and fundamental mental limits usually do not change significantly during normal lives. IQs relate to how mental EMR resonances iterate and converge to conscious solutions during life challenges.

Childhood traumas and emotional failures ingrain restrictive mental limits. Mental reconstruction processes restructure early developed mental limits to be less restrictive with kinder limits. A goal is to expand creative reasoning that has been restricted by childhood and later trauma effects. With mental reconstruction, there will be greater confidence with less uncertainties in decision making.

Social customs normally restrict thinking, emotions, and actions within social limits. We act normal. Normal conversations and interactions usually flow without activating emotional limits. We feel uncertain when approaching emotional limits.

Stresses at emotional limits release ingrained trauma energy *sensed* as small localized releases. If experiencing *brief* stress at emotional limits by practicing psychiatric exercises, we will learn effects stresses have had on us. Reasoning through, and solving, difficult problems, reduces inner stress, develops confidence, expands emotional limits, and gives a sense of accomplishment.

Weight lifting and exercising at limits followed by relaxation gives an inner sense of accomplishment and increased ability. With patience and brief limiting exercises, we may expand physical and emotional limits.

Stress from repeated bullying and abuse ingrains restrictive, rigid mental limits. Victims become and feel limited. They become reluctant or afraid to engage in new challenges.

Praying and thinking holistically about life reduces fear of limiting experiences. It is emotional and healing to be listened to by significant others and God. God listens.

Inner tensions are ingrained within neural and glial membranes from severe stresses. We re-experience uncertainties and emotions when trauma memories are stimulated too swiftly. Mental limits are necessary for humans to make decisions and survive. Listed are some events that ingrain expanded or restrictive emotional limits:

- Expecting immediate death when severely depressed to the point of not being able to think in words and *freezing in place.*
- Failing important undertakings that negatively affect self and important others.
- First time crawling, walking, or riding a bike.
- Accomplishing or failing difficult physical or mental tasks.
- Being severely injured or degraded.
- Elation after unexpectedly solving a difficult problem.
- Being left out feeling loneliness and abandonment.
- Thoughtless or careless actions or responses causing guilt.
- Fulfilling, or failure to perform, sex.
- Finding and feeling true love.
- Losing a loved one.

Care is taken in *Psychiatric Exercises and Mental Reconstruction Chapters* to understand the effects of mental limits by practicing and learning from psychiatric exercises and mental reconstruction. With understanding we expand mental limits. Without understanding stress limits, thinking becomes either more restricted or out of control depending upon how limits are approached.

Activating genetic survival limits causes extreme reactions beyond normal thinking limits. Genetic limits have evolved over generations from successful ancestor reactions to severe threats. Human genes have recorded reactions and developed human genetic structures for guiding behaviors and overcoming emotional and trauma events. Human genes store millions of human responses.

In severe traumas normal social reactions are overridden by limiting survival reactions. When trauma energy and effects are lessened through mental reconstruction, social limits become versatile and refined. Reflective brain cell membranes support long-lasting resonances for thought completion.

With good parenting, young minds become active, creative, and remain within, or gently expand, mental and social limits. Mental and physical exercises can expand emotional and physical limits.

I model trauma limits as rough, rigid nuclei membranes, which have absorbed extreme distorting emotional energy. Recall of high-energy trauma memories that have been repressed can be reactivated with high-energy frequencies similar to ingraining frequencies. Nuclei are neuron networks that act and react together with shared resonances and purpose.

Brain cell membranes increase in definition with life experiences. Current neuron activated EMR continually overlays new detailed mental hologram structure onto and within earlier membrane molecules. There must be changes in brain cell texture for human memory to continually increase. Neuron membrane reflective characteristics increase with absorption of coherent EMR. Highly reflective membranes support longer lasting resonances for constructing consciousness and greater reasoning skills.

Traumas ingrain high levels of energy within and distort brain cell membrane texture. Affected membrane surfaces become rugged with less reflective properties, shortening resonances, and constructing rugged, high energy emotional memories.

When membranes repeatedly reflect normal EMR frequencies, they become smoother. Detailed memories are constructed with higher reflections.

Different brain cell membranes have different reflective and absorption properties for various EMR frequencies and angles for creating detailed memories and thinking potentials.

Subsets of 100 billion neurons activate depending upon senses and memory recall for consciousness and reason. EMR from one firing neuron is absorbed by its own and possibly billions of other brain cell membrane molecules. Six hundred trillion synapse connections create trillions of neurotransmitter path options for organizing and sharing neuron EMR spike information. Cognizance is developed by iterating, organizing, and integrating EMR information by writing to and reading from brain cell membrane molecules. Human brains can think *infinitely* diverse thoughts.

Manic, in the Virginia Baptist Hospital psychiatric ward in Lynchburg, VA., I had just completed a session with my beloved psychiatrist, Dr. Gene Goode, deceased. As we entered a hallway, I told Dr. Goode, "I see a *flying saucer outside,*" as viewed through a large window. Dr. Goode said, "Now, be careful."

Then, I realized I was only seeing a *common sidewalk light.* What had happened within my manic mind? In mania, the energized mind overrode normal image recognition and activated my high energy emotional thinking limits. My highly energetic manic mind *searched* for *extremes.*

Dreaming limits allow actions and behaviors beyond waking limits. The dreaming mind has greater freedoms and wider limits. In dreams, we can fly and do things we cannot do while waking. We accept odd behaviors and activities in dreams we would think as impossible while waking. In mania our normal waking limits are more easily bypassed searching for extremes. Mania limits have similarities to dreaming limits. Manic *thinking* is much like dream thinking. When dreams become too emotional, we wake up.

I carefully search for limits I can activate and gain control of. One is breathing. I can breathe as deeply as I normally do and then breathe a little deeper. Doing this exercise improves lung function and posture. Begin slowly. We can expand breathing limits for our health. Think of and slowly activate and expand other limits while confident and healthy. We may make dreams possible.

Chapter 32

MENTAL HOLOGRAMS

"We are only mental holograms within another's mind."
"One mental hologram may be worth a thousand words."

H. Fulcher

Hologram: a three-dimensional image formed by the interference of light beams from a laser or other coherent light source. A photograph of an interference light pattern which, when suitably illuminated, produces a three-dimensional image on a two-dimensional surface.

Mental hologram: subconscious and conscious higher dimensional living picture electromagnetic resonances in the brain that create the mind.

M ental holograms, alphabets, and words are building blocks for human thought and language. Sensing, recalling, comparing and integrating mental hologram scenarios is basic human subconscious *picture language* for constructing conscious thought. Modeling inner mental processes for understanding improves inner communication, thought, and language. Occasionally, we become aware of mental hologram scenarios in dreams upon wakening, or if startled by expected eminent death.

Repeated thoughts and visions make related mental holograms brighter and clearer. Pondering in-depth ideas over long periods of time makes related neural networks more reflective supporting longer lasting mental resonances for thought.

Coherent neuron EMR, activated by vision, imprints higher dimensional mental holograms on complex three-dimensional neural membranes for developing memory and thought. Living brain cell membranes are the brain's *photographic medium.*

EMR from each activated neuron constructs a vague, widespread hologram as it filters through and imprints its energy and information on near, and, to some extent, far neuron membranes. EMR from one activating neuron travels complex paths as it is reflected, diffracted, and refracted, while partially and then finally being absorbed by brain cell membranes, and other less stable brain tissue.

Integrated EMR from millions of synchronized, coherent neuron activations create mental holograms in the brain. Generations of synchronized neuron firings create mental hologram scenarios for continuous consciousness, memory, cognition, and vision.

Electromagnetic radiation, from firing neurons from all angles are reflected and absorbed by brain cell membranes at all angles, constructing three and higher dimensional emotional mental holograms. Mental hologram dimensions such as levels of truth, emotion, speed of change, depth of belief, and so on, are mental hologram properties. These characteristics might be represented as overall holistic shades of *various color tints.* Mental and spiritual holograms exist within intertwined physical and spiritual dimensions. There is no precise dividing line between physical and spiritual dimensions. Any awareness or thought, greater than its physical sources, develops spiritual thoughts in spiritual dimensions. *Light* and the mind exist in both mental and spiritual dimensions. Both have greater freedoms than physical freedoms have.

When *un-focusing* and looking through a scrolling text file on my computer monitor, all letters are seen equally as the right-brain becomes dominant. There is a feeling of understanding without reading individual words. We may improve reading skills by practicing right-brain dominance exercises. This exercise improves left- and right-brain transitions. Dominance transitions occur between up-close and distant focus.

Mental holograms are our primary subconscious thinking medium. Meditating on important images or thoughts improves mental hologram details for increased reasoning.

Chapter 33

PSYCHIATRIC EXERCISES

"True enjoyment comes from activity of the mind and exercise of the body; the two are ever united."

Karl Wilhelm von Humboldt

"Exercising muscles close to the brain heals the brain and mind the most."

Hugh Fulcher

"Taking the mind to emotional limits with conflicting exercises releases trauma energy from the neck and throat and releases tensions within related areas of the brain."

Hugh Fulcher

Psychiatric Exercise: Any physical exercise that briefly extends the mind to limits and releases small *sensed* distinct trauma energy from the neck, throat and brain giving a small sense of completion. Exercising the muscles close to the brain has more effect on and heals the brain and mind the most.

n the beginning, psychiatric exercises and mental reconstruction were bold and daring. After years of practice, they have become routine.

Athletes exercise their minds and bodies to limits to receive feedback, improve abilities, and extend limits. We can improve thinking by experimenting to extend our minds to limits. I needed to practice exercises to briefly extend my mind to limits for gaining control at newly extended mental limits.

Readers will not find psychiatric exercises and their feedback sensations in medical journals. However, they have been instrumental in healing my bipolar disorder. I have experienced unusual healing sensations during twenty-eight years of mental experimentation. My exercises will be most beneficial for those with bipolar and other stress disorders.

From 1977 to 1993 after being diagnosed with bipolar disorder, psychiatric sessions and prescribed medications had not prevented sporadic manic episodes. I concluded I could not continue with medications only to prevent episodes.

During my1993 manic episode, I sensed unusual small snap-like energy releases in my neck. The more I exercised my neck the more energy releases I sensed. At that time, I thought I could energetically exercise my neck until energy releases discontinued. I have been exercising my neck since 1993 and continue to release emotional trauma energy from my throat, neck, and brainstem. Over the years, these sensations from exercises gradually have feelings of less energy. I believed releasing *mental* energy would have an effect on healing my bipolar disorder and reducing inner tensions. The brain and mind are easier to control with less energy.

With my physics background, I could only develop a physics-based *cure*. After beginning my physical and mental exercises, I have been free of episodes for twenty-eight years.

Sensations were small localized energy releases from nerves and neural networks within the upper neck, throat, and brainstem. Conflicting neck exercises increased the number of energy release sensations over normal neck exercising. I felt compelled to exercise my neck energetically to release localized sensations.

We learn more about our minds and bodies when exercised to limits. When energetically exercising my neck after my last episode, sensations felt slightly pleasant. I referred to exercising of my neck in various directions normally as non-conflicting, or simply, neck exercises. During normal exercises, tensing the throat increased energy release sensations. I *modeled* these localized sensations as traumatized nerve and neural network energy releases, for mental reconstruction and healing.

Unless experienced, it may be difficult to believe that these varying and migrating local sensations occur. Sensations from exercises were predictable in the short term. Predicting sensation changes and migrations have given some confidence in understanding the brain and mind. Psychiatric exercises release childhood, and to a lesser extent, later in life, trauma effects. Brains and minds are complex. Progress is slow and has taken years. Unfortunately, I do not have a quick bipolar disorder fix. However, it is so great not worrying about going manic.

My non-conflicting, and later conflicting, neck exercises are my most important tools for reconstructing the brain and healing the mind. Brief neck exercises extend the mind to, and expand, mental limits.

My near-death experiences and bipolar episodes had ingrained repressed trauma energy that needed to be released. When calm and relaxed with lowered mental energy, the mind is more rational and creative. My goal became to release inner stresses and develop *mind models* for understanding brain and mental changes. I believe everyone needs to release inner stresses and trauma energy, to lesser or greater extents.

We accomplish much of our best thinking and performances near emotional limits. When psychiatric exercises extend the mind to limits, energy and tensions from the most overstressed neural networks are activated and released first. After releasing ingrained energy, afflicted networks become less rigid, more elastic, and resynchronize with normal brain activities.

Baby and childhood traumas engrain highly emotional repressed memories that develop our emotional thinking limits. Young babies react at emotional limits to unexpected sounds and fast motions. We cannot recall baby repressed memories ingrained before being associated with words. Young babies think mostly with their right brains, which is more difficult to recall.

Throughout life, repressed trauma limitations affect subconscious processing and thinking. Trauma limitations remain throughout lifetimes unless purged of their excess energy through psychiatry, my psychiatric exercises and mental reconstruction, or by significant emotional events.

We have lived with trauma limitations for most of our lives and are mostly unaware of their restrictions. Some mental limits are obvious. Should we speak up or remain silent in social conflicting circumstances? Who should we respect or avoid? Who can we love and trust? It is not mentally healthy to continue to love someone who degrades us over long periods of time.

A few months after beginning exercises, I sensed that localized energy-release sensations were slowly migrating to and from the upper neck, throat, and brainstem: *the focus areas*. It was obvious that inner healing was occurring.

The focus areas are gateways connecting the body's nerves with the brain. Inner emotional limits in the focus areas gauge the energy and information transmitted to the limbic system and then to the upper brain. When experiencing traumas, the neck, throat, and *brainstem* tense severely. Localized trauma scars are ingrained within the first neural networks having resonances matching incoming nerve EMR frequencies and resonances. Ingrained trauma scars in the focused areas release energy sensations when stimulated to ingraining energy levels.

Healing sensations during exercises have been mildly pleasant and exciting to some extent. Psychiatric exercises stimulate *brain adjustments*, which are somewhat similar to chiropractic adjustments but with much less energy released. I have experienced chiropractic energy-releases when joints snap back to their normal, least stressful, positions. Manipulating joints into least tense positions also reduces joint nerve stress.

After several months of neck exercises, I referred to localized energy releases from the focus areas as <u>S</u>naps, <u>C</u>rackles, <u>A</u>nd <u>P</u>ops or **SCAPs**. In the beginning, the more I exercised, slightly more SCAP sensations were released with similar exercises. However, after a few years of practice, energy of releases and number of releases slowly decreased with the same exercises.

Trauma releases are understandable since the neck, throat, and *brainstem* tense when reacting to trauma and emotional events. When exercised to emotional limits, the most energetic SCAPS were released first.

Over the years, there have been millions upon millions of SCAP energy releases. After several years of exercises, I concluded it might be possible to purge all excess energy from traumatized neural networks and glial support cells. I defined a mind free of all trauma effects and cleared of restrictive emotional mental compartments as the *Clear Mind*. The brain should work as one unified complete subconscious and conscious system. The Clear Mind is my long-range goal. I have accepted that the Clear Mind will take years of work.

The brain and mind work better with healthy levels of certainty and uncertainty. In mania, I have had many uncertainties and needed more certainties. In raising children, we should give them levels of certainties and uncertainties by introducing reasonable challenges.

I thought releasing emotional sensations was taking so long and needed to be faster. I searched for ways to speed up my inner stress releases. I worked to discover mentally limiting physical exercises that would stimulate greater releases of trauma energy. It is healthy to briefly experience and know mental and physical limits.

Discovering and practicing resistance or conflicting neck exercises at mental limits sped up trauma energy releases. After several months, I settled on a set of conflicting neck exercises:

I use resistance with the right-hand thumb or fingers for the following repetitive exercises: head-down & back, chin-down & back, head down and right & return, head-right & return, head-back and right & return, and head-back & return.

Similar left-hand exercises were alternated after each right-hand exercise. Each exercise uses resistance of one hand such that neck muscles are rather tired after 100 repetitions. Conflicting exercises usually stimulate more trauma energy releases than non-conflicting or normal neck exercises.

There are times when non-conflicting exercises initiate rather active releases. Non-conflicting neck exercises included tensing the throat to release more trauma energy releases.

Additional repetitions are sometimes practiced for exercises releasing greater numbers of release sensations, SCAPS. Be cautious, if any psychiatric physical or mental exercise is painful discontinue it or practice it slower with less hand tension.

In the last few years, I have added an exercise. I place one hand on the front part of my chin and perform 100 repetitive conflicting exercises such that chin muscles feel rather tired. Then I use the other hand. After this exercise, feelings are rather global and there are no SCAP releases. It also builds up chin muscles for a more prominent chin.

Exercises performed depend upon number of SCAP releases and time available. Generally, exercises were practiced once or twice a week. It is important to approach mental limits slowly. Tension between hand and neck muscles should not overstress neck muscles. Repetitions do not need to be fast.

Conflicting exercises heal since they cause subconscious conflicts. It doesn't make subconscious sense for neck muscles to pull down and a hand to push up. Conflicting exercises stimulate subconscious processes to limits. Subconscious processes make fundamental changes to the brain and mind to avoid or expand limits. Similar to muscles exercised at limits, neck and glial cells break down, heal, and expand abilities.

Conflicting psychiatric exercises appear odd, so I practice in private to avoid attention and confusion. Conflicting exercises are illustrated in Figures 33.1 – 3 at the end of this chapter.

In the first conflicting exercise given above, neck muscles pull the head down and a thumb pushes the chin and head up creating a subconscious conflict that stimulates traumatized neural networks to limits, for releasing excess energy. Released neck and throat trauma energy releases trauma energy from related neurons and glia cells in the brain. With energy released, traumatized networks become less rigid, more resilient, and resynchronize with the brain's normal symphony of activities. Anything overstressed becomes brittle. A supple brain is flexible and creative.

Exercise effectiveness is assessed by the number of energy-release sensations, SCAPs, stimulated during similar exercises. Exercising muscles closest to the brain releases repressed energy from, and has the greatest healing effect within the brain.

Normally, neck movement is secondary to head control for expressing one's self or reacting to environments. Concentrating on exercising the neck is a rather reverse physical and mental process. This is one reason neck exercises and related mental processes are effective in releasing disruptive neural and brain trauma energy.

After a few months, exercises were performed rather quickly. Sensations from conflicting head-down and -up exercises feel different with different hands. Left- and right-hand neural and neuron processing paths are different.

There are differences in performing non-conflicting and conflicting neck exercises. During non-conflicting neck exercises, stiffening the neck and throat in various ways increases SCAP releases. Seldom do non-conflicting energy releases approach conflicting energy release levels. In conflicting neck exercises there is no stiffening of the throat as concentration is on conflicting tensions between the neck, hand, and arm muscles. Neck exercises are essentially a *reverse mental* activity.

It is better health wise to experience brief pulses of high-level stress than endure low levels of stress over long periods of time. Persistent stress is a killer.

Reactions to pain and trauma occur mostly in the limbic system. The limbic system represses trauma energy to protect the fragile upper brain.

Trauma energy can be released and repressed memories recalled with psychiatric counseling. Psychiatric exercises and mental reconstruction do not recall trauma memories.

We need quick defensive reactions when traumas occur. The primitive limbic system develops quick, rough fight or flight evaluations and reactions.

For most of us, the time to recall and deal with repressed trauma and emotional memories never seems to be the right time. Stimulating recall of trauma memories creates uncertainties that may feel threatening. They become less threatening when repeatedly activated. The mind normally avoids recalling repressed memories as they bring up painful feelings, guilt of being in the wrong place, and in being mentally trapped with no way out.

A goal is for everyone to have a *Clear Mind* and think as minds were designed to think. If healing processes are refined and psychiatric care is provided early on, future children will grow up with *Clear Minds*. Their future will be confident, exciting, pleasant, satisfying, and spiritual. Spiritual minds do not abuse others or cause wars.

Caveman's strenuous daily activities with fears and shrieks, at emotional limits, cleared his neck, throat, and brain of trauma effects. Cavemen had Clear Minds. They were smarter than we are today. They could travel miles into forests and find their way back. Today, we need maps when traveling on roads.

I have developed a model for understanding how caveman navigated his environments. In my last episode in 1993, I had different feelings within my brain when turning my head from north to east, and in other directions. I concluded that unusual energetic activities at limits had *magnetized* my brain with sensitivity to the earth's magnetic field or electric power lines. Brain and mind activities are electrical, magnetic, and chemical.

Caveman's *magnetic brain* was sensitive to directions and time traveled in directions. Sedentary lifestyles, complicated learning effects of speech, and suppressed guilt in later generations have overridden caveman's earlier directional abilities. Manic and Clear Minds may be able to regain these navigational abilities. My unusual awareness lasted only a few days. Animals may have this *instinctive* directional ability. Some *lost* dogs have traveled thousands of miles to find their way home. Today, we experience anxiety and embarrassment of not knowing road directions experiencing uncertainty and fear.

Exceeding mental limits causes fundamental changes within afflicted neural networks and nuclei. Beyond established inner processes, the brain and mind become reactive and iterate frantically for thought completion and sanity.

Traumatized networks absorb energy but do not release excess energy entirely like normal networks. They are less reflective than normal networks.

When suffering from bipolar disorder with high mental energy, trauma memories may be erratically recalled. This is also true for Post Traumatic Syndrome Disorder, PTSD. Unlearning processes have been developed to reduce soldiers' PTSD, high energy, emotional flashes. These processes may also be helpful to bipolar and other overstressed patients.

Criteria for practicing psychiatric exercises and mental reconstruction are uncertain. If readers are happy with their thinking confidence, I do not recommend this long adventure. The decision may be difficult since individual situations and minds are different and processes require years of patience and dedication. Bipolar patients may also benefit from facial and *Holusion* brain dominance exercises given later.

Practicing exercises and procedures has added purpose, hope, and mental stability over the years. Sanity is worth all efforts.

If practicing exercises and processes, benefits may be similar to, or different from, those I have experienced. Readers must make decisions at their own risk. Evaluate exercises to determine if sensations become *slightly* more pleasant after months of practice. Discontinue exercises if painful, or with negative feelings.

Mental healing sensations, creativity, and spiritual awakenings, may be difficult to believe unless experienced. Exercises and other healing processes require dedication and patience. This inner adventure has been worth my considerable effort.

I believe other manic depressives will also experience SCAP releases and changes if exercising their necks. I am unsure how SCAP changes will occur in *normal* people if routinely performing neck exercises. SCAP changes will probably be less and change more slowly. Readers may receive some understanding and benefits even if not *practicing* psychiatric exercises and processes. However, in any event, if practicing exercises, readers will have firmer facial and neck muscles and skin.

The next chapter, Mental Reconstruction, constructs models of the brain's reactions to exercises and other processes. Exercises and sensations are carefully presented to be my best guidance for readers. *Take it to the limit one more time.*

Figures 33.1, 2, & 3

Psychiatric Exercises

Figure 1 Head Down Resistance Exercise

Neck Muscles Pull Chin Down, Thumb Pushes Chin Up

Figure 2 Head Down & Left Resistance Exercise

Neck Muscles Pull Chin Down & Left, Thumb Pushes Up & Right

Figure 3 Head Left Resistance Exercise

Neck Muscles Pull Head Left, Hand Pushes Head Right

Chapter 34
MENTAL RECONSTRUCTION

"To know thyself is the beginning of wisdom."

Socrates, Praedrus

"We can all reprogram our brain's responses by putting ourselves into new, initially uncomfortable situations. We'll learn fear might not mean 'stop'; I've come to believe fear usually means, 'go.'"

Frances Moore Lappé

"To live a creative life, we must lose our fear of being wrong."

Joseph Chilton Pearce

"*Briefly* stressing our minds to emotional limits reveals our inner selves. Trauma scars in the brain are similar to cancers sporadically activating."

H. Fulcher

Psychiatric exercises and significant emotional events can heal the brain and mind. Engrained trauma effects can be released from neuron and glia support cells. Mind models provide understanding of trauma energy releases. It is helpful to make models to help understanding. Mental reconstruction lessens energy throughout the brain and enhances inner and decision-making processes. Brains and computers work more efficiently with less energy. After a few months, my inner research had three assumptions:

1. Local sensations, within the *upper neck, throat, and brainstem* are releases of trauma energy from nerves and also from related overstressed neural networks and glia support cells.

2. As the *upper neck, throat, and brainstem* lose energy over the years, sensations migrate within those areas. Sensations increased, peaked, and then declined over the years of exercises. Focus and control increase during emotional challenges. In my model, the brain and mind can be *cleared* of all limiting trauma effects.

3. Traumatized and overstressed neural networks and glia support cells store highly energetic repressed trauma memories that remain subconscious and hidden until reactivated by exercises or events with energies near to ingraining events. Erratic trauma memory activations cause mental dysfunctions. After releasing their energy, once traumatized brain cells resynchronize with normal brain activities and reduce emotional overreactions. The brain becomes more efficient with less energy.

Different areas of the brain are designed for different responsibilities. Neural networks compete for control and dominance of new thoughts. After energy releases from traumatized neurons, lower energy resonances are created. Other neurons with similar resonances are activated to gain mind control. With repeated exercises and related mental activities, specific neural networks and nerves become more dominant for specific ideas and actions.

My neck exercises and thought experiments activate pleasant, confident sensations. New thoughts developed during neck exercises build new neural network connections. Interfering neural networks are repressed during new emotional thoughts. Neural networks compete for controlling new thoughts and actions. Neural paths are well established for older repetitive thoughts and actions.

Everyday exercises and activities do not release emotional healing sensations. They have already released their excess emotional energy and healed their related neural networks earlier in life.

My unusual non-conflicting and conflicting neck exercises and mental reconstruction have prevented bipolar episodes for over twenty-eight years and is proof of my healing theories and processes. I no longer fear fast thinking that leads to manic episodes. Lower mental energy processes have prevented manic episodes.

Neuron emitted Light (EMR) integrates to create greater meaning than the sum of all current neuron emitted Light. Integration of Light within the brain creates spiritual consciousness in spiritual dimensions.

The mind resides in both physical and spiritual dimensions. Light is the relativistic medium between physical and spiritual dimensions. God is all *Integrated Light* and spiritual waves (defined later) throughout the universe and heaven.

Normal neural networks are flexible when reacting to high-energy emotions within mental limits. They accept and release energy normally during activities below their energy limits.

Overstressed neural networks and glia support cells do not absorb and release energy like healthy neural networks do. Overstressed neural networks degrade and become rigid with repressed trauma memories and high energy. They store energy and information at brain cell limits and release excess energy when stimulated to near ingraining levels. Trauma memories are more localized and not spread throughout the brain like normal memories.

Repressed emotional non-verbal trauma baby memories make up a majority of normal thinking limits. Early trauma memories include pain of birth, the first breath, wordless fears of being left alone, loud noises, hunger, falling, injuries, etc. Everything is new and often frightening for young babies without experience for judging activities and environments, except for nursing and cuddling. Babies have genetic thinking limits.

Repressed trauma memories are sources of dream distortions. After mental reconstruction and trauma energy releases, dreams become less distorted and less scary for building versatile waking brain and thinking structure.

After releasing trauma energy, thinking becomes more creative and confident. With fewer trauma scars, less overall brain energy is needed to override disruptive trauma effects. The brain becomes more efficient. Trauma cancers have their own identity and react independently from normal integrated brain activities. After releasing trauma energy, previously traumatized neural networks re-grow and function more normally within the brain's symphony.

Thinking and writing about the brain, mind, and God is healing in itself. Writing adds to understanding of complex ideas and builds flexible brain structure. Successively completing physical and mental challenges develop subconscious structures that destroy old and create new wider emotional limits.

I have never felt discomfort from SCAP energy releases. Pleasant feelings are proof of psychiatric healing. Normal brain reactions are processed slower with greater numbers of neuron activations than high-energy trauma reactions. Nature and the brain love energy efficiency for precise and general purposes.

After a few years of neck exercises, SCAPs were sensed as being released in shells with slowly declining energy. I would experience only a few SCAPS. Thoughts were that mental reconstruction was nearly complete. However, later while performing similar neck exercises, another shell of traumatized neural networks would rupture, releasing higher numbers of SCAPs. Trauma and emotional memories are organized by energy and energy shells.

A few highly active energy releases have caused my hair to stand on end. I delayed discussing my unusual healing processes, exercises, and sensations until I had positive results and had developed models for explaining sensations.

After trauma releases, some related less active neural networks become more active. When neurons are frequently activated, their axons and dendrites grow thicker and transmit neuro-chemicals faster for greater influence in their specialized areas.

Mental reconstruction improves communication between subconscious and conscious processes. Some subconscious processes rise to the level of feelings, and some develop semi-conscious ideas. "I know that person's name but cannot recall it." Conscious ideas are constructed from thousands of integrated, supporting subconscious processes, or sub-ideas.

Reducing the energy of the brain lowers subconscious and conscious energy barriers. Greater numbers of subconscious activations build confident conscious ideas and spiritual feelings.

Being comfortable with one's mind and thinking is a significant part of my *bipolar cure.* Anyone may become overstressed by severe trauma or continuous degradation. Psychiatric exercises and mental reconstruction increase resistance to stress. We become patient and confident.

It is important and healthy to have some understanding of how healing exercises and processes work. A reason neck exercises are important for psychiatric healing is that when speaking upper neck muscles pull the jaw down and must be coordinated with jaw muscles pulling the jaw up. Jaw and neck muscles are subconsciously coordinated within the brain and throat when speaking. Exercising muscles closest to the brain affects the brain the most. Glia cells like muscles cramp when stressed beyond limits causing headaches.

Practicing mental and physical activities gives confidence for performing them during real challenges. Meeting challenges, at limits, make the brain flexible and creative. Related neural network connections become thicker and faster when repeating routine tasks. After successes followed by relaxation, the mind feels integrated and complete. Hard fought victories make us feel complete. Stressing the mind to limits for long periods of time degrades more than heals. Psychiatric exercises briefly stress nerves and the brain to limits.

Subconscious neural processes evaluate incoming trauma information from nerves and work frantically to contain information and reactions within mental and social limits. With practice, subconscious processes gain greater control of high-energy emotional information and activities within new extended emotional and intellectual limits

Severely stressed minds become compartmentalized. Sometimes severe traumas are so stressful that brains develop compartments with separate consciousnesses to isolate fears and protect the rest of the brain. Significant emotional events and mental reconstruction break down compartments within the brain for integrated awareness and rational thinking. Feelings and ideas become more confident with integrated purpose.

Normal brains and minds are compartmentalized to lesser extents. They store scary memories in emotional closets. The Clear Mind will operate as one integrated, complete system.

Everyday exercises and activities normally do not release healing sensations. Routine neural networks have already been healed of emotional and trauma effects.

Some people age faster than others. Aging is not a consistent process. Without traumatized neural networks continually draining the brain's resources aging slows.

Healthy brain and nerve cells have communication channels to coordinate activities with nearby cells and cells with similar resonances. My goal is for brain, nerve, and muscle cells to function together creating a complete living, growing, and conscious human system. Humans love feelings of completeness. God loves completeness. The reconstructed brain and mind may renew cell division processes throughout the brain and body for slowing aging.

Early mental reconstruction may support youthful looks for long lives. I began mental reconstruction too late but have slowed aging to some small extent.

Stresses within the neck, throat, and brainstem distort incoming nerve signals. It takes complex inner processes to interpret and integrate distorted incoming nerve signals into useful brain functions.

If someone hits his thumb with a hammer, normal thoughts and awareness are temporarily overridden. In mania, *feelings* are often beyond words.

Performing psychiatric exercises and mental reconstruction gives subconscious processes increased focus and purpose. Meditate to give the subconscious mind greater freedom for iterating to completion for healing itself. Semi-awareness of inner activities and feelings cannot be easily expressed in words but give confidence of inner healing.

It takes less than a *tenth of a second* for trauma scars to become ingrained within the first specific local areas of the brain. Effects may last a lifetime.

I thank God for the wonderful sensations and feelings that have guided my healing exercises, processes, and writing. The most traumatized and energized neural networks seemed to have released their energy first. Trauma energy releases increased with exercises over time since less energy is needed to activate releases of remaining lower-energy traumatized neural networks. After several years, energy released and number of releases from traumatized networks, have lessened. Trauma release changes have occurred slowly over the years.

Mental reconstruction has been a long, yet exciting process. Being able to trust one's own thoughts is worth any price.

If anyone were to experience my inner sensations suddenly, they would be terrified. Initial sensations were perplexing. There has been no pain during traumatized neuron network energy releases. I have become accustomed to releases.

Throughout this long process of healing and change I have had only minor headaches. I am aware of headache locations. I think away and *beyond* headache locations, and my headaches subside quickly. Concentrating on a headache brings more energy to that area of the brain.

The mind strives for completion. Writing good sentences gives feelings of completion. We gain confidence when successfully completing important tasks. Unfortunately, drugs give confident feelings for doing nothing. Minds become addicted to pleasant, *false important* feelings.

Stresses within neurons and neural nuclei cause glial support cells to cramp and restrict blood flow causing headaches. Relaxing and meditating *beyond* painful areas disperses local stresses preventing headaches. Leg muscles and neural networks cramp when overstressed.

When performing psychiatric exercises, blood flow to the brain and face increase. Older faces do not sag as much and remain younger looking. With exercises, greater toxins are purged from neural networks slowing aging.

For local headaches, put an imaginary envelop around the painful area and expand it out over the entire brain. Spreading local energy throughout the brain transforms it to useful mental energy.

Let an imagined pleasant breeze carry away emotional energy throughout the brain for more holistic healing. Repeat this *dream* until there are feelings of calmness and serenity. Mental reconstruction has focused on discrete healing. Facial meditation gives more holistic healing.

Religions give feelings of belonging and completeness. Faith builds inner confidence, purpose, and influences healing and health. Religions requiring excessive memorization build rigid neural networks, beliefs, and minds, making mental reconstruction and healing difficult. Creativity is eclipsed.

I have worked toward the Clear Mind for many years. A goal has been to free my own and readers' minds of trauma effects and heal disorders. We must have patience, and faith in self and God, and not be swayed by doubters who will impede our creative adventures. My goal is to help readers have wonderful, healthy, productive, and spiritual minds and lives.

When only refined low-energy sensations remain, there is less resistance to recalling memories. With all trauma effects released and attaining the Clear Mind, one may be able to recall initial baby spiritual wisdom. Spiritual wisdom is indwelled at conception.

Unless seeing Olympic skiers jumping, twisting and flipping in the air, landing, and continuing skiing downhill, one might think no human could mentally and physically accomplish such acrobatics.

Skiers must carefully control body, arm, leg, and ski positions to be successful. Unless practicing psychiatric exercises and processes, one might think, healing sensations and feelings are not possible. We should not judge each other by our own limited experiences and abilities. Complex physical and mental activities require years of practice.

Continued research will refine healing processes in shorter times. Hopefully, we will become smarter and feel more spiritual with trauma restrictions released.

Brains, minds, souls, and God search for completeness. Overcoming our greatest obstacles gives us our greatest feelings of completeness. We work toward short- and long-term completions in things we do. We talk and write in complete sentences. Attaining eternal life is our final completion on earth. Evil is never complete.

Chapter 35

BRAIN DOMINANCE EXERCISES

Holusion: a *three-dimensional drawing* of an object or picture on a two dimensional surface created by holography using repeating lines and shades of coloring to create a three-dimensional image when focusing through the two-dimensional surface. Images furthest away, are represented by darker shades and closer images are in lighter shades. Detailed 2D patterns create a camouflage for the 3D image. The repeating small detailed 2D patterns enhance the intended depths of the hidden 3D image. The repeating pattern feeds the mind with encoded depth information. When focusing *through* and *beyond* the detailed 2D images, the eyes and brain perceive the hidden 3D images and their backgrounds.

The Holusion: "Space Ace" (26" x 22") of Snoopy on his doghouse by Nvision Grafix. Inc., is my only physical tool used for experimenting with brain dominance for healing the brain and mind. The best solution to complex problems is to collect, iterate on, and integrate all pertinent information for making complete decisions.

n this chapter, I practice alternating between left- and right-brain dominance for improving the mind's up close and depth transition abilities. Thinking is improved when different areas of the brain work together. Left- and right-brains work best when sharing and integrating information for solutions.

When viewing a Holusion, I practice alternating between up-close focused left-brain dominance and long-distance holistic right-brain vision dominance. A Holusion is my best tool for brain dominance exercises and awareness. My purpose is to integrate and improve brain dominance transitions and visual skills. My eyes and mind integrate Holusion 2D details to visualize 3D visions.

When focusing long-distance *through* the detailed 2D surface of the Holusion, the once *subconscious* 3D vision appears. The right-brain gains dominance and senses and integrates all 2D detailed lines and images on the 2D surface with equal attention for awareness of the hidden three-dimensional image, *deep within the* 2D picture.

I see three-dimensional images of Snoopy on his doghouse and their background. As I move my head side to side, the 3D images of the wolves move relative to their background similar to viewing an up-close person moving relative to a more distant background.

To practice alternating between two- and three-dimensional images, I have viewed the Snoopy Holusion while moving up and back and to the left and right for awareness of the varying 3D image with right-brain dominance.

When practicing Holusion exercises, I experience slowly changing, slightly pleasant, rather global shifts within my brain. Pleasant sensations are proof of healing. Studying the brain, mind, and God are my inner adventures.

If practicing Holusion exercises, benefits may be similar to, or different from, those I have experienced. Manic-depressives may be more sensitive to pleasant sensations. Holusion exercises have helped up-close and long-distance coordination.

Chapter 36

FACIAL MEDITATION

"Our faces tell who we have been, are, and will be, to some extent. In meditation with eyes closed, I sense the contours of my face. It is one way of thinking about and renewing one's face."

H. Fulcher

Meditate: to project into the mind; to engage in mental exercise (as concentration on one's breathing, face, or repetition of a mantra) for the purpose of reaching a level of inner calmness and a heightened subconscious and spiritual awareness.

Meditation is part of my mental healing process. It gets conscious processes out of the way so subconscious processes have greater freedom to understand and heal themselves. When meditating, we lower mental energy, and may listen for, and surrender to, God. He gives us blessings and hope when we surrender our minds and lives to Him.

Facial meditation and facial skin firming practices began twenty years after psychiatric exercises began. I meditate to see what I can learn about my inner self. Normally, subconscious processes support conscious thinking. With meditation, consciousness lessens allowing subconscious processes more ability to heal and renew themselves.

In meditation, I feel my subconscious controlled facial skin *tense* and *firm*. I use these two terms interchangeably.

Some of us never relax our minds and faces before sleeping. Faces remain narrowed, frowning, and tense even during sleep. The brain remains tense and never fully recovers from stresses of the day. Meditating and praying to relax the brain and mind before sleep may seem frightening at first, fearing recall of stressful memories, or nightmares. Frowning conceals fearful, disturbing thoughts from others. Persistent frowning confines one to an emotional prison.

Broadening the face and meditating relaxes left-brain dominance into right-brain dominance for releasing inner stresses. Relaxing the right-brain prepares the mind for in-depth pleasant and spiritual thoughts. In meditation, subconscious processes have more control of our minds. We may even feel God's presence at times.

When narrowing and tensing our faces, our brains narrow and tense. Our faces and brains are connected. The narrowed brain prepares defenses against threating physical and mental environments. Right-brain resonances are not designed for normal up-close reactions but for relaxed integrated solutions. The limbic system and, to some lesser extent, the left-brain respond to high-energy nerves that may ingrain trauma scars.

Complete recalling of repressed memories releases their emotional energy, lessens uncertainties, and is much better than letting repressed memories be partially and erratically recalled causing uncertainty and inner fears over a lifetime. Faces show if we live with persistent uncertainties. Smiling faces show confidence, build self-esteem, and accept others and their ideas.

Subconsciously, many of us keep muscles and brains tense even while sleeping. Learning to relax subconscious processes gives mental freedom for healing the brain and mind. Meditating to reduce tensions and pain heals.

It takes practice and patience to relax facial muscles so subconscious processes can renew and firm facial and facial skin muscles for a youthful appearance. The face shows pleasant emotions and relaxed thinking. Genetic influences and lifetime memories build facial, and facial skin, muscle tone. If the face is renewed, the mind and body are renewed. The face, body, and mind are closely related. God gives us our young faces. Persistent thinking is reflected in older faces.

Facial meditation is my psychiatric tool for holistic healing, slowing aging, and spiritual awareness. Similar to SCAPs, facial skin tensing migrates during meditation with lessened consciousness. After two years of practice, facial skin *firming* has become easier to initiate with a broadened face.

As we age, facial and facial skin muscles lose tension and sag. Body and skin muscles lose tone and wrinkle with age. With facial meditation, our subconscious minds renew facial skin muscle tone. Divided cells will not lose strength and prevent wrinkles. We judge people's age mostly by wrinkles and sagging faces. Cosmetic companies claim they have magic creams. Billions of dollars are spent, when all is needed is facial meditation.

Facial medication is my adventure for re-strengthening facial muscles and facial skin tone. At the beginning of facial meditation, I relaxed the face by rubbing muscles with two hands:

1. **horizontally between the eyebrows and on the bridge of the nose;**
2. **on the forehead up and down and left and right;**
3. **outward to broaden the cheeks;**
4. **outward to tighten the upper neck muscles under the chin.**

If there is subconscious *controlled* facial and scalp skin firming, related firming occurs within the brain. The face is closely and emotionally connected to the brain.

With several months of concentrating on and relaxing my face, I have experienced wide facial skin firming sensations. Later, facial skin firming was initiated by only needing to lie on my back with my face straight up and meditating on my face. Skin firming migrated from the forehead to the scalp and from the cheeks to beneath the chin.

If losing facial meditation or breathing too deeply, subconscious facial firming discontinues. I am careful to not having conscious control over facial skin and scalp muscle firming. In meditation, my face becomes my total awareness.

Facial meditation increases blood flow to the face and brain. The heartbeat is sensed within the brain at times. When meditating, conscious processes are lessened. Subconscious processes override consciousness to firm and renew the face.

Facial meditation gives feelings of self-worth. If distracted from facial meditation, mental energy increases and facial skin firming discontinues. Facial meditation sets the mind free of daily thoughts. Frowning prepares for defensive thoughts and reactions.

Frequently, I initiate facial skin firming for several minutes before sleep. Facial muscles must be relaxed to allow subconscious control of facial muscles. The face becomes pleasantly flushed.

I experiment between relaxation and concentration for skin tensing sensations During early practices, I used both hands to gently broaden my cheeks. I practiced smiling a little more and less to find my faces' most relaxed position. At times, pleasant firming sensations emerge around the crown of my forehead and the upper sides of my head. Meditating on either the forehead, nose, cheeks, or chin awakens subconscious control for skin tensing.

Sagging, loose facial skin is a prominent sign of aging. If we re-strengthen our facial skin, we slow aging. After a year or so, I only needed to relax and meditate on some area of my face to initiate skin tensing. Meditation renews facial skin from the inside out. Patience is needed.

After meditation for a few minutes, skin tensing extends to the scalp. Subconscious scalp tensing is difficult to maintain. Firming lasts only as long as meditation is maintained.

Facial and facial skin muscles are connected to related neural networks. By relaxing the face, we relax glial tensions in the brain for inner healing.

Facial skin firming provides feedback to, and firms related areas within the brain. My inner *Fountain of Youth* requires dedication. Subconscious skin firming exercises began years after of neck exercises.

Mind renewal is addressed in the Bible: Romans 12:2: "Do not conform any longer to the pattern of the world, but be transformed by the renewing of your mind . . ." This passage may refer to mental reconstruction and facial renewal.

People, who have experienced long-term stress and traumas have more wrinkles and greater facial sagging with age. Stress and frowning age the face and mind. Keys to retaining a youthful face, are releasing stress, facial meditation, and persistently feeling good about oneself. This may renew youthful heredity abilities.

We are aware of how creative some people can be. Computer designers, physicists, and engineers have designed and constructed complex useful devices. God created and organized atoms, light, space, and energy as He designed, engineered, and constructed the universe. He is the original chemist, physicist, and engineer.

Every healthy cell in the body has its activities and purpose. Clear subconscious brains will be aware of and process information from every cell in the brain and body. Without trauma effects, the brain has greater ability to influence cell divisions for restoring and maintaining youth.

After practicing facial meditation for over a year, I became aware of an inner *cosmic* noise. My inner cosmic noise may be background sounds of brain cell intercommunications or of *spiritual waves* interacting with EMR resonances within my brain. I model *spiritual waves* in later chapters to explain God's omniscience and omnipresence. This inner sound has been interesting to ponder and causes no worry.

The inner *cosmic* sound or noise is sensed within the brain and not through the ears. It was more apparent after neck exercises and facial meditation. This inner sound increases and lessens depending upon my degree of relaxation.

After a year of facial meditation and subconscious skin tensing, pleasant wave feelings were sensed throughout the brain. At times, the heartbeat is sensed within the brain. Psychiatric exercises and meditation seem to affect this inner sound. This sound lasted for a few months.

Meditation slows subconscious resonances in the brain. The heart and brain are connected by nerve and neural networks and their resonances. When resonances in the brain become long enough, they integrate with the heart's *slow* resonances. We become aware of our heartbeat in our brains.

Having loving and caring moods prepares for meditation. Loving and heartfelt caring integrate to become spiritual awareness independent of physical space and time. True love is beyond consciousness.

I cannot predict when I will discover the next mind healing activity. I work to realistically describe unusual healing sensations. My mind has become my inner laboratory.

The mind is more truthful to itself when sensing body symmetry. The body and brain have symmetry properties. When we see people's faces, we expect to see symmetry. Science discoveries have been made by recognizing symmetry properties in nature.

Symmetry is important. After symmetrically positioning arms and legs, the heartbeat is sensed more clearly in the brain. The inner mind is awakened when receiving symmetric signals. Meditation increases symmetry in brain activities, and improves quality of life.

Skin tensing of the scalp has not been easy to initiate and maintain. However, I pursue subconsciously firming the scalp.

We have a visual image of our faces when looking in a mirror. With facial meditation and eyes closed, we can sense our facial contours as a *dark inner image* of our faces. We have awareness of symmetric arm and leg positions.

A stroke is similar to a leg cramp. Leg muscles become overstressed, constrict, and stressed nerves cause pain. If older folks avoid concentration on local pain in the brain, strokes may be prevented.

Muscles atrophy if not exercised. They lose firmness and strength.

This includes neck and facial muscles. Neck exercises firm neck and facial muscles. Skin muscles are attached to facial and body muscles. We can recognize deep thinkers from their faces.

From genetics, the body, brain, and mind have been programmed to mature, loose strength and versatility, grow old and die. With mental reconstruction, facial meditation, and gene therapy, humans may break the genetic aging formula. All that is needed is persistent good health, perfect cell division, brain cell cleansing, and regrowing brain cells.

From genetics, our brains and minds focus on, recognize, and remember discrete characteristics of faces more easily than remembering peoples' names. We sometimes can recognize older faces we have not have seen for fifty years. Faces change and sag but certain characteristics remain recognizable.

Meditating on the face attracts blood to the face and brain. The brain becomes healthier and we look healthier.

Dreamers and scientists continually search for anti-aging solutions. Harvard researchers believe they are getting closer to reversing aging by testing a compound, called nicotinamide adenine dinucleotide, or NAD+ in rats. David Sinclair, co-director of the Paul F. Glenn Center for the Biology of Aging at Harvard Medical School says NAD+ is one of the most important molecules for life to exist, and without it, you're dead in 30 seconds.

By adding NAD+ to rats' drinking water they have found that older rats look and act younger. NAD+ is naturally found in humans but deceases with age. It is difficult to ensure that success with rats will be successful in humans. Human testing must be done with strict health considerations. Can divided cells be *identical* to their precursor cell? Harvard is continuing gene altering studies on dogs to slow and prevent aging.

Will integrating facial meditation processes, gene editing, and NAD+ be a solution to human aging? What will humans living for thousands of years do? Will they continue to reproduce? Will they become spiritual or controlling? Are humans worthy of living thousands of years?

Meditation can release the subconscious mind of conscious duties to renew or restore cell division processes. NAD+, meditation, and physical exercises may integrate for renewing the brain, mind, and body. With experiments and practice, scientists may do wonders for brain and body coordination. Cancer cells do not conform to integrated purposes of the mind and body.

Conflicting exercises heal local, discrete neural networks. Facial meditation heals more holistic areas of the face, scalp, and brain. SCAP sensations are more localized.

The conscious mind may relax to awaken subconscious activities. The subconscious mind is aware of threats and pleasures before the conscious mind develops awareness. We need environments that give us healthy levels of challenges and successes.

Meditation exercises clear the mind of conscious thoughts so the subconscious mind has greater ability to restructure rational thinking processes. I often extend facial meditation into less conscious black nothingness with eyes closed to allow the subconscious mind to develop more efficient less emotional conscious thinking processes. This practice often gives feelings of completeness.

We should work to understand, evaluate, and improve our minds, health, activities, and beliefs. Authorities will be quick to reject my exercises and processes until others have practiced them with success. It is great to be free of manic episodes and looking and feeling healthy.

Chapter 37

THE CLEAR MIND

"The greatest revolution of our generation is the discovery that human beings, by changing the inner attitudes of their minds, can change the outer aspects of their lives."

William James

"Open your subconscious mind." "Overcoming inner uncertainties creates greatest certainties."

H. Fulcher

The Clear Mind has been a long-range goal since 1995. In this model, the brain is cleared of all adverse trauma effects and isolated emotional compartments. The Clear Mind processes as a whole system. There will be no more trauma energy releases, or SCAPS, if continuing psychiatric exercises and processes. Ideas will have greater confidence and depth, be more inclusive, and will fly into consciousness. Once difficult to recall memories will become conscious even with low-energy stimuli. More subconscious processes integrate to construct conscience thoughts and decisions. Self-confident *clear persons* become more caring and effective.

With trauma effects purged, brains and minds work as God

designed them to do. There will be a greater awareness of one's inner self. The Clear brain's resonances make inner music as rich as a full-blown orchestra.

There is perfect communication between heredity potentials, senses, brain, mind, and soul. *The clear brain* processes with low-*refined prayer-like* energy. The Clear Mind thinks faster, simplifies and integrates complex thoughts. With Clear Minds, we will remember, integrate, and understand complex environmental data and their relationships.

When released, trauma effects in the brain connect subconscious communications with the soul. With low mental energy, spiritual communications will be received easier and clearer. *Clear* thinking is more reasonable and caring for others. The Clear Mind has greater genetic influence. Human genetic structure contains deep truths, and *secrets*, developed by emotional trials and successes of ancestors. Our emotional successes influence our genetic structure that we pass on to our children and future generations. Our lives matter.

Confident people stay calm and think with low energy. Their dreams are organized with refined low-energy and are more life-like and creative. Challenging dreams integrate inner processes for handling waking challenges and spiritual awareness.

Christian leaders preach that we only need to believe in and surrender to Jesus for everlasting lives. Jesus was the spiritual rebel of His time and forged a new spiritual path to everlasting life for those believing in Him.

My calling has taken a spiritual path less traveled. It would have been much easier to follow an accepted spiritual path. If achieved, the Clear Mind may be able to recall *wordless* baby spiritual communications and recover spiritual sensitivities. The Clear Mind is my long-range destiny. My spiritual journey has been different. Unusual creative and spiritual feelings and ideas may not be believed unless also experienced.

My beliefs have been influenced by my science and Christian backgrounds. Scientists learn about God by studying His creation and designs of an evolving universe.

Clear Minds have Clear Brains. The brain weighs less than two percent of the human body but uses twenty percent of its energy. Without it we are nothing.

It is necessary for the brain and body to remove their waste. Restful sleep cleanses brain cells of their toxins. Without efficiently cleansing toxins, brains lose abilities and age faster. Research indicates that Alzheimer's is caused by the brain not being able to efficiently remove its toxins. The Clear Brain will effectively remove its toxins.

Normal body cells share information and spiritual love with normal neighboring cells and especially cells with similar resonances and functions. They are a team supporting one another. Cancer cells do not care about normal body and brain cells. Cancer cells develop their own independent godless resonances and reasons for multiplying and growth. They do not *seem* to understand that by destroying normal cells they destroy the life that supports their own distorted lives.

From my perspective, the Clear Mind is accomplished through psychiatric exercises, and understanding itself through mental reconstruction, facial meditation, and replacing early mental limits with new, broader forgiving, versatile limits. The Clear Mind will have greater influence over cell dividing or reproduction to slow or *prevent* aging. For slowing and potentially stopping ageing, future generations need to achieve clear minds early in life. Individuals achieving Clear Minds will *prove* the value of mental reconstruction.

Achieving a Clear Mind and Being Saved requires social and spiritual dedication and responsibility. Without continued effort, faith, and spiritual purpose, *being saved may* be *squandered. Espousing being saved* without continued effort is superficial. Christians believe Jesus prepares our minds and souls for *transcending* into *everlasting spiritual life.* Christians must believe in Jesus and do our part to *be saved.* It is not spiritual to boast: "*I am saved and ask if others are saved!*" Upon death, only Jesus, integrated within God, and God judge and grant us *everlasting life, through God's grace.*

The brain is a Light, EMR, matching and integrating machine. The Clear Brain and Mind integrate greater Light resonances for a higher consciousness. Billions of neurons fire every second. Trillions of EMR reflections, and absorptions, occur each second by, and within, neural membranes.

EMR from millions of neuron spikes integrate to form subconscious resonances. With sufficient energy and reflections, neuron Light resonances construct consciousness. Humans are not aware of visions lasting less than a tenth of a second, except during a *Flash*.

Frequent ideas are more widely distributed and absorbed throughout the brain. Frequent idea resonances refine specific brain cell membrane textures for supporting memories.

Clear Mind neuron and glia membranes are more reflective and refined. They reflect longer lasting resonances for in-depth thinking. Incoming EMR is partially reflected and partially absorbed until the last membrane absorption. From one spiking neuron, membrane segments absorb the less reflected EMR before absorbing the more reflected EMR. This absorption process from firing neurons is the foundation of awareness and cognition. Coherent EMR absorptions from neurons with greater reflections builds in-depth memories.

A Clear Mind has greater spiritual sensitivity and ability for building and receiving detailed, confident spiritual ideas and making spirituel memories. Complex thoughts are simplified with more EMR iterations and integrations. Understanding *neutron* and brain cell resonances and absorption properties is important in operating nuclear reactors and the brain and mind.

Belief and Spiritual Section

Chapter 38

BELIEF

"Man is what he believes."

Anton Chekhov

"Belief gets in the way of learning."

Robert A. Heinlein

"Belief traps or frees us."

Rachel Naomi Remen,
Kitchen Table Wisdom: Stories That Heal

"If you don't stand for something you will fall for anything."
Gordon A. Eadie

"All I have seen teaches me to trust the Creator for all I have not seen."
Ralph Waldo Emerson

"Beliefs are choices. First you choose your beliefs. Then your beliefs affect your choices."

Roy T. Bennett

"Be brave to stand for what you believe in even if you stand alone."

Roy T. Bennett,
The Light in the Heart

"We are with God when creative. God was infinitely creative as He designed, engineered, and constructed the universe."

H. Fulcher

Belief: an acceptance that a statement is true or that something has happened or exists: a trust, faith, or confidence in someone or something.

Religious Belief: Strong belief in a supernatural power or powers that control or affect the universe and human destiny.

Dogma: A principle or set of principles laid down by an authority as incontrovertibly true.

Faith: Allegiance to a duty or person; something that is believed especially with strong conviction, belief and trust in, and loyalty to, God; a system of religious beliefs.

Infinite Spiritual Hologram – Living infinite higher dimensional hologram created by all electromagnetic radiation, Light, and spiritual waves in the universe and heaven. God, or God's Hologram, having infinite omnipresence, omniscience, and omnipotence

In silence and solitude, we may feel the presence, or hear the voice, of God. He gave mankind the Gift of Jesus. Jesus has spiritually changed the world. I believe each of us has the opportunity to make a spiritual change in the world for mankind, Jesus, and God. Many of us have developed strong beliefs after surviving difficult or survival experiences.

From genetics, babies innately believe soft gentle touches and soft sounds comfort and protect them. They believe in their mother's softness and innately believe that quick movements and loud sounds are threatening.

In childhood, it is emotionally healing to be listened to by caring parents. It is calming and healing for believers to be listened to by a caring Jesus and a caring God.

As children, most of us had faith and believed our parents would take care of us. As adults, we believe in physical laws and our abilities to navigate and control our environments. Many of us believe in God and that spiritual lives will lead to a blissful *life* after death. We live and die according to what we believe.

Children are indoctrinated early on by parental and social behaviors and sometimes by religious practices and influences. Children should be taught to learn and reason about what they learn.

What promotes beliefs in later life? We observe and learn what works and does not work for us and others, and what is comforting and confidence building, or is threatening, to us. Beliefs may be positive for our wellbeing or negative for us. Most of us believe what parents, religious leaders, doctors, and trusted others say and do. We develop beliefs in our own and others' skills, and sometimes believe we can improve our skills. We learn to believe in and trust our own judgment, and to trust or distrust others.

Science discoveries and engineered devices give us beliefs in technologies helpful to us. Using technology has become routine without needing to understand how devices work. One of my goals is to bring science and religion closer together and both more understandable.

Some of us have received strong spiritual messages that have framed our beliefs in God, His love, and His abilities. Strong spiritual messages *force* us to believe in and serve God. Consistent beliefs, religions and dogma spiritually guide our lives.

Religious values and practices are usually centered on teachings of a spiritual leader or leaders. Belief in Jesus by Christians has lasted for over two thousand years. The Bible's absolute truthfulness is not questioned by Fundamental Christians, even though some Christian dogma has been disproven by science. Fundamental Christian leaders go to great lengths to support the Bible as God's *perfect word*. This belief has benefited many Christians for over two thousand years.

Over the centuries, Christian scholars have selected what should be, and should not be, in the Bible while declaring the Bible to be perfect. Jesus disciples' writings are an important part of the New Testament.

Human words and decisions are never perfect. Meanings of words depend on individual experiences and emotions that change with time. Meaning is altered by interpretations and translations. Interpreters and translators are never perfect. However, I believe Biblical writers were amazing toward Jesus' and God's Truths.

Before traditional religious eras, worshippers created, and believed in, their own gods. Some even believed they could deceive their gods. Early believers worshiped idols, their leaders, and events they did not understand. Most people need to believe in and worship something different from, and greater than, themselves. We had an emotional need to believe in parents' guidance early in life.

Without checks and balances, humans tend to exaggerate to gain influence and power over others. Even today, people tend to believe greater lies more readily than small lies. Bernard L. Madoff, with his Wall Street Ponzi scheme, scammed investors out of $20 billion dollars. Investors *believed* in him but he was a heartless, scheming liar.

Christians believe in Jesus, one God, and have cultured beliefs with strict spiritual dogma. America, with its Christian heritage and human rights and ethics, supports spiritual and humanitarian needs throughout the world.

Beliefs are formed by genetics, experience, study, science, philosophy, emotions, and religion. Philosophers reason about their beliefs and knowledge to disavow false beliefs. I hope my philosophy models may have some influence in bringing religions closer together for integration of truthful, moral, and spiritual lives. In developing my reasoning, I had to use words defined by those who have written before me.

We develop beliefs from the things we hear, see, and think

about. With different abilities, experiences, and emotions, people develop unique individual beliefs and talents. Words are interpreted differently by each of us. I may believe a person is wonderful. With different backgrounds and experiences, another might distrust that person. If we believe liars and repeat their lies, we have become liars and deceive innocent people. We become less believable.

Forceful speakers use emotional self-centered and exciting rhetoric to influence and brainwash listeners. High-energy sermons and political speeches appeal to audience's self-serving interests and emotions, giving them elevated expectations, with little reason.

Truthful spiritual and political speakers appeal to, and encourage, listener's own reasoning toward discovering historical and current truths. Beliefs should be founded on truths and reason, not on short-term, self-centered emotions and greed.

Belief in ourselves and our environments allow us to walk, talk, and do many things. Without believing in ourselves and our abilities, we can do nothing. Spiritual beliefs give feelings of being loved and cared for by God. Worshipers search for self-worth and meaning beyond their *earthly* reasoning experiences by believing in and worshipping God.

Some of us become brainwashed, believe in, and follow false spiritual leaders who demand adherence to their dogma and way of life. We must reason about and evaluate our beliefs to follow true spiritual leaders and avoid power hungry *false spiritual* leaders.

We are *forced* to believe in the value of science, technology, and engineering application. Our cars, planes, electricity, buildings, and phones would not be possible without science and engineering. We believe our engineered devises will work when needed.

About two-thirds of scientists believe in God. Studies show that science is more compatible with religion today. Those in the social sciences are more likely to believe in God and attend religious services than researchers in natural sciences. I was raised a Christian and have escaped *expected imminent death*. Uncertainties and struggles have forced many of us to become more spiritual and believe beyond our reasoning ability. Christianity today has a level of mystery. We are unable to understand an infinite God.

Science has forced many of us to change some of our early spiritual beliefs:

Science Fact: An observation in nature that has been repeatedly confirmed through experiment as true and a fact, or a *confirmed belief*. A science fact shows consistency but may never be final.

Scientific method: A way to ask and answer scientific questions by making observations and performing experiments. Methods were developed to discover God's *physical* truths. Scientific method steps are:

- Ask a Question?
- Do Background Research in Social or Natural Sciences;
- Construct a Hypothesis of What You believe to be True;
- Test Your Hypothesis by Doing an Experiment or Study;
- Analyze Your Data and Draw a Conclusion as to whether your hypothesis was true or false;
- Communicate Your Results and expected use of your results.

Through religion and science, we should work to understand and practice the truth in everything we do. Traditionally, early philosophers did not address religion since many historical governments were, and some still are, ruled by religious leaders.

Early religious leaders would not allow philosophers or scientists to question their *perfect* beliefs. It would be dangerous to question their *absolute* authority. Many people strive for and then abuse authority. Many religions consider their Spiritual Leaders and Spiritual Books as perfect. Manmade words are never perfect and are interpreted and translated differently by people with different experiences.

Intelligent people should question their beliefs and search for truths in their spiritual books and leaders, political leaders, and in their own lives. Science and religions should search for physical and spiritual truths together. They are intertwined. Searching for physical and spiritual truths in science and religion attracts God's blessings. God reveals His physical truths through science, for Man's beliefs and benefits.

Today, we believe in and trust science and technology. Science and technology will improve spiritual communication technology for discovering God's physical laws and spiritual truths in how He designed, engineered, and constructed the universe beginning fourteen billion years ago.

Scientists have performed wonders in discovering and using physical principles for advancing the human experiment. Thomas Jefferson applied science and reasoning in interpreting the Bible and Christianity and separated the American government from religious control. Independence from religious domination allowed science and philosophical reason to thrive and has advanced America socially and spiritually.

American religions and their denominations have been versatile in serving American spiritual needs. Governments based on one spiritual leader's interpretations or on one dictator's rule have not always been good for their citizen's social and spiritual development.

Jesus gave *the world* spiritual technology in presenting and teaching the Lord's Prayer, Matthew Chapter 6:5-14. Jesus taught love for one another and God.

God gave humans free wills to choose worldly and spiritual destinies. If believers analyze their religions as scientists have analyzed the physical universe, the world will become a better, safer place. Some *misguided religious* leaders teach beliefs that it is spiritual to kill believers of other religions.

An important principle is to admit errors and learn from mistakes. This applies to politics, science, and religion.

If a religion promotes a loving God, gives comfort and confidence, and does not promote hurting or degrading anyone, that religion has merit. God *listens* to and *learns* from our prayers. If that were not true, we would be wasting our time praying. God gave us free will for His and our benefits. *Demanding religions* ingrain false superior dogma in their believers that stifle their creativity and spiritual value.

I attempt to smile and show caring for and acceptance of everyone I meet, when reasonable. Dr. Jerry Falwell was good at this.

It is difficult to love those who degrade, injure, and want to kill us. Brainwashed, prejudiced people degrade those they do not even know. If we believe we are spiritually superior, we are spiritually inferior with little spiritual purpose. We learn of God's Love and Truths from true religions and our spiritual messages received from Jesus and God.

In John 14:6, Jesus told His disciplines He is the only way to heaven. Believers of other religions do not believe this. Jesus is my guide for acceptance by God. After His death and resurrection, Jesus' Spirit continues to guide and save lives and souls of those believing in Him.

Moses lived before Jesus' time. He was *chosen by* God to free and save God's chosen people. Moses saved His righteous Jewish *family* from bondage. This was before Jesus' time. They did not know Jesus. I believe *God accepted them* for Eternal Life.

Beliefs, confidence, and life styles are important for mental health, peace of mind, and eternal life. Jesus, Christian leaders, the Bible, my philosophy and quasi-physics interpretations, and my spiritual messages received have framed my spiritual beliefs. We should interpret and reason about religious books and leaders for framing our beliefs.

Spiritual books and *science* help us reason about and praise God. He created the universe and heaven. The better our models are of the universe and God; the better we can communicate with, and worship, Him. No human could design such a majestic universe.

We should contemplate science facts and spiritual interpretations, to frame our beliefs. Scientists learning the architecture of the universe *learn about God's work* for human benefit. Religions help us believe our lives have meaning and matter to an all-powerful, all knowing, God. Few seldom significantly change spiritual beliefs, unless having experienced a significant emotional event such as a near death experience.

Inquiring people search to discover their origins. As, we get older, many of us work to understand and praise our mothers and fathers even more. Some of us work to discover our ancestry, and even Man's and God's *origins*.

In early traditional religious eras, spiritual leaders pondered to understand their origins. Who, in those times, would believe Man began as simple cells in the ocean, and over millions of years evolved as humans? Today, some believe there are still missing links in the trail of Man's evolution. In traditional religious eras, who would have believed in evolution, and that their great, great - - - great grandfather and grandmother began as *amoebas*?

Scientists study evolution to discover Man's origin. From the Bible, God created Adam and then created Eve from Adam's rib. A *man* must have interpreted, and *men* repeated, this version of Man's creation. Adam and Eve were created with developed language. This story has satisfied explanation of Man's origin for thousands of years. Since God *created* Adam, the *process* did not need be understood or questioned. Few ask how God created Adam. *Creation* in Genesis took *six eons*, or *six spiritual days*. Adam's and Eve's creation and lives were very different from our lives today. Some scientists believe this biblical story was a parable to explain Man's origin. Many believe the story of Jonah swallowed by the whale was also a parable to emphasize that Man cannot escape from God.

God has not yet created a species on earth with greater intelligence than Man. If so, humans may be relegated to the *animal* kingdom.

Many of us believe in spiritual communication and that Jesus and God hear and react to our prayers or we would not pray. With our prayers, we may enhance our deceased loved ones' spiritual activities and responsibilities in heaven. Recursively, they may improve our lives on earth, and, hopefully, later on in heaven. I have a strong belief my deceased loved ones in heaven hear my prayers.

Religions, science, and experience develop lifetime beliefs needed for acceptance by God. We have free will for learning and accepting spiritual beliefs. We must accept God's physical laws, and the truthfulness of science? Spiritual, mental, and physical truths are intertwined.

When celebrating exciting victories, many of us believe our beloved deceased are looking down from heaven and celebrating with us. When highly emotional and lying on an emergency room table expecting imminent death, I *sensed* and *saw* my beloved parents and deceased uncles and aunts looking down on me and concentrating to return my soul to my fragile mind and body. My awareness, *soul*, was floating above my feet. I *believe* they and God returned my soul to a fragile mind and saved my life. I celebrate life every day.

In times of great need the subconscious mind becomes conscious. Subconscious minds are spiritually connected to God through our souls. Scientists will advance spiritual communication technology to assist our lives and God in the future. God needs our prayers.

When loved ones pass on, tradition is to pray for our loved one's soul to: *Rest in Peace.* I interpret this to mean for the body to rest in peace. Some *life* remains in deceased bodies for some time. Hair continues to grow! I do not normally recommend cremation. There may be residual spiritual communication between the *dead* body and the soul, or with their spirits in heaven. I pray every night that God grants my beloved spirits: "Wonderful, exciting activities and responsibilities in heaven." This is the best I can do for them. I feel good when praying for my spirits in heaven. We may continue to grow spiritually until we die.

From life experiences, we develop beliefs about everything we encounter. We make judgments about things and people that we believe would be good or bad for us. We develop faith in our cars and in trusted people. Many of us have faith in Jesus and God and strongly feel *Their* presence throughout our beings. I have faith in my beloved saints in heaven. Their spiritual resonances are integrated within God and I believe they *listen* to my prayers.

Most of us have pride and joy in thinking of and doing exciting, helpful, and spiritual things. *Accepted* souls ascend into heaven to become complete beyond worldly dimensions and integrated within God's Infinite Hologram. Spiritual believers have pride in surrendering to God's Will for our and God's benefit. Beyond our lives on earth, our heavenly activities will accelerate in scope and depth. If our spirits were to rest in peace forever, heaven would become eternal boredom. God is infinite and has infinite spiritual purposes and needs for our beloved spirits to accomplish.

My spiritual thoughts on death have been cultivated through my experiences in confronting death and *experiencing* images of beloved spirits guiding my escaping soul to return to a fragile mind, with love and concern. In my unexpected spiritual experiences, I felt no pain, but had hopes for life *on earth or in heaven.*

Being spiritual may be simple. Sharing anything with positive intent, without expecting anything in return, is spiritual. A smile can be spiritual. Praising God is spiritual.

Chapter 39

NOTHING BEFORE TIME

Nothing: not anything; no single thing

Infinity: limitless or endless in space, energy, speed, size. ability and knowledge. God's love and power is beyond human ability to understand, measure, or calculate.

"My model of the first *Existence* is *Nothing Before Time*. It represents the simplest mathematical terms – a point existence alternating faster and faster with an infinite homogeneous existence. It explodes from nothing into the infinite – Baby God.

H Fulcher

I n my first and severe manic episode, I *needed* to understand existence before God and needed to make a dramatic model of God and then for God to create the universe. I used my physics background. To model creation of God, I used the *Reverse* Heisenberg Uncertainty Principle to give me a feeling of existence before God and the universe. I begin with an imaginative model of *Nothing before Time*.

I *dreamed* a model of *Nothing before Time* that had properties to transition into God and His infinite spiritual existence. Something dramatic had to happen to create God and then for Him to create the universe.

My model of *Nothing before Time* began with the simplest concepts I could imagine. A point alternating with a perfectly infinite homogenized existence. The infinite existence was not space and did not allow or have movement. Neither can be represented separately by mathematics. Mathematics can only relate these two existences to each other. These two existences randomly alternated faster until it fused - a cataclysmic event - into one entity. It exploded from nothing to an infinite Baby God. Within zero or infinite pre-spiritual time this existence transcended into an infinite Baby God as the first awareness of self with infinite power over a new existence. After zero or infinite spiritual time, Baby God created heaven with spiritual time and the universe with physical time. There is no reason to believe spiritual time is anything like physical time.

God's power was so great that He needed to create a universe to reduce his power so He as *Light* could have consistent properties. In fractions of a second, He created space and all hydrogen atoms with freedoms to travel in space.

God created heaven to store memories forever of all good thoughts and things that occurred in the universe and heaven. In heaven God had and has abilities to relate memories of all good things to all other good things to make spiritual completeness. Heaven has awareness of all living souls including those of spiritual humans on earth that have transcended into heaven upon death. Upon death, souls change polarity to become heavenly spirits. God was and is always complete in a very different spiritual time and existence.

God created confined energy as atoms from His highest Light energy waves. Atoms also have traveling energy or momentum. This is my model of *Nothing before Time* that transcended into God. And then He created the heavens, the universe, and the earth with living things including potentials for humans.

Nothing before Time was very different from the physical time and space we know today. My manic mind was briefly extended to emotional limits to create the simplest model of existence and God. There must have been a cataclysmic polarity change in existence to create God and His spiritual energy and awareness. Then another polarity change must have occurred for God to create the energy and space of the universe from Nothing before Time.

I assumed the Reverse Heisenberg Uncertainty Principle, given earlier, existed in *primordial time.* In my reverse model, *Nothing* and spiritual energy transitions were limited to values *below* h/(2π) which is less than any physically measurable energy transition after creation of the universe. This primordial model supports transition to God and spiritual existence. There were no fixed laws in *Nothing before Time. But it* had probability to create spiritual time and existence.

Light *or EMR laws* did not exist in *Nothing before Time.* Light became the medium between spiritual and physical time and existence.

In my first dramatic manic episode, I lost sense of self and physical existence. An uncertain mind drifted into the uncertainties of *Nothing before Time.* I had a need to understand the beginning of existence. Physical space, energy, and time did not exist as we now know them. There was no spiritual or mental awareness in *Nothing before Time.* The timing of point and infinite existence vibrations randomly increased without meaning, consistency, or purpose. There was no movement in primordial existence. Random primordial existence existed in negative, imaginary time.

Later in my more normal times, I worked to recall my *manic dream of Nothing before Time* that transitioned into an *infinite spiritual reality – Baby God.*

Existence in premortal random negative time, transitioned into perfectly organized, spiritual time and *Perfectly Organized Spiritual Energy and Light at zero* time. Spiritual time is very different from God's later created physical time with created atoms. At the moment of the Big Bang, after *zero or infinite* spiritual time, Virgin Light was created at the beginning of the Big Bang. Virgin Light is light that came from the Big Bang and not from fusion of hydrogen atoms in stars. Virgin light expands space at the edges of the universe at the speed of light.

Spiritual time existed before physical time and cannot be measured from a physical or human viewpoint. Probability existed in *Nothing before Time* to transition into God and His infinite spiritual energy and expanding space. God is the definition of infinite awareness and existence. Infinite is a term for existence, thinking, and power beyond human imagination.

Negative primordial time *changed polarity* to become organized spiritual time. The transition between primordial and spiritual existence occurred at random *zero or infinite spiritual time*. Spiritual time is very different from human sensed physical time. God's thoughts and actions must be much faster than Light to be aware of and *control* the entire universe and an infinite heaven.

Primordial time was random without laws or awareness. Primordial random uncertainties had a change of polarity and became perfectly organized spiritual waves and spiritual time. Primordial uncertainties and randomness transcended into God and stable spiritual waves and heaven. God was the first awareness of self and all spiritual existence.

Spiritual space came from a point and an infinite homogeneous existence. There were no measurable differences in infinite spiritual existence. All changes occurred throughout an infinite spiritual existence. Who would restrict God's space and time to physical space and time?

Cosmology studies and models the early universe. Cosmologists believe scientists will never scientifically learn anything before the Big Bang or before physical space and time. This is true unless God informs believers of His existence before creation of the universe.

Primordial space may have existed in only two dimensions. Primordial time may have been slow or fast depending upon dimension vibrations and may have varied along only one or two *primordial* dimensions. There were no relationships in primordial existence, which is different from both spiritual and physical space and time.

God *controls* a very different spiritual time. He emotionally needs physical time and space to complete Himself. He does *infinite* spiritual activities simultaneously throughout the universe and heaven. Spiritual histories last forever.

God is the awareness in spiritual existence. He controlled infinite spiritual energy and *needed* to create a very different existence, a universe, from within Himself to stabilize His spiritual foundation. Universal dimensions were created as a subset of God's infinite spiritual dimensions. The universe was created to support God's spiritual Light energy and information.

Shortly after creation of the universe, God fused His highest energy spiritual waves to create all atoms of the universe. Creating all atoms gave God His *constant* speed of light, and consistent physical laws and properties. God continually travels at the speed of light relative to all physical things. In heaven, He travels at spiritual speeds. He learns about the universe with His very fast spiritual waves. Unusual things happen at the speed of light. Space contracts. God sees the universe differently than humans do.

Distance and time are *consistent* on earth today but are very different near or within very dense black holes. Matter curves light and condenses space. Space expands at large distances from galaxies. Space and time at the very beginning of the Big Bang had properties much greater than that in black holes. The universe was created from a single spiritual point expanding at the speed of light.

The first moment of physical existence was a completely organized *infinite* black hole without physical space. Early existence was very different from current space and time, on the earth. Will understanding time and space in black holes give insight into spiritual time and space?

God created a perfectly organized heaven, and an initial perfectly organized universe with zero entropy. God became completely organized by reducing His energy and by creating the universe with consistently organized physical space, time, energy, and probability laws. Uranium atoms decay at a constant probably rate. However, scientists cannot predict which atoms will decay when. Probably is a random physical law. Probability allows for the universe and man to have a future. Man, the universe, and God are not predestined. There is a future to learn about.

The universe evolves and becomes less organized in physical time. God is perfectly *aware* of all spiritual and physical histories of the universe and heaven. He existed before the physical universe and will exist forever in spiritual time.

God integrates all physical and spiritual information to be omniscient and omnipresent. Spiritual information is in *integration dimensions*. His awareness of all information at the beginning point of the universe is integrated and then reflected back to each point in the universe for God to be omniscient and up to date.

God is all *Light* and spiritual waves throughout the universe and heaven. His spiritual awareness over a great big universe, requires communication speeds much, much faster than the speed of light. It would take billions of years for light to travel from one boundary of the universe to the opposite boundary.

God organizes and controls activities in the universe with His physical and probability laws. God could control Man but gives him free will to think and act on his own. God needs our prayers and learns from our free wills. Man has a purpose. Humans may choose to think or not to think, or to pray or not to pray. In my first manic episode, imaginative *Nothing before Time* and spiritual models gave feelings of time, space, hope and spiritual understanding.

Chapter 40

CREATION

⸙

"In the beginning, God created the heavens and the earth."

(Genesis 1:1)

"A simple model of Creation was a random vibration of *Nothing Before Time* – a very fast resonating point existence and infinite perfectly homogenized existence that created a polarity in existence – God. He then created the heavens and the universe in His spiritual time. The universe expanded from a point *toward* an infinite physical existence at the limiting speed of Light."

H Fulcher

Christians accept with awe, but do not attempt to understand, God's *Creation* of the universe. Scientists and philosophers develop theories about God's Creation. Thinking about and making models of Creation gives a spiritual feeling of belonging in the universe. In the future, Clear Minds may receive some understanding of Creation from God.

Philosophers and cosmologists ponder the unchanging physical and probability laws of an evolving universe. Some philosophers ponder the existence of God and the structure of heaven. God needed structure for His spiritual existence and reality. Heaven is everywhere the same and independent of space. All spiritual activities affect all of heaven and God equally. Spiritual energy is very different from physical energy. God created the universe with physical differences to support His infinite spiritual wave, space, and integration dimensions.

In 1977 with manic sensitivities, I pondered Creation. After initial amazement, spiritual feelings and thoughts seemed as if known for a long time.

I have worked to recall and write about spiritual messages received during early manic times to construct spiritual models. My philosophical, spiritual models are based upon science, the Bible, and spiritual messages received. Manic spiritual ideas are like dreams and too often quickly forgotten.

My Creation model transitioned from my *Nothing before Time* model. Random primordial existence transitioned into a perfectly organized, highly energetic spiritual *point* or *near point* at zero or infinite spiritual time. Baby God, as the first awareness with ability to organize, was *born* into existence. The spiritual *point* resonated or repeatedly *exploded* as a boundless infinite existence and then fused again with infinite potential to explode again or continue to resonate. Undefined spiritual time between vibrations could have been zero or infinite.

In *spiritual time*, God created the repelling unified field force, which caused the Big Bang to explode into three spatial dimensions, and created physical space and time. In a fraction of a second, the unified field force reversed polarity to become an attractive gravity and other field forces, as they are today.

The Big Bang was initially all *Light*. In a fraction of a second the most energetic Light waves imploded into hydrogen atoms.

Big Bang spiritual reverberations travel from the center of the universe to its expanding boundaries and back every 10^{-106} seconds giving God omniscient and omnipresent abilities. As the universe expands at the speed of light, God's awareness resonates at *near infinite* speed. It became *certain* that God and the universe existed.

Very Fast Spiritual Wave reverberations are reflected at the universe's expanding boundaries. Spiritual information from each point in the universe is recorded and focused toward the center of the universe. All information is integrated *within* the origin, spiritual, point of the universe and reflected outward to every point in the universe every 10^{-106} seconds giving God omniscience and omnipresence at every point in the universe.

Spiritual waves interact only with Light, not atoms. They travel so fast relative to Light that possibly Light travels only one quantum of space between spiritual wave reverberations. Spiritual resonances at near infinite speeds update God's infinite wisdom every 10^{-106} seconds, creating His omniscience and omnipresence. Space varies in massive matter such as black holes. The universe was initially like a huge black hole.

After God's transition from *Nothing before Time*, He existed as resonating Light and spiritual waves in spiritual dimensions as complete organized existence. God's original spiritual energy became too strong to control spiritually. He fused His highest energy spiritual waves into physical energy and hydrogen atoms. God fused His most energetic spiritual waves to create 10^{82} confined quantum energy resonances, or hydrogen atoms, in less than 10^{-35} seconds after the beginning of creation. Physical time and space gave atoms freedom to travel.

Virgin Light, or EMR, was created directly from the Big Bang and not from atom excitations. Virgin Light continually expands the universe at the speed of light.

God transitioned from *Nothing before Time* as spiritually perfect. Perfect cannot be understood or maintained without understanding imperfect. Man has a purpose!

God and heaven were and are perfectly organized after transcending from the randomness of *Nothing before Time*. God was lonely and created the universe with uncertainties and organization potentials to have something to nurture, love, and reflect information back to Him. This might be similar to living beings needing to nurture their offspring for them to become reflections of themselves in body and spirit. Humans are God's offspring.

Energy is continually shared between *Light and Spiritual Waves, God,* and matter within the universe: $E = mc^2$. Light is the medium between physical and spiritual existences. Discrete changes continue throughout the universe, and holistic changes continue throughout heaven.

Changes in the universe keep heaven perfectly organized. The universe becomes less organized in time, and God in Heaven becomes more organized to keep track of all activities in the universe and heaven. The universe has probability laws and uncertainties. God learns from and responds to physical, mental, and spiritual activities. Physical activities are controlled by God's constant physical and probability laws. He has spiritual influence in physical and *spiritual time.* God's spiritual and relativity time are very different from human observed physical time.

Conflict continues between Light and matter. Will the universe end as integrated *Light* resonating holistically in spiritual dimensions or as collapsed black motionless *frozen* matter as a *point devoid of Light or energy*? Will all Light become frozen matter, or will all matter become Light? If all matter becomes *Light,* Existence would become entirely spiritual again.

God, the universe, and Man are not predestined. By creating uncertainties, God's loneliness turned to emotions and Love for the universe, and then Man. He created Man on earth, and beings on other planets, for them to receive His love and reflect it back to Him, with free wills.

God created Adam or Man in a spiritual day that could have been millions of now 24-hour earthly days. Days were undefined back then. *Biblical creation* models relate to spiritual time and not to earthly time. Spiritual and physical time are very different but are intricately connected.

God constantly communicates throughout, and controls, the universe. Man is controlled by gravity, light, and other forces, but has free will to think independently of God and His *spiritual laws.*

Pets have free wills but give humans something to care for and love, and from being lonely. Humans are God's pets?

Light energy is created by physical fusion and fission of atom nuclei in stars and the sun, and by chemical reactions. Light, EMR, have freedoms to travel throughout space at relativistic speeds. Atoms travel slower. God travels at the speed of light, and His awareness of information throughout the universe and heaven travels at the speed of spiritual waves. Christians refer to spiritual waves as the Holy Spirit. God is *Light*.

Perfect spiritual books are interpreted differently by different religions and their denominations. Intelligent believers must reason about their own and other spiritual leaders and their spiritual books to separate enlightenment from control. Thomas Jefferson's beliefs were responsible for preventing religious control over the American people. With freedom of religion, American religions are less controlling than those of many countries.

Spiritual feelings and enlightenment give us comfort, completeness, and freedom of thought. With spiritual meditation, we isolate ourselves from outside influences so only God and our minds matter in our personal spiritual time. We must strive to know our inner selves to truly love ourselves, those close to us, and God.

Spiritual models give a sense of adventure, comfort, and inner confidence. Hopefully, my models of God will inspire science research of my and others' spiritual messages. God's complete wisdom is available everywhere in the universe. Humans can improve their individual spiritual technology and skills. God usually only gives spiritual information believers are able to understand. A fundamental goal for mankind is to learn from God, and reflect His Love and Truths back to Him and to people we meet.

We must continue to improve spiritual technology for receiving spiritual wisdom. Inner healing sensations and spiritual messages are intuitive. Spiritual communication is different from normal human communication. We learn about God by studying and analyzing His universe and by being sensitive to His spiritual messages directly, from the Bible, and from other believers. Many historical messages have been written in spiritual books. The universe is God's body. Light and spiritual waves relate to His mind. God is the universe's integrated *Mind*. Without minds, brains and bodies have no purpose. Without God, the universe has no purpose.

At the moment of creation, the universe was perfectly organized. Minds are drawn to *perfect* organization and structure. Organized dancing is inspiring. If dancers show synchronized movements, they display purpose, even spiritual purpose. We strive for organization in the things we do. Computers help organize our minds.

Heaven is an organized, integrated higher dimensional existence and is home for God's Infinite Spiritual Hologram. All information from all activities in the universe is integrated within heaven and affects all of heaven equally.

The beginning universe was completely organized and much simpler for God to keep track of than it is today. Baby God, ruling over the young universe, had much, much less to be aware of, to learn and control. The universe evolves. God integrates Light, learns, and evolves His continuing perfect completeness.

Evolution of the universe has nuclear and chemical potentials for organizing atoms and molecules with potentials to create Man – a bunch of organized atoms and molecules. The universe and Man's origin and organizing abilities were and are from God.

A particle of mass attracted by a massive black hole is accelerated faster that light in vacuum as it approaches the black hole's event horizon. An event horizon is a sphere around a black hole in which incoming matter has no chance of escape. Time as matter nears a black hole's event horizon becomes slow and then *stops*. The universe has differences in time. Spiritual time is very different from physical time, which man lives with and partially understands.

In early stages of creation, the very, very massive and dense universe would have acted even more drastically than actions near and within black holes. Time would have been very different within different areas of the very young universe. God, observed by man within the evolving universe, would appear as having existed forever. At the beginning of the universe, Baby God was less infinite than He is today. God and His spiritual laws are, and will continue being more, perfect. He receives feedback from the universe and human prayers. God's perfection continues to grow in spiritual time. He is the continued definition of infinite from a human viewpoint.

There is no existence, awareness, or thought without uncertainties. God has certainties, probabilities, and future uncertainties. He has perfect awareness of all physical and spiritual histories. God and humans must have uncertainties, or they cannot make decisions for control of Their futures. Otherwise, existence would be predestined. No *real* decisions could be made without uncertainties. God would not create Man and deceive him. Humans make real decisions. The greatest accomplishments are when scientists and heroes make the greatest uncertainties, certain, to learn more of God and His universe.

Humans' purpose on earth is to assist God in building spiritual certainty and overcoming uncertainties in the universe. The evolving configuration of the universe constructs God's perfect continuous *awareness* of all spiritual and physical history.

God was the first awareness created from *Nothing before Time*. He created the universe to share and preserve His spiritual energy, information, and Truths. He created living beings with ability to share His Will and Love. God has given Man free will for Him to learn from and love. He needs our prayers.

He created probability laws in the universe so details of the future are never completely known. God and Man have a future to look forward to and improve. Without uncertainties there would be no future. Everything would be predestined. With probability laws, God knows the overall or integrated future of heaven and the universe but not the future of all individual events.

I praise God for creating the universe and heaven, for His infinite abilities, and for listening to prayers. Many of my prayers are for loved ones in heaven. I pray for God to give them wonderful activities and responsibilities. These prayers give me pleasant feelings of completion.

My models and ideas are not meant to be perfect or even consistent. They began as manic ideas and are intended to make readers think and imagine.

Chapter 41

JESUS

"A new commandment I give to you, that you love one another, even as I have loved you, that you also love one another."

John: 13:34

"Blessed are the poor in spirit, for theirs is the kingdom of heaven.
Blessed are those who mourn, for they shall be comforted.
Blessed are the gentle, for they shall inherit the earth.
Blessed are those who hunger and thirst for righteousness, for they shall be satisfied.
Blessed are the merciful, for they shall receive mercy.
Blessed are the pure in heart, for they shall see God.
Blessed are the peacemakers, for they shall be called sons of God.
Blessed are those who have been persecuted for the sake of righteousness, for theirs is the kingdom of heaven."

Matthew 5:3-10

"At the end of the day, the most important relationship we can have is the one with our lord and savior Jesus Christ."

Unknown

J esus' peaceful, loving, and spiritual teachings are foundations of my beliefs and worship. He prepared *thirty* years for His spiritual work and developed skills to love, teach, heal, do miracles, and save souls.

We must develop foundations and reasons for our beliefs and question them at times. The world changes over time. God listens and responds to our prayers in His spiritual time. His wisdom increases as the universe expands and becomes more complex. However, His spiritual, physical, and probability laws are constant and do not change.

We can predict the overall probably of uranium atoms decaying but we cannot predict which individual atoms will decay when. In the same way, God can predict overall, integrated purpose of the earth, universe, and heaven but may not entirely predict all individual events. Humans have free wills. The universe and God have a future. Existence is not predestined!

After receiving my life-changing spiritual message: "Don't Leave God Out," I was unable to distinguish whether my spiritual messages came from Jesus or directly from God. Jesus' spirit is integrated within God's Eternal Hologram so I conclude spiritual messages have come from both Jesus and God.

Many have experienced unusual demanding messages from God. Moses, experienced God's *burning bush* as a demanding message from God. I pray my work serves Jesus, God, my beloved ones in heaven, and readers on earth.

Before His three years of teaching, Jesus' Mind had become integrated with, and part of, God. God spoke through Him. In John Chapter 14:6 Jesus answered, "I am the way and the truth and the life. No one (*from the earth?*) comes to the Father except through me." Was Jesus talking to His disciples, or to all of humanity, including those who may have never heard of Him? Jesus was born Son of God. All babies have God's complete wisdom but lose recall of that wisdom due to baby and childhood trauma scars.

Are only Christians saved for eternal life in heaven? Are all other believers deceived and wasting their time for attaining spiritual lives in heaven? Were Noah and Moses, who lived before Jesus' times and obeyed God, accepted for Eternal life?

Jesus ascended into heaven and formed a Holy Trinity with God and the Holy Spirit. Jesus' spiritual resonances became integrated within God's higher dimensional Eternal Infinite Hologram Resonances. All saved souls' spiritual resonances integrate within, and add to, God's Eternal Infinite Hologram. Jesus and God only accept those into heaven who believe in Them. Existence in heaven is very different from life on earth.

What spiritual purpose, blessings, and freedoms will we share in heaven? We must have responsibilities and tasks in heaven or spiritual existence would be Eternal meaningless and boredom. To experience spiritual activities, decisions, and goals in heaven, we must overcome spiritual uncertainties and challenges on earth. All changes in heaven are holistic. Understanding and solving holistic uncertainties and challenges on earth require holistic spiritual beliefs and skills. God's physics laws are holistic and unchanging throughout the universe.

Jesus prayed often and received guidance from God. He did not let His spiritual achievements corrupt His search for spiritual Truth and His love for mankind.

Many of us have an inherent desire to be with good amazing *perfect* people. Jesus was amazing in His love, teaching, and spiritual influence. People have been attracted to Him and His teachings for over two thousand years.

Jesus needs our reflections, love, and praises. Loving mothers and fathers need their children's love and reflections. God and our parents made us. To truthfully love ourselves we must love God, others, and do things to be loved. We must reflect love and respect to God as earthly mothers and fathers hope their children will reflect love and respect to them.

If Jesus is perfect for all times, would there be no pain or sorrow? It is difficult to define perfect lives. However, Christians believe Jesus lived a perfect three years of teaching. I believe Jesus developed a *Clear Mind* free of trauma scars, or sins, to accomplish the spiritual things He accomplished. Early in life, He must have experienced severe emotions and pressure from such high expectations.

Christians believe Jesus was conceived by the Holy Spirit and born of Mary, a virgin. God must have male DNA. Would Jesus' DNA have been very different proving He was the Son of God? We are sons and daughters of God!

To understand the needs of the poor and heal the sick, Jesus must have experienced difficult and painful times earlier in life. Anyone during Jesus' times with mental disorders would have been put in a closet and stigmatized. This may be why there was little history of most of His life. It is no sin to have mental disorders. We learn the most about ourselves and God when overcoming adversity at emotional limits.

Jesus told His disciples, John and James, they must become servants in order to lead. How many political and spiritual leaders today think of themselves as servants to their constituents and congregations?

Using the words *perfect* and *genius* has kept many, even today, from questioning religions. Would you question someone who has been called a *genius*?

Definition of *perfection* changes over time. *Perfect* is difficult to define. A *test* of Jesus' *perfection* was that His disciples, and those who judged Him could find no fault in Him. Did this prove Jesus never sinned?

Suffering makes us aware of blessings we have had, and upon recovery, makes us humble, thankful, and less self-centered. Suffers often seek spiritual guidance and goals.

An all-knowing, all-powerful God is aware of evil on earth but continues to nurture human free wills. Spiritual *perfection* is difficult to understand. Could Jesus have been more perfect or spiritual by beginning His teaching earlier and saving more lives? We humans do not understand spiritual perfection.

During Jesus' life, few people were literate. Elders told stories to pass down their way of life, for controlling their children, and for entertainment. Much of the New Testament was written sixty years after Jesus' death. After sixty years with the best of notes, it would be difficult to write perfectly, unless they were in *complete awe* of Jesus, His work, and God. Biblical writers were amazing. Did they write perfectly?

There was little science and technology two thousand years ago. People would more readily believe in miracles. Many of Jesus' miracles were observed by many. I belief in Jesus and His miracles.

In His era, Jesus was the *modern* radical preaching *radical ideas* and performing miracles. He healed the sick but did not explain His medical miracles. Scientists and medical doctors today explain and document their healing technologies. Future *miracle* technologies will reduce suffering and make lives better. Jesus made lives meaningful and better. I pray for the Ukrainian people.

We must strive to learn from Jesus and God; They learn from our prayers and free wills. We have a purpose. For Eternal life, our soul's resonances, constructed by our genetics and lifetime of thoughts and actions, *must* synchronize with Jesus' and God's spiritual resonances in heaven to be accepted.

I met a lady on my way to a nursing home. She surprisingly asked my name. I asked who she was. She said she was the chaplain of this nursing home. I asked her the purpose of her visit? She said she was there to tell residents that she loves them and that Jesus loves them. She came to bring comfort and purpose to elderly and sick residents. She gave me a needed lesson of hope and spiritual comfort.

Many Christians promote: *not I, but Christ.* I aspire to do this. This chapter is brief. For more information, read the Bible and attend a church. I love Jesus but I am not able to love those who have been extremely and continually evil to me. God gave us emotions to love others and to protect ourselves.

Chapter 42

PRAYER

⌒∞⌒

"I believe in prayer. It's the best way we have to draw strength from heaven."

Josephine Baker

"Therefore, I tell you, whatever you ask for in prayer, believe that you have received it, and it will be yours."

Mark 11:24 | NIV

"May your sins and troubles be few and your spiritual dreams come true."

H. Fulcher

Knowing God, with Infinite Power, is listening to my prayers, makes me humble and smile.

H. Fulcher

Prayer: a solemn request for help or an expression of praise and joy addressed to God or to an object or person of worship.

Most spiritual messages received are like diamonds in the rough. They have deep hidden meaning and beauty. We must cut and polish spiritual diamonds for them to reflect their inner beauty and sparkle for all. Spiritual diamonds have reverberating resonances that reflect inner truths to the *subconscious mind*, and, sometimes, directly to consciousness. It is our duty to translate our spiritual messages into *human made words*.

Be happy and anxious to pray. In good times, praying should be fun. I am happiest when praying for God to give my beloved spirits in heaven wonderful activities and responsibilities. "Make a joyful noise unto the LORD, all the earth: make a loud noise, and rejoice, and sing praise." Psalms – 98:4 KJV.

We must calm our minds to receive spiritual wisdom from God and interpret His spiritual waves. God is omnipresent and His spiritual waves are constantly around and through us and throughout the universe. We must be either very *calm* or *highly emotional* to receive God's highest blessings. Normal mental energy levels are for responding to earthly activities and needs.

When depressed and giving up on life, we no longer focus on earthly goals. Our holistic right-brains become dominant for communicating with and surrendering to God. Humble prayers have very low mental energy. High frequency mental waves also synchronize with God's infinite spiritual waves to become integrated within God's Perfect Infinite Spiritual Hologram. Our prayers aren't accepted in part, but holistically by God in spiritual dimensions that are entwined with the universe's physical dimensions.

God gave humans, and other living beings, with souls, free will. We have free will for selecting and achieving daily tasks. We can do this or that. It is spiritual to think about, help, and give confidence to others. Nurturing and loving our children, spouses, and all who are good to us is spiritual. Praising God for what we have and enjoy is spiritual.

It is preposterous to believe God creates *spiritual* humans to kill other humans, who have done nothing to them but worship differently. At times, God demands us to do spiritual duties. He asked me not to leave Him out of my first book twenty-eight years ago. That is why this book is spiritual. We have freedom to choose between earthly and spiritual purposes.

Demanding spiritual leaders emotionally brainwash rather than teach and lead. Brainwashing destroys free will and limits thinking. The brainwashed become prisoners within their own minds. Brainwashed victims regurgitate memorized dogma rather than reasoning about their lives and God's purpose for them.

Surrendering to God in prayer is important for receiving His blessings. Our souls are worth nothing without God's love and caring.

Many Christians repeat those old hymns praising Jesus and God with a sense of love and purpose. God *senses* our praises and reflects them throughout the universe and heaven. We have a spiritual purpose.

We might pray holistic, unselfish prayers for every living being in the universe with a soul. We should think about our prayers to ensure they serve God's needs. He needs us to praise Him for He has prepared the universe and heaven for us. Praising God should be similar to how we should praise good mothers and fathers for the good things they have done in preparing us for life.

Current physical configurations within the universe and spiritual structures in heaven depend upon their entire histories. God's wisdom includes all historical and present activities in the universe and heaven. God's omniscience and omnipresence is complete and intertwined with physical space and time. Human memories have chemical structures on brain membranes that store historical events in sequential and emotional energy order.

I meditate and surrender conscious control for awakening subconscious inner processes. My body and environment no longer matter when feeling God's presence, love, and consistency.

When loved ones are lost in tragedies, community and spiritual leaders ask everyone to pray for their families. I pray that *lost* loved ones in heaven have wonderful spiritual awareness, interactions, activities, and responsibilities for serving God. It is the best I can do for them. Doing nothing in heaven would be eternal boredom, and next to Hell.

I and others, when experiencing expected imminent death, have received visions of deceased loved ones giving hope to hold on to life. Our beloved spirits in heaven and God answer our prayers, when we surrender to God. I pray that Jesus and God make my beloved spirits in heaven spiritually strong to serve Them and communicate with believers on earth in need.

I pray to Jesus and God and to my revered deceased parents, uncles and aunts, and heroes: "You are wonderful. I praise you and humbly ask for your blessings." Our beloved saints, resonate as everlasting spiritual holograms, synchronized, and integrated within God's Infinite Hologram. Spiritual existence in heaven is very different from physical and spiritual existence on earth.

We can improve our personal prayer technology by reading the Bible. Spiritual waves received by our souls, have traveled across the universe and heaven in a small fraction of a second. We are part of God's universe and our souls are interwoven within heaven's infinite dimensions. Our souls are freed from our bodies upon death to live a *complete spiritual existence.*

Changes in religions has been slow and difficult, because they espouse that their leaders have led, or are leading, *perfect* spiritual lives. Some believers claim their religion espouses perfect beliefs. No one can improve perfect.

Will there ever be peace on earth with *biased, perfect religions?* Hopefully, spiritual leaders will improve and expand prayer technology to unite all religions with God's love and truth. When humble before God our subconscious minds may improve our prayer technology.

God's spiritual time is very different from physical time on earth. God *processes spiritual wisdom trillion times trillions* of *times faster* in spiritual time than humans do in physical time. With differences between physical and spiritual times, we must be patient to receive God's responses to our prayers. He is in a very different time zone. He judges us on earth by our potentials for eternal life in heaven.

I pray readers will benefit from my work and receive God's blessings. God, Jesus, the Holy Spirit, heavenly spirits, and God's angels are a team. I hope to become part of that team. As insignificant as I may be, at times, I pray for *every creature, who has a soul,* within the universe, and who loves and does good things for God and the down trodden. I pray for all heavenly spirits to have wonderful activities in heaven. Heaven will not be boring. Our prayers should assist God in His purposes and help worshipers be less biased and spiritual for all.

Our prayers must be truthful. If we pray against someone or some group either for our protection or for retribution, we must be truthful that that person or group has been persistently evil and damaging to us. We should analyze our behaviors and interactions toward being spiritual and truthful.

Praying for God to give my beloved *saints* wonderful activities in heaven gives me pleasant, confirming sensations around the forehead and sometimes over the scalp. I pray for God to help me communicate stronger and in greater detail with my *saints* in heaven. I also pray for God to give all spiritual people on earth stronger communications with Him and *their loved ones* in heaven.

I receive feelings of comfort, completeness, and hope when praising God for His creations and wonders, and ask for His guidance in improving my prayers. I receive the most joy when asking God to give my beloved saints in heaven wonderful activities and responsibilities. It is the best I can do for them. My prayers are mostly simple and personal. I praise God for light and my eyes and for air and my hearing and breathing. I experiment in prayer until receiving inner joy. I have not been called upon to be evangelical except through my books.

I praise God for all the stars, planets, and moons, space and movement, gravity, and electromagnetic radiation. I pray for all activities that make the earth livable, and for evaporation from the oceans that give us clouds and rain. I pray my work will be helpful to readers.

We do not need to love those who continually bully and degrade us, but pray that God will change their minds and behaviors. Loving those who continue degrading us will cause us to lose our health. I pray for *all* people who love those different from themselves and for them to have inner peace. I thank God for everyone who has been good to me and for those who would be good to me if we were to interact. Jesus is my Savior. I pray for forgiveness of my sins. I am a sinner who tries to improve.

Chapter 43

ALPHA AND OMEGA OF PRAYER

Earlier, I proposed a theory that upon conception *babies* are aware of God and His Infinite wisdom and power. God is omniscient, omnipresent, and near completely omnipotent. God gives living things some minute' amount of power.

Early mental challenges and traumas eclipse spiritual awareness and wisdom as life progresses. Spiritual awareness and wisdom have very low holistic spiritual energy that is below and usually independent of Man's normal mental energy for consciousness and everyday tasks. Without spiritual wisdom, humans become short sighted in their knowledge and activities in space and time. God's infinite awareness and wisdom span from His beginning in spiritual time before, and beyond, physical time.

God's awareness and wisdom are integrations of all physical, mental, and spiritual thoughts and activities throughout the universe and heaven in spiritual time. God's awareness and wisdom exists in every point of vacuum or *spiritual* space. Human memory and wisdom are very limited and shortsighted.

From heredity, human souls include survival and spiritual wisdom from all of our direct ancestors' lives. Our soul's wisdom begins with our earliest ancestors' souls, continues to our recent ancestors' souls, and includes our own earthly spiritual thoughts and activities. Our heredity wisdom in our souls may have begun with our first *amoeba*. In a spiritual sense, we have inherited responsibility for the survival and spiritual activities and thoughts of our complete line of ancestors. God is aware of our inherited lives through our souls. He judges inherited and lifetime thoughts and activities within our souls. Spiritually, we have our ancestors,' and our own, histories. We have extended spiritual responsibilities.

God judges our soul's integrated histories. We should praise our *ancestors* for the good within our souls and ask for God to forgive us for evil near the edges of our souls. Our souls are integrals of all of our ancestors' souls with awareness of our lifetime events within our souls. We inherit and only borrow our souls. Hopefully, we will give them back to God. We should praise God and pray for forgiveness of our and all our descendants' future transgressions. Spiritual power comes from our goodness, our ancestors' goodness, and the potential goodness of all future descendants. Hopefully, we have trained our children well. Our activities influence our and our descendants' DNA and souls. Spiritually we have integrated responsibilities. Spiritual time is very different than human dream, mental, and sensed physical time.

Some conflicting religions on earth compete with and degrade one another. With Clear Minds and if prepared to receive God's wisdom, we may receive wisdom from all souls with DNA or spiritual resonances similar to that of our own soul. God usually gives us only information we are prepared to understand. To be accepted into heaven, we need genetic spiritual purpose beyond our own spiritual purpose.

Hopefully, true religions with spiritual wisdom from God will unite to create one religion that is good for everyone on the earth and in the universe. It would be the spiritual thing to do. Spiritual purposes must unite to continue God's purposes. Spiritually, saved people will praise God and all spiritual believers in heaven upon ascending into heaven. Saved spirits will not be self-centered. God gave humans, and *possibly* aliens, souls to be spiritual for supporting and praising Him. God has a purpose for Man's and Aliens' spiritual free wills.

In prayer, I often praise God for His mercy, goodness; my body and mind, fusions in the sun, Light, air, space, gravity, and my life. I ask God to bless all of my ancestors and loved ones. I live and pray. May our *spiritual* human descendants continue until the earth and sun no longer support human life, or until God no longer needs human lives. I pray for everyone I have loved or will love and for everyone who loves me or will love me.

PRAISES

Jesus and God thank you for the Lord's Prayer and having interest in human minds, lives, and prayers. Jesus, integrated within God, thank you for loving us sinners. Thank you for the universe and heaven - places for us to live and exist. May all people in the world praise you for their lives and spiritual successes. I praise you for the earth, continents, ocean, water, and life. Thank you for physics, chemistry, biology, and other sciences that make our lives better and easier. Thank you, Jesus, integrated within God's Infinite Spiritual Hologram, for giving me the mission to write this healing and spiritual book for you. I could not write spiritually without your guidance. Thank you for all my direct ancestors, grandparents, and parents for without them I would not exist. Thank you for the structure of heaven that supports your omniscience, omnipresence, and omnipotence.

Thank you Lord and Jesus for being You and saving human lives.

HELP

Lord help humans improve our prayer technology so we can praise and love your more deeply. Help everyone to be pain free, have healthy lives, and achieve spiritual missions. Help us listen for you better and learn from Your love, and praise You more. Help everyone on earth to love one another. We sinners need your help. Teach me to pray as you would have me pray to renew my life. Be with your churches and have them worship you as you would have them worship you. Have all people, and all beings with souls, love and praise you as you need to be praised. Have the earth support human life as long as you need it to. Give everyone spiritual missions to make the world a better place.

Dear God please be with the Ukrainian people who *are* being attacked by Vladimir Putin and his Russian military forces. People have a right to be free and choose their own leaders.

Chapter 44

RELIGION

Religion: the belief in and worship of a spiritual leader, and especially God, or personal gods.

"Children must be taught how to think, not what to think."

Margaret Mead.

"Any religion or philosophy which is not based on a respect for life is not a true religion or philosophy."

Albert Schweitzer

"It is an overwhelming thought to realize that as we degenerate in morality, we increase in force."

Dr. David Jeremiah,
"The Handwriting on the Wall,
Secrets from the Prophecies of DANIEL," 1992

My beliefs are as a Scientist and a Christian. Historically, societies were governed by religious leaders. Scientists were logical and a threat to religious leaders. Science and religion became separated early on. Scientists are only discovering God's work and learning about God. Science and religion should complement one another.

The quote above, by Dr. Jeremiah, reminds me of the fiery sermons my family attended when I was young. These sermons were described as "Hell, Fire, and Brimstone." The more forceful sermons became; the scarier they were to me. Calm, encouraging voices build love, reason and confidence.

Powerful speakers stir up selfish emotions to control listeners. Speakers' ideas and interests become more important than listeners' own ideas and interests.

I continue to be an outsider to science and religious authorities. Science discoveries and everyday interactions can be discussed logically without emotion. Religious leaders often refer to their founders as perfect to influence or brainwash listeners. *Perfect* religions teach emotionally, beyond logic. Emotional religious and political differences are difficult for many to discuss.

Manic-depressives experience emotional highs and lows, and, sometimes, receive spiritual information and purpose. Depressed individuals may be too weak, and manic individuals too excited and disorganized, to consistently communicate spiritually. *Normal* mental energy levels are for performing daily activities and are usually less sensitive to lower energy spiritual communications. However, in an *instant*, a powerful spiritual communication, above normal emotional energy, may be life changing. Practice speaking with calmness and reason before sharing.

Cultures must work together to develop spiritual technology for a spiritual future with opportunities and freedom for all. With communication technology advances throughout the world, spiritual beliefs may become integrated to develop heaven on earth.

Imagine how wonderful the world would be if everyone worked physically and spiritually together for each other's benefit. Everyone would feel spiritually equal to each other. There would be no more preparing for wars, or wars. World social, economic, and spiritual accomplishments would be many times greater. There would be no hunger, and there would be an earthly and spiritual purpose for everyone. With today's communications, we may become united in a smaller world.

Christian services teach about Jesus and God, spiritual interactions, and to be humble before God. We become selfish if we remain to ourselves. Christianity encourages spiritually sharing.

Believers should develop principles from their own experiences and not lose self-identity. Religions should integrate God's truths but retain believers' individualities to nurture spiritual truths, and not brainwash. God made us different.

Emotional reaction to my powerful spiritual waves from God, "Don't leave God out!" was *instant and precise.* My mind and soul immediately understood this astonishing spiritual message *in words.* I have had to work to choose words for less forceful spiritual messages. We must receive and accept that which God gives us. If we learn more about the universe, we may receive more spiritual information from God. God and the universe are intertwined.

Spiritual waves overwhelmed my normal thinking, creating an abrupt spiritual consciousness. His message was as attention getting as hitting my thumb with a hammer. Gentle spiritual messages emerge like diamonds in the rough giving us freedom to mold them into spiritual feelings and words.

God informed me *holistically* in general terms in what to do without giving details. He has given me spiritual seeds to write using my spiritual experiences, creativity, and free will.

As science progresses and increases the understanding of God's universe, religions must accept current science discoveries to be more meaningful. Humans can only build simple models of God and physical reality. Spiritual books are only interpretations of God's perfect spiritual waves, using fragile and often ambiguous human words. Religions only make models of God's reality.

God is aware of the universe and even our prayers. He loves us. Religions should include that humans and God advance over time. God speaks to us today as strongly as in traditional religious times.

God has spoken strongly inspiring spiritual leaders and even sinners like me. God forgives sins.

In emergency health crises, faith is important. With failing health and only confidence in self, critical patients have less chance of survival. With faith in and surrendering to God, patients remain calmer and have greater chances of survival. Calm attitudes and belief in God heal and save lives.

A few years ago, when attending Timberlake United Methodist Church, in the Lynchburg, VA area, I received an amazing *flash* of my *entire* spiritual purpose. I experienced a brief moment of spiritual completion. However, as in dreams, my spiritual message was quickly *lost*. I have recalled little of that spiritual flash. One purpose was to help all children and adults release their trauma effects and recover their spiritual wisdom and communication skills received upon conception. Trauma scars remain repressed until activated by similar energy levels that ingrained them. When *forcefully* released by psychiatric exercises, or a significant emotional event, disruptive trauma energy is purged, and renewed neural networks resynchronize with normal brain functions for the mind to gain spiritual purpose.

Science, Christianity, philosophy, meditation, and spiritual messages received have nurtured my spiritual beliefs and writings. Spiritual feelings are holistic and often difficult to express in words.

Chapter 45

SPIRITUAL MESSAGES

"Spiritual messages *drift* into consciousness at unexpected times and soothe the soul."

H Fulcher

When severely depressed in 1977 for a brief time, I could not think of, or speak, a single word. The energy of my brain and body was so low I became aware of flowing spiritual feelings that seemed more important than words. However, when regaining mental energy, I could only recall having received strong spiritual feelings. This experience was similar to remembering having dreamed but not remembering the dream.

During high-energy manic episodes, spiritual messages became so strong and overrode my normal awareness and thinking. I appeared as if losing worldly sanity. My thinking varied wildly in reacting to spiritual messages. If receiving messages from God, we must have patience, humility, and pray for guidance in organizing our gifts before presenting them to others. One becomes highly emotional and feels empowered, without knowing what to do.

Some spiritual feelings become conscious with refined low energy. Feelings are like that of a pleasant dream. Without writing them down they vanish as if blown from the mind with a gentle breeze. I have lost so many spiritual ideas without writing them down quickly enough. However, during *expected* imminent death, spiritual ideas strike like lightening.

We should refine spiritual thoughts before discussing spiritual messages with a minister or psychiatrist as they will be skeptical. We are in awe when receiving spiritual messages. If God asks us to do something for Him, we must commit to His request. One brief message from God may inspire a lifetime of dedication. Ministers receive callings.

In October 1993 during my last manic episode, I saw a silver lining in the clouds one day and began believing I could reason through anything. Dreaming while awake, I joyfully ran through my beautiful field receiving *words* from God. We became *buddies* that day during my *worldly* insanities. I would romp in the tall grass and think of something to say and clear my mind of all thoughts.

I would wait, and God's words would emerge as either with comforting feelings or as a boom in the distant thunder. I was elated when God responded. His responses were deep and sometimes funnier than my questions. Surrendering worldly cares opened my mind and soul to God's communications.

Manic, spiritual words were similar to dreams and difficult to recall. Here are a few interactions recalled from that beautiful sunny day, with clouds in the distance:

H. "Why is the sky blue?" G. "Physics."

H. "Why can't I see you?" G. "I am the Light that you see with."

H. "Who are you?" G. "I am the *Light* through which all things are seen and done."

H. "You neglect me." G. "Who are you?"

H. "You make me laugh." [The earth shook as God laughed. I fell in the tall grass laughing.]

H. "Do you like my writing?" G. "About what?"

H. "Not making earthly sense." G. "Makes sense."

H. "Who created me.?" G. "Me."

H. "Do you love me? G. "Yes."

H. "Why?" G. "You are me."

Spiritual communications continued on and on. I was a two-year old spending time with and enjoying a childish game with my Father. There was more reflection than response. We reflected feelings and words back and forth. Often, the simplest times are the most meaningful. I had never felt more spiritual and joyful. Observers would have thought I had lost my mind. I was communicating, learning, and having fun with God.

One spiritual message may benefit an individual, one religion, or all of humanity. It is our responsibility to promote God's messages to benefit others. I wish everyone could be as happy as I was on that special spiritual day. Traditional spiritual leaders may not believe strong spiritual messages can be received by those who are not religious scholars. They may have interpreted messages differently or have an issue in not listening to an *average* person's spiritual messages.

Not responding to God's messages limits us and those who would listen to us. We must be servants before we can lead. Jesus remained a servant, and a leader.

Language and communication skills are specialized for science, medicine, spiritual, and other disciplines. Will scientists, medical professionals, and spiritual leaders improve spiritual communication skills? Memorized spiritual dogma increases importance when repeated. Spiritual leaders must communicate God's truths.

In 1995, I was attempting to hurriedly finish my first healing book and received an astounding spiritual message, "Don't leave God out!" from all *inner* directions. At that time, my healing book became spiritual. Other spiritual messages received have been with low calm or high manic energy. I will be thinking of everyday thoughts and a gentle *harmonic* of my astounding spiritual message, evolves into my reality.

Receiving spiritual messages can be life changing. We have been chosen as servants of God. It is an honor to be selected for a mission as a servant and writer for God. Writing spiritual messages down and obeying them can be demanding. Receiving and obeying spiritual Truths give spiritual rewards. Ideas given here were inspired by God. However, I make mistakes.

God spoke to traditional spiritual leaders as He speaks to us today. We must be prepared to *listen*. Jesus had *perfect* spiritual communication with God.

God answers prayers and gives blessings of responsibility. Man's greatest honor is serving God and those in need. However, we must keep in touch with physical *realities*. There are challenges and rewards in a new focus and direction.

I have had difficulties distinguishing if my spiritual messages come from Jesus or directly from God. Traditional Christian writers did not understand integration but believed that Jesus became one within God and the Holy Spirit. This is integration. My feeling is that Jesus' Perfect Spiritual Hologram became integrated within God's Infinite Spiritual Hologram.

The earth is not the center of the universe. Spiritual humans have some very, very small ability to influence God's Perfect Infinite Hologram. Humans are born with spiritual purpose but must work to recall and serve. We must meditate and lower the energy of our brains and minds to accept God's wisdom with humility.

Chapter 46

SOUL

"Music in the soul can be heard by the universe."
"To the mind that is still, the whole universe surrenders."

Lao Tzu

"I simply believe that some part of the human Self or Soul is not subject to the laws of space and time."

Carl Jung

"The body and mind are temporary. Souls *are meant to be* immortal. An evil mind buries its soul in the grave."

H Fulcher

Soul: the spiritual or immaterial part of a human being, regarded as immortal and consisting of all integrated emotional, spiritual, and limiting thoughts, decisions, and actions with the belief they transcend into a heavenly spirit. (Our souls may include integrated *souls* of direct ancestors through genetics.)

God gives us genetic, or handed down, souls from our direct ancestors, with perfect spiritual potentials in spiritual dimensions, at the moment of conception. We must build spiritual love and truth within our souls to gain influence for Eternity. Christians pray that at the time of our deaths Jesus will receive and prepare our souls for acceptance by God's Grace. Our souls exist in spiritual space and time dimensions, have perfect communication with God, and are independent of physical space and time.

Our souls are focused on and record spiritual thoughts and actions with synchronized mental and spiritual resonances. Upon death, souls lose connections with dying minds to become free spirits with spiritual freedoms in heaven.

Trauma and emotional scars within our brains eclipse our minds' communications with our own souls. Truthful minds are intertwined with their souls through synchronized mental and spiritual resonances.

Millions of synchronized neuron Light resonances integrate to construct our consciousness. The soul compares our mental resonances to God's Truths and *His Eternal Infinite Spiritual Hologram Resonances.*

Our souls record and integrate our spiritual thoughts and actions over lifetimes including God's reflections of our thoughts and prayers. Good works and God's reactions and blessings build our souls within spiritual dimensions. God continually receives spiritual communications of our lives through our souls. He judges our life's completeness and truth.

Upon death, accepted spiritual memory resonances are activated within our souls and integrate to form *everlasting heavenly resonances.* Spiritual time and space are very different from earthly time and space. Souls from elderly human deaths will gain strength and youth in spiritual time. Souls will become more integrated and organized in heaven. Thoughts of good worldly activities will become spiritually integrated.

Depending upon attitudes and morals, the soul contains, or is void of, spiritual wisdom. In my model, spiritual worth is multiplicative.

One evil thought or activity may negate many spiritual thoughts or activities. For example, the worst evil activity may have a spiritual value factor of: 1/1,000,000. The best spiritual accomplishment may have a value of 1000. In this simple model, it would take one thousand spiritual thoughts and activities to overcome one horrible evil transgression. In this spiritual model, spiritual ratings must be one or above for souls to be accepted into heaven at the moment of death with God's Grace. Sincerely expressing remorse and asking God for forgiveness may improve spiritual ratings. Transitioning from life on earth to freed souls and spiritual life is a very different concept for God than for Man. Life and life after death are God's miracles. God is aware of a smooth transition.

We have a guiding light to live by. Spiritual wisdom is constantly reflected between God and our souls. High energy trauma effects within the brain eclipse spiritual communications, possibly, for life unless humans remain spiritually humble. We must reconstruct our minds to be reborn for communicating with our souls. Newborn babies have pure communications with their souls and God.

The soul absorbs wisdom from God's resonances in spiritual dimensions, which are independent of physical space and time. Integrated spiritual wisdom consists of truthful relationships between minds, souls, and God. In severe trauma, we may surrender our free wills to God as babies and young children surrender to parents in times of need. The *Flash* was my intense emotional spiritual surrender of my life to God.

With humbleness and low mental energy, our long-range right-brains may become synchronized with our souls. At the end of our lives, we must accept God for Him to accept us. We get to heaven only by God's grace.

We can only translate God's perfect spiritual resonances and feelings with fragile words and language. God's perfect spiritual wave language can be truthfully translated in different languages if translators remain *calm, honest and unbiased*. Minds and words are never sufficient to perfectly interpret God's perfect wisdom.

For God to be everywhere and *instantly* know everything about the universe, higher integration dimensions exist beyond Man's understanding of Light, space, and time. Science and relativity may assist spiritual understanding. God may be aware of every atom in the universe. His spiritual waves transmit their status, location, and connections *instantly* throughout the universe and heaven. God knows each hair on our heads and each atom of our faces. God may be aware of atoms of living things more than those of inanimate things. The brain creates its own Light, has awareness, and is alive. The sun and stars create their own Light, may have awareness, and be alive.

Our souls include our entire life's history including spiritual feedback from God. Upon physical death, if accepted, our soul's wisdom is absorbed by God's Higher Dimensional Infinite Spiritual Hologram, for Him to become slightly more complete. Spiritual Holograms are always complete but become brighter with new and greater spiritual wisdom

We are not aware of God and His higher dimensions with our senses or devices but through our souls. We sometimes hear that someone is *soul searching* while making tough decisions. We must relax and get our conscious minds out of the way. During spiritual openness, God and our souls reflect confident ideas to us that are better than we thought we could have had on our own.

Upon death, souls escape bodies and minds to become integrated within God's Infinite Spiritual Hologram Dimensions. With freedom from our bodies, our souls transcend to become heavenly spirits throughout heaven's existence independent of physical space. Our heavenly spirits sometimes reflect their images to loved ones on earth for saving them in time of great need.

At times, our souls receive God's resonances and guidance that briefly eclipse our free wills. The purpose of life and free will is to grow physically and spiritually for giving God something to look forward to and nurture that He does not need to directly control. This is similar to parents raising children.

Upon death, our spiritual resonances and souls in heaven will be more real than our brief minds and bodies on earth. We have a purpose on earth and in heaven.

God indwells within our souls at the moment of conception. We borrow our souls for recording our spiritual thoughts and works.

There is no beginning or ending to our spiritual souls. They have access to God's spiritual wisdom. We are entrusted to add our brief spiritual histories to our souls as our direct ancestors have done. Our genes are powerful and include wisdom of our ancestors.

If we lose our souls, our histories and ability to communicate with God are lost. We no longer receive spiritual guidance. If we are spiritual and our souls accepted, we will experience joy in all things we do, and in good things others do for us. Sincerely expressing remorse for our sins may lift burdens from our souls.

Upon death, our heavenly spirits relate to Jesus, God, and heavenly spirits with similar DNA. They support God with their spiritual histories developed while living on earth. Everything is related in heaven. All spiritual waves and wisdom are integrated in heaven independent of space and physical time. God and His wisdom are integrated in heaven independent of physical space and time.

Chapter 47

SPIRITUAL MODELS

"The miracles on earth are the laws of heaven."

Jean Paul

"Heaven means to be one with God."

Confucius

"You have to grow from the inside out. None can teach you; none can make you spiritual. There is no other teacher but your own soul."

Swami Vivekananda

"True prayer is neither a mere mental exercise nor a vocal performance. It is far deeper than that - it is a spiritual transaction with the Creator of Heaven and Earth."

Charles Spurgeon

"The structures of Heaven and the vacuum of space are one and the same."

H. Fulcher

My spiritual models integrate science, Christianity, and my spiritual experiences. Christianity, physics, bipolar disorder, expected imminent death, and spiritual messages received have given spiritual feelings with a vague insight into spiritual dimensions.

Without certainties and uncertainties, human life could not exist. Without uncertainties God and humans could not make decisions. Genetics brings a level of organization and certainty to human life. We are never absolutely certain what our next thought or action might be. God created all beings with souls to help build spiritual certainty.

Reasoning through and integrating lifetime uncertainties builds spiritual certainty. Discovering a physics law is both physical and spiritual in recognizing God's perfect work. We study physics and other sciences to discover God's reasoning in designing, engineering, and constructing the universe.

Scientists have calculated the shortest physical time as around 10^{-43} seconds for light to travel the shortest length, 10^{-35} meters. These values were calculated by scientists using God's fundamental physics constants and laws. God integrates physical time for creating spiritual time and His Completeness. I do not believe God's spiritual time is anything like physical time.

Caring for and worshiping God varies by individuals, but integrated caring for God throughout the world gives greater blessings and reflections to God. He needs human worship and praises to continually refine His spiritual perfection. God is perfect and becomes more perfect in spiritual dimensions over spiritual time.

Through God, in spiritual dimensions, our lives affect the entire universe and heaven to some very, very small extent. We have free will to have or not have a relationship with God. Some sense God strongly and some ignore Him.

All spiritual thoughts are saved within our souls, which interface with spiritual dimensions that integrate our spiritual thoughts evenly throughout the universe and heaven. Unlike memories, our souls' wisdom does not degrade with time.

Scientists have proven that laws governing overall galaxy behaviors have an amazing consistency. With very, very large distances between galaxies, there are consistencies in physical, probability, and spiritual laws, God controls a very big expanding universe with His physical, probably, and spiritual laws.

Scientists have developed strict criteria for discovering and proving physical facts or laws. An explosion of useful machines and technical devices enhances human lives. No recent religious awakening or discoveries have radically advanced overall spiritual communication skills and lives. However, some individuals experience lifesaving miracles. Believers are taught their religion is *perfect* for all times. Some religions believe God cannot improve over time.

Religions that promote peace for, and love of, all humans do a spiritual service for God. Religions that divide people have little spiritual value.

To integrate science with religion, we must distinguish between belief and fact:

Fact - something that exists, interacts, or happens and has objective reality as understood by a perceptive, reasoning mind, or as *repetitively* and consistently proven through scientific tests. Three facts are:

- Humans have limited understanding of reality.
- Humans can understand some physical properties and predict events.
- Physics and other science laws control the universe.

Belief - a mental acceptance of something as real or true. Beliefs may or may not imply certitude in the believer. Faith implies trust and confidence even when there is no evidence or proof. Beliefs imply intellectual acceptance without proof.

Two spiritual beliefs are:

- God *receives* spiritual information from prayers and transmits all spiritual wisdom equally throughout the universe and heaven. God is omnipresent.
- After death, spiritual histories in souls from human thought and activity on earth become independent of physical time and space, to have constant spiritual structure throughout heaven for Eternity.

Humans must obey God's physical laws but have free will to obey or disobey His spiritual laws and will. Overcoming suffering tends to make humans more spiritual.

Traditional religions look mostly to the past and often restrict future thinking and actions. Churches give spiritual guidance. We must remember the past to make reasonable decisions for the future.

Should we worship the same as our ancestors worshiped two and six thousand years ago? Christians believe we are most spiritual when following and praising Jesus and His teachings. Can we improve our spiritual lives using today's communication technologies?

God and heaven become more organized over time by recording activities of an increasingly disorganizing and complex universe. Cosmologists may discover related physical and spiritual properties for Man's benefit.

Christians believe God is omnipresent and omniscient. We can pray anywhere and anytime and God is there to listen to our prayers and pleas. Otherwise, we would be wasting our time praying. "I can't pray today because God is on the other side of the universe." Christians do not believe this. There *must be* very fast *spiritual waves* for God to be omnipresent and omniscient throughout a very big universe and an infinite heaven.

Light does not lose energy when traveling through the vacuum of outer space, but is not independent of gravity. Spiritual wave energy and information are exchanged with Light throughout the universe.

Light and Virgin Light appear nearly stationary relative to very fast spiritual waves from the Big Bang Explosion needed to explain God's omnipresence and omniscience. The speed of spiritual waves is nearly infinite, or spiritually fast, for God to have updated information *instantly* from the entire universe and heaven. The speed of spiritual waves traveling from the center to the expanding edges of the universe and back may correspond to the speed for light traveling one quantum of space.

Here is my omniscient and omnipresence model:

> **Spiritual waves are reflected at the expanding boundaries of the universe by the back side of much slower expanding Virgin Light (at light speed). Spiritual waves capture information from all Light in the universe as they travel back toward the origin of the universe. All incoming spiritual wave information is Integrated within the Spiritual Point of the Big Bang origin or center of the universe. All integrated, updated spiritual waves are reflected outward to share their complete,** integrated **spiritual information with each point of the universe and within dimensions of heaven. Spiritual resonances vibrate from the center to the expanding boundaries of the universe every 10^{-106} seconds. God's information is updated instantly from a human viewpoint for creating His omniscient and omnipresent properties. From a biblical viewpoint, spiritual waves are the Holy Spirit.**

We have constructed a quasi-science omnipresent and omniscient model. This model makes me feel as if I have some spiritual understanding. Something very unusual and powerful had to occur to create the Big Bang Creation of the universe.

Beyond the expanding borders of the universe are ruminants of *Nothing before Time* without space and time. There is no difference between an inch and a billion miles in Nothing beyond the universe. One would not know if he was being still or flying at the speed of light. Virgin Light interacts with the *Boundaries of Nothing* to create quanta of space and time as it expands the universe.

Scientists will never be able to detect and measure fundamental spiritual waves. Speed of spiritual waves is only a rough estimate. I have made only a beginning. Spiritual information must travel very, very fast for God to be omnipresent and omniscient over a big universe. Spiritual wave resonances must last long enough in the brain for our minds to receive God's wisdom.

If God is omniscient, does He know everything that will occur in the universe's and heaven's futures? In that case, we would not need to pray because God already knows our needs and praises. God and humans would have no future to look forward to. God and we would be predestined. God and humans would not be making real decisions.

I do not think this is the case. God is perfectly aware of the complete integrated history of heaven and the universe in spiritual time. He may or may not need to know the activity of each atom.

Having historical knowledge of all activities in the universe, God may predict far into the future, but gives humans free will to think about and do creative things. We know so little about spiritual activities in God's time frame.

Prayer is the medium between spiritual and mental realities. We sometimes sense, and *hear from,* God when our minds and souls are calm, clear and surrendering. Manic minds in crises become sensitive to God's spiritual information at times. Spiritual time may go slow or very fast.

Spiritual waves are very fast shock waves from the Big Bang Creation. Spiritual waves are super-relativistic to Light. They share spiritual energy and information with *Light* throughout the universe and a holistic heaven in a very different spiritual space and time. Spiritual waves, the Holy Spirit, is God's medium for transmitting, reflecting, absorbing, and controlling perfect spiritual wisdom throughout heaven and the universe. The Holy Spirit is the communication medium between God, heaven, and the universe.

God created the universe and is more real than the universe. The universe is His mirror and reflection. In error when reasoning within the universe, humans believe God is the mirror and the physical universe is reality. Inside a relativistic recursive relationship, it is difficult to determine between reality and reflections of reality. The universe and human minds respond to God.

Without uncertainties, God could not make judgments. Overcoming our greatest uncertainties create our greatest successes and certainties.

Heaven is the higher dimensional spiritual structure supporting God, His angels, and saved souls. Heaven's resonating structures integrate information from very fast spiritual wave and *Light* resonances for sharing spiritual information between God, spirits in heaven and, to some extent, spiritual beings with souls in the universe.

From the Bible, heaven has many *rooms* for human souls. My belief is that infinite spiritual resonances will be homes for human souls that transform into everlasting spirits in heaven. Our spirits will have perfect everlasting spiritual activities and responsibilities in heaven. There is no resistance to spiritual activities in heaven. This is similar to perfect guitar strings resonating in vacuum for an infinite time.

Integrated spiritual wisdom and *Light* information create God and to some small extent the subconscious mind. All spiritual information in heaven is integrated within the completeness of God's Infinite Hologram. God has infinite action potentials to control heaven and the universe. Human minds have potentials for thoughts, beliefs, emotions, actions, and spiritual communications.

My model is that heaven resides either within the vacuum of space, the vacuum of space resides within heaven, or they coexist as being intertwined. God, heaven, and the vacuum of space are everywhere the same, omnipresent, and *infinite*. God is separate from mass but is influenced by gravity and Light from atoms.

We do not know all of space's and God's characteristics. We live within space. Heaven and God are within us. God's potentials move mountains and create galaxies. God is aware of all physical and spiritual activities down to some small degree.

With limited abilities, human minds can only relate spiritual activities and dimensions to physical activities and dimensions. Heaven includes higher spiritual relativity and integration dimensions. At spiritual times on earth, human free wills become spiritually integrated within God's Will. God cultivates human minds in prayer at times.

God hears and strengthens our prayers and reflects them back to us. We get to know our true selves from God's reflections.

Remembered mental images are not as precise as mirror reflections. However, responses include deeper spiritual meaning within self. Humans can be initiators and responders. God is a perfect initiator, reflector, and responder in spiritual dimensions and time. He interacts with human minds in physical and spiritual time through our souls.

Everything in heaven is relative to everything else in heaven and is reflected throughout the universe. God, heaven, and the vacuum of space are perfect. Humble minds are attracted to God.

Human thinking has three phases:

1. Concentration is on, use or avoidance of, material things encountered and on every-day and future security, survival, and material advancement for the benefit of self.

2. Doing things for others and God expecting no personal benefit is spiritual. Light within the brain creating the mind can be spiritual. The spiritual and physical can communicate. Spiritual is devoted to kindness, love, and building confidence within others. God's *Light Waves* resonate and synchronize with, and influence, human brain waves. Truthful prayers interact with and influence God. Humans have ability to think and communicate spiritually.

3. Continued concentration on, preparing for, and permeating evil for material or psychological gain forfeits Eternal Life. A lost soul stays connected to the physical brain and is buried with the dead body.

Upon physical death, our spiritual holograms resonate within our souls to become integrated and complete in everlasting spiritual dimensions as a very, very small part of God. When severely ill and near death, we may *sense or see* our beloved spirits in heaven, especially those having a *need* to save our lives. Heaven is just *next door.*

Our beloved heavenly spirits strengthen our souls for them to return to our fragile bodies when expecting death at times. Heavenly spirit resonances last long enough to synchronize and integrate with our mental resonances and our souls to save our lives when expecting death at times. We hope to meet our deceased loved ones in heaven when it is our time of *Glory.* Heaven is about relativistic and spiritual relationships. Light and spiritual waves are relativistic to physical things.

My models of heaven began during expected, imminent death. When alone and expecting death, only God matters. We grasp for His attention, understanding, and forgiveness.

Normally souls escape minds, brains, and physical bodies into spiritual space and time quickly after physical death. Spiritually deceased souls become integrated within God's Infinite Spiritual Hologram. Death frees our souls from earthly bodies and responsibilities. Our souls respond to all accepted spirits in heaven and sometimes to minds and souls on earth.

I do not believe God would create a universe He could not be aware of and not control. His control of the universe and heaven are very different from human control of minds and environments. God organizes and manages activities between heaven and earth.

We must do our part on earth to be accepted by God's grace. Humans and God love organization and completions. Spiritual people assist God by sharing spiritual activities on earth. Human souls and minds grow when receiving and sharing God's Blessings. As we grow spiritually, we learn more of God's Wisdom and receive greater spiritual responsibility. Our purpose is to serve God in His chosen and integrated way.

I pray nightly for my beloved spirits in heaven to have wonderful activities, responsibilities, and purpose. Our beloved spirits in heaven influence our lives in times of great need. I and others have sensed beloved spirits in heaven when *expecting* death. We need to get the conscious mind out of the way at times to give our subconscious processes spiritual freedom to heal and strengthen with God's help.

Reflections from our spiritual holograms in our souls make God's Infinite Spiritual Hologram a little bit brighter. We have a purpose. God becomes more complete and more infinite every day. We know little about what infinite means.

The spiritually humble on earth will have spiritual power in heaven. The arrogant deceased were not seen in my *expected death visions.*

God judges us strongly by those we have treated the worst. If a husband is cruel to his wife but treats everyone else well, he is judged mostly by his treatment of his wife.

I pray for forgiveness for being insensitive to others. If remorseful and asking for forgiveness, God may adjust spiritual values. Christians believe Jesus had and has perfect spiritual values.

There are many everlasting spiritual resonances in heaven for our soul's holograms to *resonate* within spiritual *space* forever and ever. God prepares a place for our souls' resonances within His Infinite Hologram Resonances and Harmonics. Spiritual holograms are higher dimensions of spiritual reality.

Upon death, our integrated life memories and souls become spiritual holograms independent of physical space and time. Spiritual holograms become more real and lasting than the physical brains and spiritual minds from which they were constructed. A great picture is greater than all it parts. Our spiritual existence is freed of physical responsibilities to become integrated within God's spiritual dimensions for accepting spiritual responsibilities.

For some, special places on earth enhance spiritual communication, make believers feel spiritually whole and in *awe* of Jesus and God. Jesus and God *cuddle* us in our special spiritual places. In these places, spiritual feelings and thoughts strengthen minds and souls.

A perfect love makes us feel complete mentally and spiritually. God does not separate our souls in heaven from our lives on earth. Otherwise, our work on earth would have been meaningless.

Our souls' resonances are independent of physical space. Our spiritual thoughts and souls are the same next to us and on the other side of the universe through God's Infinite Spiritual Hologram communications. In heaven as spirits, we will always have time to do everything in spiritual time God asks us to do, and all spiritual things we wish to do. Very fast spiritual resonances can integrate and resonate long enough to communicate with relatively slow Light resonances in human minds.

Spirits in heaven will have access to all spiritual wisdom and will perfectly communicate with, understand, and love one another. There is harmony in heaven. Memories of human spiritual thoughts and activities become integrated within God's completeness. Only souls prepared to love *all spirits* in heaven will be accepted. It may not be so easy to attain heaven. Praying for God's forgiveness and grace helps. All heavenly spirits will have separate identities but exist in harmony with all others.

Most of us have a sense of how intricate and detailed electricity can be as the working medium within computers and the internet. Spiritual communications and activities are trillion times trillions of times more intricate and faster than electricity within the internet.

God's Heavenly Spiritual Hologram structure is much, much more intricate than structures within human brains. God's Hologram fabric and spiritual waves become more detailed by His continued learning in spiritual time. God has spiritual wisdom of all human souls.

God has an unbelievable, *or infinite*, number of abilities to monitor and control the universe and heaven. God is the universe's and heaven's perfect, *totally conscious, mind.*

Each minute' EMR change within the brain affects the mind. Low-energy, refined EMR changes within the brain has more spiritual importance than a lightning bolt.

Fixed written words have some similarity to God's unchanging spiritual waves and physical laws. However, words have different meaning to different people. God's perfect spiritual wave language is constant throughout the universe but may be interpreted differently with imprecise human words.

If religions truthfully interpret, accept, and communicate God's spiritual truths, believers would strive for peace and love throughout the world. God gave us free will and made each of us different for Him to learn from and love.

If we have lived spiritual lives, cared as much for others as ourselves, and crossed that spiritual Bar, each moment of spiritual time will be more exciting and rewarding than our best times on earth. Heavenly *lives and activities* will relate to earthly spiritual activities and accomplishments.

God is aware of, and loves all who love, or will love, Him. Accepted souls in heaven are aware of and love those on earth who have loved them.

True religions preach God's love and His desire for all people to love Him and to love all peoples on earth. At times, I pray for all people, including *everyone* from *all* religions, who wish to love, care, and nurture all peoples on earth. We do not need to love and support those who continually abuse us or cause others to abuse us. If we do, we will lose our health.

I continued to be good to and supported my former wife who abused me for years. Her continued degrading behaviors made no sense and stressed me beyond ability to cope. I became bipolar. Her abuse caused me loss of health and almost caused my death when severely depressed. The Living God, my loving parents, loving and deceased aunts and uncles saved my life. If someone begins to abuse us, we should work for some time to interact with abusers to change abuse into support and love. However, some relationships are impossible for us to change. We may need to distance ourselves from evil people. Love everyone you can.

Chapter 48

PROOF OF GOD'S EXISTENCE

Existence: the fact or state of living or having objective reality

Proof: evidence or argument establishing or helping to establish a fact or truth of a statement or activity

Proving God exists or even that our minds exist is a difficult task. Humans can only make models of physical and spiritual realities. Our eyes are only sensitive to light and not the entire electromagnetic spectrum. Humans are limited. Only God knows reality and is sensitive to and learns all information within all electromagnetic radiation and spiritual waves in the universe and heaven.

In my first severe depression, I had strong feeling of imminent death and had lost all hope of life. Unexpectedly, I felt an inner strength beyond my physical and mental abilities that saved my life.

German philosopher Immanuel Kant attempted to prove the existence of God. He *proved* reality is beyond human experience. He concluded if God exists, humans cannot know Him as he really is.

Proving God and heaven exists, with God having great wisdom of, and power over, a great big universe is difficult but may be accomplished at some point by believers. I believe God needs reflections from imperfect *spiritual* lives to make Him more perfect and complete. God is continually the definition of perfection and the *Infinite*. God's Infinite Spiritual Hologram is always complete, and continually more complete with greater detail in physical and spiritual time.

The universe was perfectly designed with certainties, uncertainties, and probability for an evolving future. God gave the universe potentials to organize and disorganize.

We cannot directly prove that minds exist. We can only infer something is controlling and organizing our thoughts, bodies, and speech. We must also infer something is controlling and organizing the universe. The mind is spiritual beyond the neuron Light and the chemical and physical processes that created it. Integration of Light in the brain creates the mind.

God and the universe exist in a recursive relationship. He created the universe and it supports His existence and power. He controls spiritual and physical time, and minds when *spiritually needed*. Normally, He honors human's free wills.

We should not limit God to human sensed and understood dimensions. Scientists are just beginning to understand the universe - God's physical reality. Scientists' understanding relates to a few pieces of sand. God relates to and controls the entire universe.

The Second Law of Thermodynamics states that physical systems become more random and disorganized over time. Crystals and living things seem to violate this law. However, it takes energy to organize. Our minds become more organized with memories as we experience life. The body, brain, and mind need outside energy to organize and control their activities. We eat.

God designed prefect probability laws for atoms to give the universe uncertainties for a future to look forward to. God and Man have *organization* abilities beyond that of a disorganizing physical universe. Without probabilities, *future* of the universe would be certain and predictable. There would be nothing to look forward to.

With uncertainties in the universe, God and humans continue to have challenges to learn about and make decisions on.

God is relativistic to humans through Light. Science and general relativity prove the universe does not adhere to everyday human reason.

Aspiring to be perfect accelerates good and bad behaviors. Thinking, of oneself as spiritually superior, twists minds toward selfish thoughts and behaviors. Anyone believing he is spiritually perfect is spiritually inferior.

In any argument for or against the existence of God, we must make and understand our assumptions. Without assumptions, we must model the entire universe and God. Many scientists and philosophers are unaware of, do not know, and do not define their assumptions in their physical and spiritual models of reality.

The past cannot be *truthfully* changed. We live in a certain and an uncertain present. The future is influenced by the past but is never entirely predictable. Time changes all things physical. Thinking about the past and predicting the future is a current activity. The better our predictions the more control we may have over our lives.

God predicts the future of the universe to a much greater extent than humans can. God limits His ability to predict the future to allow a future for heaven, the universe, and Man. They are spiritually intertwined. Without probability laws God would know the entire future. Mankind and their prayers would not be needed. God would not really judge humans and other living things. Existence would be predefined. God has a continuous infinite purpose. Humans have short- and long-range purposes for supporting God in prayer. Humans are born, live, and die.

God is the Truth and nurtures the Truth throughout the universe and heaven. Probability is a part of God's Truth and Existence. Humans make models of reality and truth for their earthly and spiritual purposes.

Human spiritual thoughts and achievements influence God's decisions to some very small extent. He *listens* to our prayers. He has a purpose for us humans.

Observers traveling toward a light source at very different speeds observe light as having the same speed. Relativity has proven that light has this unusual property. Light properties seem unreasonable without understanding relativity. Light speed and God are consistent to each of us no matter our speed in the universe. The earth travels at great speeds in the universe. God's awareness of physical activities is very different than human awareness of those activities. Our understanding of God must include understanding Light, integration, and relativity.

Scientists cannot detect spiritual waves because their frequencies are too fast, their wavelengths are too short, and their information is too detailed and refined. Spiritual waves resonate perfectly between the Big Bang origin and the expanding boundaries of the universe, without losing spiritual energy and knowledge.

Spiritual energy is independent of space, is never lost, and lasts forever. Virgin Light absorbed by *Nothing beyond the Universe* continually transforms it into space and the expanding universe. Virgin Light is directly from the Big Bang explosion and travels at the speed of light.

General relativity is difficult for most of us to understand but may be a step toward understanding God. Our souls have access to God's complete spiritual wisdom wherever we happen to be. Our mental trauma scars prevent us from accessing God's infinite wisdom. Our mental resonances are sensitive to God's infinite spiritual resonances in times of great need. Clear minds, free of trauma scar restrictions, may receive greater spiritual wisdom. Jesus' mind was free of trauma scars.

There is no physical or spiritual reality without God's awareness. Here are my models toward proofing God exists:

1. I received an astounding spiritual message from God: "Don't Leave God Out." This message was so alarming and powerful that I immediately knew it was from God. This message proved God existed to me.

2. Jesus performed miracles and healed the sick and lame. He was seen by many people after He arose from the dead. This proves God's existence for Christians and me. Jesus and the Bible are Christians most important proof of God's existence.

3. From several miles away, I received a highly emotional inner message from my son, as he experienced a traumatic car accident. *"Light,* God" transmitted an unexpected, highly emotional message of love directly from my beloved son's mind to my mind. I immediately knew he was in trouble. I do not believe brain EMR waves were strong enough to send this urgent message over this distance. This unusual awareness transmission proves God and spiritual waves transmit emotional information spiritually at near instant, spiritual speeds throughout the universe.

   Emotional mental energy above normal everyday mental energy/emotional limits are amplified by spiritual waves. My most rewarding prayers have been when experiencing very high emotional mental and spiritual energy. God exists.

4. Experiencing the feel and smell of death and not being able to recall, or think in, words, I had lost all hope of life continuing. I could not have recovered without God's assistance. To my satisfaction, I have personally proven God exists. I live.

5. I awoke in the middle of the night with the shocking awareness of a friend dying several miles away. Emotional spiritual messages were transmitted by God and His spiritual waves. Being beyond emotional limits at times has given me unusual awareness.

6. I have a strong feeling that God hears and reacts to my prayers.

My efforts proving God exists is compelling for me. Christians believe God exists and the Father, Son, and Holy Spirit exist. It may be difficult for some to know God and prove He exists. I yearn to receive more wisdom from God.

Chapter 49

MODEL OF THE LIVING GOD

"The whole problem with the world is that fools and fanatics are always so certain of themselves and wiser people so full of doubts."

Bertrand Russell, Philosopher

"God is *Light*; in Him there is no darkness at all."

1 John, 1:5

"Do you not know that you are a temple of God and that the Spirit of God dwells in you?"

1 Corinthians 3:16

Spiritually, we are our minds. God made Man's mind in His image.

H Fulcher

The universe is within God. *Infinite* is beyond human understanding."

H Fulcher

1. **God:** (in Christianity and other monotheistic religions) the creator and ruler of the universe and source of all moral authority; the supreme being.

2. **God:** (in certain other religions) a superhuman being or spirit worshiped as having power over nature or human fortunes; a deity.

Spiritual Waves: A model to support God's omniscience and omnipresence. Derived from the inverse Heisenberg Uncertainty Principle. Spiritual waves travel across the universe and back every 10^{-106} seconds or possibly the time for light to travel one quantum of space. Known as the Holy Spirit in the Bible.

Spiritual waves reflecting from the edges of the universe read all Light information in the universe. All Light information is integrated at the spiritual point of the Big Bang. All updated integrated spiritual wave information in the universe is again reflected back to all Light at each point in the universe. God is omnipresent and omniscient at every point in the universe.

God is an Infinitely Dimensioned Spiritual Hologram. Humans dream and our subconscious minds develop multi-dimensional mental holograms. In the Flash, I experienced very fast scenarios of three-dimensional emotional images that moved relative to backgrounds.

There are additional dimensions we do not visualize in dreams. Two of these dimensions are the rate of change of images and the emotions felt in dreams. The speeds of Light and spiritual waves allowed my mind to think very fast in the *Flash* and leads me to construct my model of God as an Infinite Higher Dimensional Spiritual Hologram.

Before creation of the universe, God was *infinite spiritual waves*. He had a purpose for creating atoms and the universe to store His energy and give Him something to think about, control, and love. After God created the universe, *Light* activities of the universe and spiritual waves maintain God, and He controls the universe with His physical and probability laws and infinite spiritual power and wisdom. This is similar to activities of the brain creating the mind and the mind controlling the brain and body.

God is the same in each quantum of spiritual space with infinite spiritual resonances and infinite spiritual dimensions and perspectives. His spiritual resonances and wisdom are updated every 10^{-106} seconds. Spiritual space and time are very different from physical space and time.

Humans might be thought of as God's pets. God influences us but gives us free will most of the time. At times God gives us spiritual and physical purpose. This model of God gives me comfort, and makes me feel spiritual. I feel I am doing something for God in describing Him for others.

Is it not amazing that coordination of billions of firing neurons in the brain, the filtering of Light through neuron membranes, and the integration of Light construct integrated light images we see in dreams? Humans think by the brain and mind controlling changing mental images, scenarios, and words. Conscious thinking begins as subconscious visualization. I can close my eyes and *visualize* an image of my parents' house I lived in long ago. We have mental hologram images in memory.

Activities in the brain create the mind. All EMR activities in the universe and spiritual waves create and maintain God in heaven. God is aware of the entire universe and heaven. My models are certainly not perfect but hopefully good enough to help readers think and possibly inspire some to make more detailed models.

We may think of certainties and uncertainties of the past and cope with the uncertainties of the present and future. Scientists cannot determine when an individual uranium atom will decay but can predict the overall decay rate. This *leads* me to believe uranium-235 atoms have *communications* with other uranium-235 atoms for such a constant decay rate.

Similarly, we do not know which neurons in our brains will fire when but know that the integrated effect of all activating neurons will develop conscious thoughts that we can control at times. God may not be aware of all future individual atom activities but *is aware* of the overall future of the universe and heaven. God allows uncertainties throughout the universe but knows the integrated purpose of the universe.

I believe in Jesus and God and accept those who don't. We are free to nurture our beliefs with our free wills. In traditional religious times, spiritual leaders mostly received information they could understand. Today, science explains diverse relationships in nature. God may give us more science related spiritual wisdom today that we can now understand. It makes little sense for God to give us information we cannot understand.

God must have had a need and reason for creating the universe and then humans. In my model, He created the universe for it to reflect His Truths back to, and renew, Himself. Spiritual and physical existences are very different. Atoms are *batteries* that emit Light energy. God is *Light* and shares wisdom and spiritual energy throughout the universe. He is the overall, holistic purpose for the universe. Our brains and bodies are *batteries* that provide energy for our minds and souls.

Who would believe God restricts Himself to physical time and space? Even in dreams, time and movement is not restricted to physical time, energy, and spatial laws. God is spiritually alive, which is much greater than being physically alive. Our minds can be spiritually alive when we pray and do good things. Unlike physical life, God is infinite pure oneness and does not need to reproduce Himself. God has no beginning and ending in physical time. There was no physical time and space until God created the universe.

God integrates Light (EMR) information from physical and spiritual dimensions. Integration of Light from activities of the entire universe constructs God's Spiritual awareness, decisions, and actions. On earth, spiritual love comes from integration of two minds for one spiritual life.

Without the brain, the mind is *nothing*. Without the mind, the brain is *nothing*. Without the universe, God is *less*. Without God, the universe is nothing.

When experiencing expected immediate death, we learn about our inner selves and God. It may take the rest of our lives to recall and interpret God's perfect wisdom we received in one *spiritual flash*. We can only use imprecise manmade words to describe God's perfect spiritual wave information from within His Infinite Spiritual Hologram.

God is *Light (EMR)* and *spiritual waves* that influence us through our souls and *normally* through our subconscious minds. He influences our subconscious waves that integrate to construct the words we think, speak, and write. God receives our prayers, makes judgments, and responds in His spiritual time. He views physical death very differently than humans do. Human death is only a change of venue to God.

Humans can only make theories about, and models of, God. Properties of the universe, relativity, spiritual books, prayer, and traumatic spiritual messages from God construct my *elementary* model of God.

A three-dimensional commercial hologram is seen differently from different perspectives. God's infinite wisdom is the same throughout the universe and heaven but different from different perspectives. His infinite spiritual information is transmitted through near *infinitely* fast *spiritual* waves with infinite perspectives, frequencies, and resonances. Our minds and souls have unique resonances for receiving spiritual frequencies and perspectives of God's wisdom. Each of us have different DNA and spiritual resonances to receive aspects of God's wisdom. God is aware of and judges us by our entire lives and not by each moment.

I have mentally experimented and made theories to understand God. Scientists will never be able to detect or measure God since He is the same throughout the universe. Manmade instruments only measure physical differences.

God has symmetric, probability, integration, and consistent spiritual purpose. God's *Perfect Wisdom is* integrated and permeates heaven and the universe.

God may not predict individual human *free will* thoughts and prayers but may predict overall integrated human information and activities throughout the world. Nuclear engineers cannot predict absorption and decay of individual uranium atoms but can predict overall probability of uranium absorption and decay rates in nuclear reactors. God made different laws for organizing and governing very small and very big things. He gave Man abilities to organize and control some physical properties. God listens and learns from human *organized* thoughts and prayers, or we would be wasting our time praying.

God needed spiritual blueprints, materials, skills and energy to construct the universe. *Create* is a term for building something new but omitting thoughts and details of the building process. Scientists study how God designed and constructed the universe but do not know why He designed and created the universe and heaven.

God learns and creates. We can pray anywhere and God hears our prayers. God is *Light* and His relativistic speed is always measured the same independent of believer's speeds. God is amazing to keep up with us on the earth with all our varied speeds and directions as we travel through the universe.

God's spiritual waves are intertwined at boundaries between physical and spiritual dimensions and can be on the edges of human consciousness. Low and high mental energy levels are more sensitive to spiritual thinking. Normal mental energies are for humans interacting with and surviving physical existence. When praying, we pray to God within us. We do not need to go anywhere. God and heavenly dimensions are consistent everywhere throughout the universe intertwined with physical dimensions. Spiritual places may open minds to receive spiritually.

If we wish to learn about a creative artist, we study her work. A great artwork is greater than the sum of its parts. Visual meaning is relative and integrated. Scientists work to understand the laws of the universe and to understand more of God.

The Bible is the *Word of God* as *translated* by biased human writers. If we truly analyzed our lives in depth relative to others in the world, we would realize how biased we and our writings are toward our way of life and beliefs. Different Bibles have different interpretations. What is considered infinite to Man is routine for God.

Space and time would contract to *zero* if it were possible for Man to travel at the speed of light. From relativity of Light, God observes the universe as a *near point* containing all integrated physical existence and information. God's reality is very different from Man's reality. Spiritual space is very different from physical space. We should not judge God by limited human senses and abilities.

No one surrendering to Jesus and God degrades or destroys others. Espousing spiritual superiority is rejecting others and God. However, it is thrilling to be on a humble path toward acceptance by God. God, *All Integrated Light*, transforms human spiritual thoughts into integrated spiritual waves within heaven.

Without uncertainties, there is no purpose for doing anything. The future needs uncertainty. Best physical and spiritual successes are organizing and converting difficult uncertainties into certainties.

Humans see through a small spectrum of electromagnetic radiation, light, and hear with limited air frequencies. God is, and *sees* through, all electromagnetic spectra and spiritual waves.

God and spiritual dimensions are more real than the universe and physical dimensions. Humans understand more of their inner selves when working to understand God. Christians and other religions love to repeat their meaningful verses and songs for praising God.

God's communication structures are *constant* over time. He communicates with us today as strongly as in traditional religious eras. My unusual awareness of spiritual feelings and messages began in 1977 when manic, helpless, near death, and surrendering to God. I have worked to recall spiritual meaning received when manic in 1977. I can only make models of God.

God's spiritual waves are *infinitely* more detailed and precise than Man's best science and mathematics. Each vacuum point of the universe contains God's perfect spiritual wisdom. God sees all reality.

Like the bullet that travels so fast that we cannot see it, God's activities are usually so very fast that our minds cannot sense them. However, when He chooses, He creates resonances that last long enough for much, much slower human minds to receive and become aware of. "Don't leave God out!" was a resonating message from God that lasted long enough for me to become aware of in great awe with immediate belief to obey.

Throughout history, God has revealed Himself and His Purposes to His Chosen Disciples. God told Moses: "I am that I am." He simply said He *existed*. He did not tell Moses in greater detail or in scientific terms about Himself. Moses would not have understood. God usually gives us only Wisdom we can understand. With science and faith, we may understand more about Light, *Spiritual Integration Dimensions*, and God.

Spiritual waves in higher dimensions interact only with Light. Light then affects atoms and matter. Spiritual waves are not slowed with interactions with matter.

God has information from, and responds to, our entire integrated life experiences through our souls. Scientists and engineers divide things into components to analyze them. After understanding all parts, they integrate individual components together to understand the functionality of some devise or aspect of nature.

God analyzes the status and purpose of entire galaxies in one *complete thought*. Each of us has ability to be an important child of God with our innate and cultured prayers. We must nurture our inner spiritual sensitivities to increase spiritual communication skills and value.

Our senses and minds are normally oriented to engage physical, social, and work activities, more than sensing spiritual awareness. Spiritual information is received holistically, and sometimes suddenly. We receive spiritual information to serve God more at or near low or high emotional limits. When beyond mental limits, we cannot trust our minds but must trust in God.

Our genes have unique spiritual resonances that make our spiritual communications unique to and from God. Parents and relatives have similar genes and receive similar spiritual resonances. Upon death, we will have closer awareness and communications with deceased parents and supportive relatives in heaven. God integrates an *infinite* diversity of spiritual resonances for constructing His bright detailed Infinite Spiritual Hologram *within heaven and empty space.*

The universe exists within God's Infinite Spiritual Hologram. His Infinite Spiritual Hologram is detailed and everywhere the same independent of space.

Each human heavenly spirit exists as specific spiritual resonances integrated within God's and heaven's spiritual dimensions that are intertwined with the universe's physical dimensions. Humans can only relate spiritual dimensions to mental and physical dimensions for understanding. God's sense of relativity and physical size is much different than that of humans. Human souls are holistic throughout heaven.

Our subconscious minds and souls are sensitive to unique spiritual wave frequencies in a manner similar to radios receiving specific EMR channels. Each human has unique DNA that is sensitive to unique spiritual resonances. Radio stations have unique frequencies. God has infinite spiritual frequencies. Possibly more than one for each of us. Emotional activities we experience affect our DNA and the DNA of our babies and their babies.

Limited human eyes and minds *integrate* vision to understand and negotiate our environments. Otherwise, we would see all atoms in our vision, or feel atoms when we touch. Instead, we see and feel integrations of atoms. Humans do not need to see small details such as atoms to engage our environments. Human senses integrate details to fit their purposes. Our sensitivities and understanding are size adjusted. God integrates very small and large details to fit His infinite integrated purposes.

God *is aware of and understands the purpose of* integrated atoms in each galaxy. We should not believe God *sees* things as humans do. God *sees* all atoms of our faces.

Christians believe in the Father (God,) Son (Jesus,) and the Holy Spirit (spiritual waves) integrated into spiritual oneness. An integrated spiritual model may also be God, Jesus, the Holy Spirit, angels, and *all* saved *souls* in heaven. The Holy Spirit is God's spiritual technology for communicating with all living beings, and *human* spirits, souls, and minds.

Jesus' spiritual resonances, integrated within God's Infinite Hologram, are powerful enough to attract, love, and cuddle His believers and then save their souls into His Spiritual dimensions. Jesus' spiritual resonances continue to save Christians for Eternal Spiritual Existence.

To know Jesus and God is to love Them. A reason to love ourselves is that God is within us. When sharing prayers with God, we are blessed when realizing God is our Father and best Friend. Christian believers have a *friend* in Jesus.

God has given Man abilities and tools to benefit from His physical laws and structures that permeate the universe. Engineers have constructed complex machines and structures for human benefit using Light, gravity, and God's earthly materials.

God gave Jesus spiritual abilities. Moses received God's Ten Commandments. Humans benefit spiritually as we learn God's spiritual laws. To God, all living beings are spiritually related.

We communicate spiritually with our *unique spiritual radio waves*. The more we learn about spiritual laws, dimensions, and structures, the better we can communicate with and praise God, and receive His blessings.

We should vary our emotions, at times, to become sensitive to receiving God's perfect spiritual communications. We may improve our spiritual communications by lowering mental energy and surrendering to God in prayer.

In trauma, God often gives us life-saving communications and a redirected purpose. Humans may learn of God's love and spiritual laws and communications throughout their lives and strongly at the moment of death. With mental reconstruction and spiritual awakening, we may benefit from God's spiritual laws similar to learning details of and benefiting from His physical laws.

We must reconstruct our minds, at times, to discover who we are spiritually. Look where current *superior* religions have gotten the world today. Religions develop strict, unforgiving dogma to either teach or brainwash young and adult believers. Believers of each religion *are certain* that their communications with God give them salvation.

Christianity needs to be inclusive, *versatile*, creative, and global. It may need to relate Jesus' and God's love to other religions at times.

Scientists and engineers make models of physical laws and devices and believe their models and devices can be improved. Religions teach their dogma as perfect and cannot be improved.

We should love ourselves and God since He is within us. We have a perfect reason to love ourselves. Do not only ask what God can do for you but also ask what you can do for God. We have ability to love and praise our parents and God. We have senses, brains, and minds, to love environments, those close to us, and God.

Spiritual models do not need to be exact to be useful to Man and God. They can be improved later. We need to judge if our models are in the right direction and giving us some sense of spiritual completion. Human minds are never exact and cannot translate God's perfect spiritual waves into human words perfectly. I pray mostly consistent prayers that give me a sense of completion.

Spiritual waves travel so very fast they must travel in higher spiritual dimensions. Light travels in both physical and spiritual dimensions. God, *Light*, shares His Truths from the beginning of Creation when we learn to *listen* spiritually. There is no resistance to spiritual ideas and wisdom in heaven.

To understand God's control over the universe we must study science and probability. Spiritual and physical laws are intertwined. God may not need to predict and control every atom in the universe but predicts and controls large integrated numbers of atoms for His integrated purpose. Human minds cannot control the firing of any one neuron but controls the integration of many firing neurons to think and live. God has given our minds free wills through His probability laws for integrated conscious thinking. It may be helpful at times to consider God as *A Perfect Parent*.

From human perspectives within the universe, it is difficult to understand or explain God's existence in spiritual dimensions. We may not see the forest or the trees.

I pray for God's guidance for me to *love* and *care for* Him and people more. I wish to be a small part of his *team*. He listens to all who love and pray to and *for* Him. My knowledge of spiritual time and space is so limited.

God likes organization even though the universe becomes more disorganized overtime. Man's purpose is to help God organize spiritual thinking through prayer. Spiritual ideas give feelings of completion.

We may think of understanding our subconscious and conscious potentials as a starting point in understanding God. *Loving, needy* subconscious minds receive spiritual miracles. Spiritual feelings cannot always be put into words. Spiritual thoughts we receive are part of God to some very small extent.

This work is meant to assist readers in evaluating and improving their beliefs. We consider our religious practices, science, philosophy, and spiritual messages received when working to discover and refine our beliefs. Christianity is a wonderful religion to believe in and work within for building foundations of spiritual beliefs.

Every now and then, I call God a Genius. It praises Him and makes me happy. We can have fun with God and enjoy Him more at times. He has, and has given humans, a sense of humor.

I love, respect, and praise all of my direct ancestors for without them I would not exist. They have evolved for me to be who I am. I love my Mom's and Dad's memories and their spirits in heaven; they and God have created me and nurtured my life. I love and respect God, His universe, and my ancestors.

From my experiences, I would like to further define God:

God: a living omniscient, omnipresent, *nearly* omnipotent, and Infinite Spiritual Hologram consisting of all Light activities in the universe and heaven, and either consisting of spiritual waves or controlling all spiritual waves with power to control an expanding universe and an infinite heaven with His physical and spiritual laws.

I do not know physical or spiritual reality. I can only make humble models of reality. I used manic notes and memory to make my model of God. All truths are God's; all errors are mine.

CONCLUSION SECTION

Chapter 50

CONCLUSION

"Those who are able to see beyond the shadows and lies of their culture will never be understood by the masses."

Plato

THE LORD'S PRAYER

Our Father, which art in heaven,
Hallowed be thy Name.
Thy Kingdom come.
Thy will be done on earth,
As it is in heaven.
Give us this day our daily bread.
And forgive us our trespasses,
As we forgive those who trespass against us.
And lead us not into temptation,
But deliver us from evil.
For thine is the kingdom,
The power, and the glory,
For ever and ever.
Amen.

TWENTY-THIRD PSALM

> "The LORD is my shepherd; I shall not want.
> ² He maketh me to lie down in green pastures: he leadeth me beside the still waters.
> ³ He restoreth my soul: he leadeth me in the paths of righteousness for His name's sake.
> ⁴ Yea, though I walk through the valley of the shadow of death, I will fear no evil: for thou art with me; thy rod and thy staff they comfort me.
> ⁵ Thou preparest a table before me in the presence of mine enemies: thou anointest my head with oil; my cup runneth over.
> ⁶ Surely goodness and mercy shall follow me all the days of my life: and I will dwell in the house of the LORD, forever."
>
> Matthew 6:9–13, King James Version (KJV)

The Lord's Prayer is spiritual technology Jesus gave to His disciples. The Twenty-third Psalm is believed to be written by David. These two passages have been comforting to Christians in need of prayer for over two thousand years. With science, technical, and spiritual advances, we may receive additional spiritual information we are able to understand. God *technically* created or designed, engineered, and constructed the universe and heaven.

I wrote about everyday normal activities and thoughts in some depth in beginning Chapters to demonstrate normal thinking. I wrote a chapter on modeling. Later models in following chapters may not be completely correct. However, models that help thinking about the mind and God in a positive light have healing and spiritual benefits.

In manic episodes I have felt confident of spiritual communications. Everyday thinking did not feel complete. From psychiatric exercises and mental reconstruction, I have had confidence in preventing manic episodes. I hope to receive further responsibilities from God?

After having severe sporadic episodes for 17 years, with medications I began my conflicting psychiatric neck exercises and continued medications. I have been manic free for 28 years. It is fantastic not worrying about going manic and losing control.

I was as surprised as anyone would be when God asked me to write for Him. I could only use words defined earlier by others and information I knew, or could learn, to write for God. I have practiced my psychiatric exercises and processes that have healed and *renewed* my mind and spirit. My goal is to continue mental reconstruction until I have feelings of completion. There have been billions of SCAP energy releases from billions of overstressed nerve cells, neurons, and glia cells. Readers have an option to practice exercises and processes to help heal their stress disorders.

I kept my healing and spiritual work separate from health care professionals and spiritual leaders. My work was so unusual that psychiatrists, medical doctors, and spiritual leaders would have claimed I was manic and discouraged my work and writing.

All *healing* practices, ideas, and experiences are my own except spiritual assistance from Jesus and God. I am thankful and blessed to have had and been healed of bipolar disorder. I have accomplished a persistent sanity.

Psychiatrists and spiritual leaders should help mental patients regain control of their lives. They must ask what caused their depression and disorder? They should help patients understand the origins of their disorders. Throughout history, authorities have discredited new creative ideas and discoveries. They want to continue their authority on how things *are* and *should be*.

Childhood and later traumas slow, distort, bias, and limit thinking. Mental limitations continue throughout lives unless we receive dramatic spiritual messages, have successful psychiatric counseling, practice my healing processes, or experience a significant emotional event.

It is devastating not being able to trust one's own mind. In 1977, manic insanities and an unexpected spiritual awakening distracted me from daily activities. Worldly activities had less importance during emotional survival thinking. I appeared lost when experiencing manic uncertainties and spiritual communications. I had no alternative but to turn to God.

Conflicting and non-conflicting neck exercises continue to purge disruptive energy from overstressed nerves and neural networks. I have been blessed with an amazing success, and a passion for writing for God and those in need of psychiatric healing.

My brain and mind are more stable and efficient with less energy. We all have emotional limits to lesser or greater extent due to trauma creating high levels of inner stress.

Trauma effects or scars in the brain eclipse spiritual communications until their disruptive high energy is released. Without trauma effects, with improved spiritual communication skills, and with patience and dedication, people throughout the world will be more confident, understanding, and supportive of one another.

My spiritual models and beliefs are founded upon Christianity, spiritual messages I have received, science, and philosophy. The better our spiritual technology becomes, the better we can receive and understand God's Truths. Light is the medium between physical and spiritual dimensions.

My healing and spiritual adventure has not been easy. It is a miracle to be alive. I have survived severe childhood bullying, a deceptive, degrading wife, severe depression, and severe manic episodes. Healing has been a long journey toward a not well-defined destination.

Neck and brain energy releases, SCAPS, from psychiatric exercises continue to give slight pleasant feelings. This makes me *confident* of healing and spiritual blessings. Energy released from fewer individual SCAPS has lessened over the years. This gives hope for the Clear Mind and *unusual* mental and spiritual blessings. My work is not finished.

One firing neuron does not create an idea. Light from millions of firing neurons integrate to construct a conscious mind that can focus on one thing, or on diverse ideas. Integration of Light is an important concept for understanding the mind and God. To be omnipresent and omniscient, God must integrate all information from throughout the universe and heaven into completeness.

Conflicting neck exercises release trauma energy from nerves in the upper throat, in the upper neck, and from brainstem neurons at emotional limits. Subconsciously, we wish to *express* emotional experiences. The brainstem and limbic system must interpret distorted information passing through traumatized nerves in the upper neck and back of the throat. Releasing trauma scars lowers the energy of the brain for increased mind control. With trauma nerve and related neuron energy released, nerve signals passing through the back of the throat and upper neck are easier for the brain to interpret. Minds heal when carefully experiencing mental limits.

I have been blessed to experiment and write independently about my mental healing and beliefs. I hope this work will help readers heal their stress disorders and build their own truthful beliefs.

God gives us freedoms to either love or not love others. We should expect to love everyone, but do not need to love those who continually abuse us. We will lose our health if we do! God has given us emotions for us to love others and for us to protect ourselves.

Psychiatric medications may be quick and simple but may have mind slowing and negative side effects. Some side effects may last a lifetime if not resolved. Psychiatrists must be aware of and correct medications with mind slowing side effects.

Psychiatrists should calm spiritually inspired patients down and learn causes of anxieties and fears. They might say: "Slow down and organize your thoughts so together we can resolve your difficulties." Spiritual awareness is common when feeling uncertain, manic, or near death.

Take your time and organize your spiritual thoughts. You are not *alone*. Make your writing make sense to you first and then to others. Disorganized spiritual thoughts are difficult to understand.

Healing is discovering, understanding, and expanding mental limits. We must work for feelings of completion in thoughts we have and activities we do.

Normal mental energy levels are for daily activities, such as keeping ourselves safe, and is greater than dream and normal spiritual energy levels, otherwise spiritual thoughts and dreams interfere with daily activities. In extreme need, God takes over our free-will minds with *high spiritual energy* to save us from imminent death. When traumas cause us to momentarily lose control, God saves us.

Children will benefit from mental reconstruction, with less time and effort. Their mental restrictions are less ingrained. With counseling, mental reconstruction, and extended prayer, future generations may have Clear Minds free of trauma effects for most of their lives.

Psychiatrists may eventually include processes given here as additional treatment in helping children and adults through mental difficulties. Future generations will be smarter, more spiritual, live longer, and be more considerate of one another. In the future, all children should be evaluated by psychiatrists to discover and reduce trauma effects early on. Trauma effects are more easily released at young ages. Society should be aware that everyone has levels of trauma scars and should benefit from psychiatry to lesser or greater extents.

America was founded upon freedom of religion, which has spawned amazing technologies. My conflicting physical exercises and mental and spiritual models, while continuing medication, have healed my disorder. I see no need for discontinuing medication. I do not sense mind slowing side effects.

After high energy is released from trauma scars, neuron electromagnetic spikes and energy levels will be more even throughout the brain. Neuron Light will interact with each other, and integrate, more. Similar neuron electromagnetic resonances will integrate to produce more in-depth confident thinking.

God is the perfect integration of all *Light* and *spiritual wave* information in the universe and heaven constructing His perfect, infinite wisdom. His creation and control of all universal forces and spiritual potentials give Him omniscience, omnipresence, and near omnipotence. Humans have free will control over some very, very small fraction of the universe's energy.

When relaxing facial muscles and meditating on the face, pleasant tensing sensations occur around the sides of the forehead and scalp. Tensing is with subconscious control. The face and brain are closely connected. I sense slight brain tensing with facial tensing.

I believe trauma energy releases are more probable for manic-depressives and older persons. Research on neck energy releases and exercises should be continued.

My healing work is long and involved. I believe individuals having frequent manic or other mental episodes while taking prescribed medications would benefit from my psychiatric exercises and processes. I have faith in my work for helping overstressed minds.

God created the universe and is more real than the universe. He rules the universe with His constant physical laws, *Light*, gravity, other field forces, and spiritual waves. God's control of spiritual time and energy is very different from Man's concepts of physical time and energy.

God is *Light* always traveling at light speed relative to physical things and Man. Light from neurons in the brain is slower than Light in the vacuum of space. Neuron Light in the brain is reflected by, and deposits its energy and information on, neural membranes. Integrated *Light* from neuron activations creates the mind and spiritual wisdom.

God made Man's *mind* in His image. Minds consist of integrated Light and spiritual waves within the brain when praying. God learns from prayers and spiritual waves throughout the universe. Our minds are tiny subsets of God. We are *children* of God. I cannot imagine God as a Big Man in outer space.

Spiritual waves reverberating between the origin of the Big Bang and the expanding boundaries of the universe travel much, much faster than light and integrate spiritual wisdom from all *Light* throughout the universe. I model spiritual waves to explain God's omnipresence and omniscience. They are referred to as the Holy Spirit in the Bible. Models help us think and can be improved.

Religions and parents must teach children how to think, and not just what to think. It is spiritual to teach children to believe in and love Jesus and God, and to respect others spiritual traditions and cultures. God gives us unique abilities to think differently. We have unique spiritual *radio* frequencies.

Jesus did not conform to the religious culture of His era. He developed His own spiritual practices. Healing and faith are foundations of Christianity.

When meditating and lowering mental energy, we may become aware of heavenly spiritual resonances similar to that of our own souls' unique spiritual resonances or *spiritual radio channels*. Jesus' wide spiritual resonances or *channels* can be received by all who believe in Him. Spiritual communications do not lessen over distance and are independent of physical space.

Jesus integrated within God has *infinite* spiritual communication channels – one or more for each of us. When we were conceived, God created unique spiritual channels for our minds and souls. With patience and spiritual practice, we may broaden our spiritual channels. If we understand the *vacuum of space*, we will understand more of God.

God sees life and death differently than humans do. He sees the transition of the mind and soul from life to spiritual life after death as a continuous process. The soul is the integration of good, and possibly bad, mental activities during life. Upon death the soul transcends into heavenly spirits retaining only positive spiritual information for heaven. There are no sins or evil in heaven.

Physical dimensions are a subset of spiritual dimensions. From expected imminent death experiences and receiving inner spiritual communications, we gain spiritual purpose.

God performs miracles in His very different spiritual time. Jesus and God love and nurture us while we are *briefly* on earth and nurture our loving spirits in heaven forever. I pray nightly that God gives my beloved deceased Mother, Father, my beloved deceased aunts and uncles, and deceased others who have loved me wonderful activities, responsibilities, and purposes in heaven. It is the best I can do for them. I get wonderful feelings when I feel I have honored and helped my beloved ones in Heaven.

God had a reason for creating the universe and heaven. His purpose was to advance spiritual energy, information, and lives. Human thinking is the controlling of mental energy and information. Prayer is sending and receiving spiritual energy.

God created the universe and heaven to support mental and spiritual resonances for sharing love. Love is spiritual and completes God and humans. Love connects and integrates; hate divides. Heaven is Jesus', God's and loving spirits' everlasting home.

God's purpose for granting free wills and souls is for humans to grow spiritually and give Him something to care about He normally does not need to control. God desires His love to be reflected, and added to, by humans.

God's spiritual waves are so fast that His awareness of the universe and heaven is independent of space. God hears prayers from everywhere in the universe.

I praise Jesus for saving my life. His dying on the cross has forgiven sins of those who believe in Him. I trust in Jesus.

I could not have had so many creative ideas without God's guidance. I have *listened* carefully. Thank you for your interest in this healing and spiritual endeavor. I hope readers will build upon my elementary efforts and models for a positive, spiritual world. When humble, we feel God cuddling us.

Years after her passing, I still hear my mother singing in Ivy Hill United Methodist Church: *This is my story; this is my song; praising my Savior all the day long.*

This is *my* story and my song. I continue searching for mental and spiritual realities. I am proud to have been bipolar, experienced unusual ideas and beliefs, and to have been healed of my disorder. Bipolar disorder forced me to be creative *and* spiritual for inner healing.

I am blessed for receiving this *mission to write for God. All truthful ideas are from God; all errors are mine.* I praise God for giving me so many ideas for writing this book. I pray for Jesus and God to forgive my shortcomings and sins. In God I trust.

ABOUT THE AUTHOR

A physicist and nuclear engineer became bipolar due to bullying throughout childhood but mostly due to a degrading wife. He experienced 17 years of severe sporadic manic episodes even with medications. With his conflicting physical exercises, he carefully and briefly extends his mind to emotional limits to release trauma energy from the brain. Exercising muscles closest to the brain affects and heals the brain the most. His facial meditation practices reduce mental energy and calm the mind and body. Briefly extending the brain and mind to limits heals the brain and mind and maintains control at expanded emotional limits. He has healed his disorder with conflicting physical exercises at mental limits. The subconscious mind learns to heal itself when briefly experiencing mental limits. Athletes extend minds and bodies to limits to be all they can be. He has practiced conflicting psychiatric exercises for 28 years with medications – One Bipolar Cure!

Bipolar disorder is caused by stress beyond ability to cope with feelings of no way out. Normal everyday interactions and coping skills are overridden by high-energy emotional survival thinking. Survival thoughts override reasoning with others. The manic mind goes out of control.

In the author's first manic episode, he had a need to learn of God's origin. His imaginary manic model explains God's origin. While working on his first healing book, he received a traumatic inner voice:

"Don't Leave God Out." His writing became spiritual. Jesus and God are important in his healing and beliefs.

One Bipolar Cure! / 28 Years without an Episode! Teaser! And Why Read?

Do you have bipolar, or other mental, disorder, or want to understand and help someone who has? Learn how a physicist/ nuclear engineer has healed his bipolar disorder using conflicting exercises for extending his mind to emotional survival limits, and meditation to calm back down. Exercising muscles closest to the brain affects and heals the brain the most. It is life changing not worrying about going manic.

The author experienced 17 years of sporadic manic episodes even with psychiatric medications. He has been mania free for 28 years.

Bipolar Disorder is caused by stress beyond ability to cope with feelings of no way out. Normal thinking within social and challenging limits is overridden by high energy survival thinking. The manic mind goes out of control beyond emotional limits. Experience manic thinking.

With conflicting exercises, the mind learns to control itself at limits. We learn the most about our minds at limits. Exercises release small discrete trauma scar energy from the neck, throat, and brainstem, releasing tensions in related areas of the brain. The mind becomes less emotional and easier to control.

Trauma scars are like cancers sporadically firing and causing the overall energy of the brain to remain at high levels. Athletes extend minds and bodies to limits to be all they can be.

Facial meditation reduces mental energy and subconsciously tenses muscles on the sides of the temple and scalp renewing facial, and facial skin, muscles. The face looks and feels younger.

In the author's first manic episode, he needed to learn of God's origin. His imaginary manic models explain God's origin and his infinite abilities. Working to finish his first healing book, he received an inner voice: "Don't Leave God Out." His first book became and later books were spiritual. Christianity and science were important in mental healing and spiritual beliefs.

Printed in the United States
by Baker & Taylor Publisher Services